TO PROFESSOR STACY,

WITH GRATITUDE FOR HER

SUPPORT ALL THESE YEARS!!

THE POLICY OF LAW

The book focuses on the relationship between law and politics as perceived by the legal community and more specifically, the transformation of politics into law. After exploring the relationship between law and politics as considered by the major modern schools of legal theory, the focus moves to the regions of interaction in which law and politics meet, termed the 'policy of law'. The policy of law is characterised in this work as the stage of the law-making process at which values entrenched in political decisions are transformed into legal concepts in order to fit the existing legal system. The space labelled as policy of law is today mainly (but not exclusively) the domain of legal actors. Consequently, the identification of a branch of the legal discipline specifically devoted to the investigation of the transformations of values into law is given: the policy of law analysis. Finally, whether and to what extent the policy of law analysis can be encompassed within the traditional legal discipline and, more particularly, as a part of jurisprudence, is explored.

European Academy of Legal Theory Series: Volume 8

EUROPEAN ACADEMY OF LEGAL THEORY
MONOGRAPH SERIES

General Editors

Professor Mark Van Hoecke
Professor François Ost
Professor Luc Wintgens

The Policy of Law

A Legal Theoretical Framework

Mauro Zamboni

·HART·
PUBLISHING

OXFORD AND PORTLAND, OREGON
2007

Published in North America (US and Canada) by
Hart Publishing
c/o International Specialized Book Services
920 NE 58th Avenue, Suite 300
Portland, OR 97213–3786
USA
Tel: +1 503 287 3093 or toll-free: (1) 800 944 6190
Fax: +1 503 280 8832
E-mail: orders@isbs.com
Website: www.isbs.com

Hart Publishing, 16C Worcester Place, OX1 2JW
Telephone: +44 (0)1865 517530 Fax: +44 (0)1865 510710
E-mail: mail@hartpub.co.uk
Website: http://www.hartpub.co.uk

British Library Cataloguing in Publication Data
Data Available

ISBN-13: 978–1-84113–723–0

Typeset by Columns Design Ltd, Reading
Printed and bound in Great Britain by
TJI Digital, Padstow, Cornwall

A Tiziana, la mia compagna di viaggio

Acknowledgments

My first thanks go to Jes Bjarup and Laura Carlson for reading the entirety of the manuscript and providing me with invaluable comments. I am also deeply indebted to Bruce Anderson, Reza Banakar, Brian Bix, Kaarlo Tuori and David Wood for taking the time to read the manuscript and giving me insightful and valued comments. I would also like to thank Roger Cotterrell, Åke Frändberg, Torben Spaak and Jori Munukka who gave me very helpful comments on earlier drafts of this work. I am very grateful to Luc Wintgens and Mark Van Hoecke, for their friendship and their support, and to Lawrence Friedman for sponsoring my year as a visiting scholar at Stanford University, where this book took its final shape. Last, but not least, I would like to thank Enrico Pattaro, for showing me the beauty of legal theory.

Contents

The obvious is our business; making sense (or nonsense) of the obvious is what philosophers do. We are the ones who examine cause-and effect, the reality of the external world, personal identity, and our ability as humans to argue about value.

Jeremy Waldron, The Dignity of Legislation 126 (1999).

Introduction:

'Not Law but
Politics-Smuggled-into-Law'

I N 1996, THE UNITED States Supreme Court found the Common-
wealth of Virginia in violation of the Equal Protection Clause of the
Fourteenth Amendment due to its state support of a military college
exclusively for males. Justice Antonin Scalia wrote in his dissenting
opinion:

> The tradition of having government-funded military schools for men is as well
> rooted in the traditions of this country as the tradition of sending only men into
> military combat. *The people may decide to change the one tradition, like the
> other, through democratic processes; but the assertion that either tradition has
> been unconstitutional through the centuries is not law, but politics-smuggled-
> into-law.*[1] (emphasis added)

Scalia's words reveal the complexity faced by scholars and practitioners
when dealing with such an issue. While espousing a duty for judges to avoid
political decisions masquerading in legal dress, proclaiming that traditions
may only be changed through a *democratic* process, Scalia actually tackles
and decides highly political issues. Scalia implicity smuggles into the political
ideology the idea that it is better that certain basic societal decisions be made
by elected legislatures, rather than by unelected judges.

Moreover, Scalia's dissent typifies the central role that the relationship
between law and politics has been delegated in modern legal thinking and
practice. In one way or another, every legal practitioner as well as every
modern legal theory is confronted with the issue of how the legal and
political phenomena interact with each other.[2]

This work frames, from a normative perspective, a field where politics
and law meet: the policy of law. By defining the borders of one of the
places where law and politics meet, the goal is not simply to offer a stable
theoretical ground from which a journey to find solution(s) to the complex

---

[1] *United States v Virginia et al*, 518 U.S. 569 (1996).
[2] See K Klare, 'The Politics of Duncan Kennedy's Critique' (2001) 22 *Cardozo Law
Review* 1076; and N Duxbury, 'The Theory and History of American Law and Politics'
(1993) 13 *OJLS* 249.

of problems revealed by Justice Scalia's dissent can depart. The hope is also that this work, by focusing on the central role played by the legal actors in the passage from politics to law, defined as the policy of law, will be able to contribute to the theoretical debate as to the centrality of the law-making process, not only for the understanding, but also for the interpretation and creation, of the law.[3]

I. THE THEORETICAL BACKGROUND

The justices sitting in the US Supreme Court are certainly not alone in grappling with the relationship of law and politics. From the very birth of the nation state, and particularly after its transformation into the modern welfare state, attention has specifically been devoted to explaining the interrelationship of legal and political phenomena. Niccolò Machiavelli and Thomas Hobbes stand out clearly for their early lucid and penetrating analyses of the law-politics issues in modern times. This theoretical interest has its roots in the fact that, as pointed out by Jürgen Habermas, the very 'complex of law and political power characterizes the transition from societies organized by kinship to those early societies already organized around states'.[4]

Nearer to the present, Rudolph von Jhering has a central position among legal scholars attempting to understand and depict the relations between law and politics. In particular, according to von Jhering, the law not only has the central function of reconciling clashing social and individual values and ideals, its very origins and nature are rooted in and mirror such conflicts.[5]

Despite so much attention, this issue of positioning the law with respect to the political realm is far from being settled around generally accepted propositions, as can be seen from the discordant opinions of the US Supreme Court. Just the opposite is the case, as the distances between opinions as to issues of law and politics have widened considerably with time, in particular after the birth of the welfare state and its dissemination in the Western part of the world. This disagreement as to the relation of law and politics has increased, in part due to the fact that the welfare state form of political organisation requires as one of its fundamental features the very use of the law as an instrument of social engineering. This feature,

---

[3] See J Waldron, The *Dignity of Legislation* (Cambridge, Cambridge University Press, 1999) 129.

[4] J Habermas, *Between Facts and Norms: Contributions to a Discourse Theory of Law and Democracy* (Cambridge, The MIT Press, 1998) 137. See also N Machiavelli, *The Prince* (London, JM Dent and Sons, 1908) chs V, XII (reprint 1532); and T Hobbes, Leviathan (London, Penguin Books, 1985) ch XXVI (reprint 1660).

[5] See R von Jhering, *The Struggle for Law* (J Lalor (tr), 2nd edn, Chicago, Callaghan, 1915) 1–2, 25–9, 61–3.

in its turn, has given birth to the phenomenon of a 'systems conflict', an aspect of the more general 'dilemmas of law in the Welfare State'.[6]

This phenomenon arises due to the co-existence in the contemporary age of two systemic forces towing the law in opposite directions, affecting the very nature of the legal phenomenon. One force pulls in the direction of concentrating the law into the hands of politicians, therefore requiring a law more obedient in nature to reasons of politics than, for example, to those of systematic legal development. The content of the law hence cannot be viewed as completely independent from politics, as the modern state is characterised by the very fact that the law is a tool available to Parliaments or governments in order to realise programmes within a certain community. In other words, law becomes structurally more flexible to the reasons of politics.[7]

The increasing complexity and number of areas the political world recognises as its domain, and therefore regulates by law, in their turn cause a second force pulling the law in the opposite direction. This increasing politicisation of the community life produces a force towing the legal phenomenon in the direction of a more specialised and therefore more autonomous law with respect to politics. This further encourages the development of the idea of law as autonomous from outside reality, with its own rules as monopolised by a group of professionals. As a result, the distances between the legal phenomenon and the political world tend to widen.[8]

These tendencies, by which the law is politicised and framed in spaces of autonomy, certainly are not typical only of our time.[9] However, the simultaneous and increasing intensity of the forces pulling law towards and away from politics, almost equal in strength, consequently creating a tension within the legal phenomenon, are elements that characterise today's systems conflict. The recent shifting of many Western countries to a more deregulated or weaker version of the welfare state does not appear to

---

[6] G Teubner, 'The Transformation of Law in the Welfare State' in G Teubner (ed), *Dilemmas of Law in the Welfare State* (Berlin, Walter de Gruyter, 1986) 6–7. See also L Friedman, 'Introduction' (2003) 4 *Theoretical Inquiries in Law* 446; and K Tuori, 'Legislation between Politics and Law' in LJ Wintgens (ed), Legisprudence: a New Theoretical Approach to Legislation (Oxford, Hart Publishing, 2002) 100–1.

[7] See R Cotterrell, *The Sociology of Law: an Introduction* (2nd edn, London, Butterworths, 1992) 44; and R Posner, 'The Decline of Law as an Autonomous Discipline: 1962–1987' (1987) 100 *Harvard Law Review* 766, 767, 773–4.

[8] See N Luhmann, *Law as a Social System* (Oxford, Oxford University Press, 2004) 187–9.

[9] See M Weber, *Economy and Society* (G Roth and C Wittich (eds), Berkeley, University of California Press, 1978) 775–6, 789–92; D Trubek, 'Max Weber on Law and the Rise of Capitalism' (1972) *Wisconsin Law Review* 750; and J O'Neill, 'The Disciplinary Society: from Weber to Foucault' (1986) 37 *British Journal of Sociology* 57.

affect the strength of these two pulling and divergent systemic forces. On the contrary, the importance and use of the law as a tool in the hands of politicians has increased.[10]

Political authorities usually promote and implement deregulations of the welfare state through the law. Almost paradoxically, new and often extremely detailed legal measures are now required from the state for regulating the services freed from the state monopoly and now offered by the private sector. The complex and highly technical nature of the deregulating legal measures relegates a leading role then to such legal actors as legal consultants or administrative judges and, more importantly, to their methods of reasoning.[11]

II. A MAP OF THE PRESENT WORK

Chapter one explores, based on this background, the relationship between law and politics as considered and interpreted by the major contemporary schools or movements of legal theory. The approaches of the different legal theoretical streams are classified in accordance with their responses to the following issues: how these contemporary legal scholars view the law in relation to politics (the 'static aspect'), how the law-making relates to the political order (the 'dynamic aspect') and the degree of relation of legal discipline to the political material (the 'epistemological aspect').

Three ideal-typical models are proposed according to the answers given to these questions: the autonomous model, the embedded model and the intersecting model. These provide an ideal-typical classification of the different ways the legal and political phenomena's relations work for the various contemporary legal theories. Each of the models, however, mirrors the peculiar situation of modern law: law and politics tend to keep the features of being two different phenomena as well as of presenting regions of interaction, although with differences as to extent and intensity.

Chapters two and three analyse one of the regions of interaction in which law and politics meet, the transformational moment. This moment is defined as the stage in the law-making process at which the values produced inside the political arena are transformed into legal categories and concepts. This moment, on one hand, has been given a crucial role in the images of the relationship between law and politics by most contemporary legal theories. On the other hand, most legal scholars for different

---

[10] See MDA Freeman, *Lloyd's Introduction to Jurisprudence* (7th edn, London, Sweet and Maxwell, 2001) 1047. See also Habermas, *Between Facts and Norms* (n 4 above) 152.
[11] See N Luhmann, 'The Self-Reproduction of Law and its Limits' in Teubner, *Dilemmas of Law* (n 6 above) 120–1; eg M Ruggie, 'The Paradox of Liberal Intervention: Health Policy and the American Welfare State' (1992) 97 *American Journal of Sociology* 927.

reasons have not fully developed any systematic investigation of this transformational moment in their legal-theoretical proposals.

The possibility of filling in this theoretical vacancy in investigating the transformational moment by employing the conceptual apparatus as developed within political science is explored in chapter three. Attention is focused on the distinction made by political scientists between the *politics* and the *policy* dimensions of the process of the formation and the implementation of political decisions. In particular, the definition of policy by political scientists as a network of processes and decisions with a conversional function is examined. Finally, the normative perspective of policy in general is scrutinised: how legal actors usually have perceived the idea of policy in general and, in particular, how they fit it into their idea of law.

Chapter four investigates the possibility of defining, from a normative point of view, the transformational moment as the stage of the law-making process at which the policy of law takes place. A model for explaining the position and functions of the transformational moments in the law-making process is presented, the result of a progressive refinement of basic ideas as to how the law-making process works. This model demonstrates how a space can be opened in the law-making activities between the formation of values in the political world and the impact of the newly-made law on the community. This space is defined as the *policy of law*. The policy of law is then characterised as the stage of the law-making process in which the values entrenched in political decisions are transformed into legal categories and concepts in order to modify the existing legal system. The space labelled as policy of law today is mainly the domain for the work and the reasoning of the legal actors.

The identification of a branch of knowledge specifically devoted to the investigation of the transformations of values into law is made in chapter five: the *policy of law analysis*. The work of the policy of law analyst is characterised, both in its object and its investigative tools, in such a way as to distinguish it from the other two neighbouring types of studies: the politics of law analysis and the sociology of law. Finally, whether and to what extent the policy of law analysis can be encompassed within the traditional legal discipline and, more particularly, as a part of jurisprudence, is explored.

After summarising the work and results presented here, chapter six proposes possible further investigations for the policy of law and its analysis. The framework of policy of law spaces in the national legal system can be extended to national law-making processes heavily influenced or even determined by local, supranational and international legal-political organisations (eg the European Union or agencies of the United Nations), allowing for new applications of the current investigation. In addition, possible contributions which can be derived through a policy of law analysis are presented, particularly with respect to two current compelling problems as faced by contemporary legal systems, globalisation and gender. Finally the essential elements for a future modelling of the policy of law processes and results are posited.

III. KEY CONCEPTS

A terminological clarification as to certain key concepts used throughout this work is required before starting the investigation.

A. Law, Law-Making and Legal Discipline

This work has adopted a very broad definition as to the concept of *law*. By *law* is meant the complex of norms (ie standards, maxims, principles and rules) which have a binding character, a character generally accepted by the members of the community to whom they are addressed, and whose enforcement is guaranteed by specialised enforcement agencies employing coercive measures. This definition is mainly derived from Max Weber's works, inter alia, and one can trace a basic similarity to Neil MacCormick's enlargement of Herbert LA Hart's idea of law, in addition to legal rules, to also include legal principles and legal standards.[12]

The concept of *law-making* is also used here in a broad context. Law-making encompasses the mechanisms and procedures having legal recognition and directed to the production and enforcement of the law. This also includes the institutional actors participating in such production and enforcement. In other words, law-making refers to the operational aspects of the legal phenomenon, that is the mechanisms that make certain moral propositions or political declarations directly relevant, either in legislative or judicial forms, for the legal world and its actors.[13]

As with the other two concepts, the *legal discipline* or legal scholarship is here also characterised by its ample space, identifying a wide range of understandings and educational activities as developed by legal scholars

---

[12] See Weber, *Economy and Society* (n 9 above) 34; M Weber, *Critique of Stammler* (New York, The Free Press, 1977) 131–4; N MacCormick, *H.L.A. Hart* (Stanford, Stanford University Press, 1981) 126–30; and N MacCormick, *Legal Reasoning and Legal Theory* (Oxford, Clarendon Press, 1997) chs VIII–IX.

[13] See eg, J Raz, *The Concept of a Legal System: An Introduction to the Theory of Legal System* (2nd edn, Oxford, Clarendon Press, 1980) 156–66; and the Hartian idea of legal system as interpreted by MacCormick, *H.L.A. Hart* (n 12 above) 20–4.

and directed at investigating, explaining and teaching the law and law-making from a normative perspective.[14] Finally, *jurisprudence* is used as identifying that part of the legal discipline which investigates the nature of law, its production and its working.[15]

The meanings here attributed to *law, law-making, legal discipline* and *jurisprudence* naturally also entail limitations. First, they are all grounded on perceptions of the legal phenomenon as shared mostly in Western legal cultures and, in particular, those in democratic forms of political organisation.[16] This limit, however, brings with it an opportunity largely exploited in this work. Once the analysis is restricted to Western democracies, it is then possible to make use of certain generic explanatory examples without having to specifically ascribe them to one or another national legal system. Such generic examples expose the problems (and solutions) with which most Western lawyers and scholars are quite familiar. The linguistic distinction between *politics* and *policy* is, however, not as strong in other Western languages as in English. Consequently, the examples used often reflect actual cases and problems of the legal theoretical discussion and legal practice arising in the United States and, to a much lesser extent, the United Kingdom.

Secondly, for the sake of clarity and space, *law, law-making, legal discipline* and *jurisprudence* as considered here are those typical for a contemporary nation state organisational form, and postulated as closed to international and supranational legal, political and social influences. However, the possibility of applying the results reached in this investigation to a more actual reality of a nation state open to such influences, is presented in chapter six.

Finally, as stated above, these meanings as adopted are very broad, and therefore sometimes tend to overlap; it is often difficult to distinguish one from the other.[17] Moreover, these definitions as set forth here are primarily valid for the entire work except chapter one; there the primary criteria for classifying the different contemporary legal theories under the different

---

[14] See O Weinberger, 'The Norm as Thought and as Reality' in N MacCormick and O Weinberger (eds), *An Institutional Theory of Law: New Approaches to Legal Positivism* (Dordrecht, D Reidel Publishing, 1986) 44–6.

[15] See H McCoubrey and N White, *Textbook on Jurisprudence* (3rd edn, London, Blackstone Press, 1999) 1; and Freeman, *Lloyd's Introduction to Jurisprudence* (n 10 above) 3. In this work, jurisprudence also encompasses legal theory. See R Dreier and R Alexy, 'The Concept of Jurisprudence' (1990) 3 *Ratio Juris* 1.

[16] For a comprehensive definition of 'legal phenomenon' from a Western perspective as adopted in this work, see R Summers, 'On Giving Legal Forms its Due: a Sketch' (2003) 7 *Associations: Journal for Legal and Social Theory* 201.

[17] See eg, the triple nature of law as a system of norms, a system of action and a system of knowledge as exposed by Habermas, *Between Facts and Norms* (n 4 above) 79–81.

ideal-types model are the very differences stemming from what the various theories mean when speaking about law, law-making and legal discipline, in particular in relation to politics.

These certainly are relevant limitations. Nevertheless, the main goal of this work is to offer a framework within which to develop a possible *middle-range theory* concerning the law-making process, a theory that takes its start from the assumption that the entirety of a phenomenon, ie how the law, law-making and legal discipline relate to politics, cannot be explained by recourse to *one* theoretical system giving (or assuming) *one* specific definition.[18] As a consequence, the efforts here are mostly directed at the explanation and analysis of only segments of the legal phenomenon, eg the segment of the policy or transformational moment in the law-making process, moving the macro-dimensions of the legal phenomenon (ie law, law-making, legal discipline and jurisprudence) and their in-depth outlining temporarily to the horizon of the investigation.

B. Politics, Political Order and Political Material

In contrast to law, law-making and legal discipline, the use of the concepts 'politics', 'political order' and 'political material' focuses around a more restricted range of meanings. This methodological choice of capturing the political concepts within a very narrow range of meanings is based on the observation of the ideas the different contemporary legal theories have of the political phenomenon. If it is true that the meanings assigned to the law by the different legal scholars vary radically, it is also true that the different legal movements tend to perceive the political phenomenon in a quite similar way.

The commonly accepted meaning of *politics* as perceived by the legal world is that it is a complex of values (of an economic, social or moral nature), as well as the processes through which such values are then chosen to be implemented by the public authoritative apparatus into the community using the law-making.[19] Values, in their turn, are:

---

[18] This concept was developed within sociology, see eg, R Merton, 'The Role-Set: Problems in Sociological Theory' (1957) 28 *British Journal of Sociology* 108. See also J Coleman, *The Practice of Principle: in Defence of a Pragmatist Approach to Legal Theory* (Oxford, Oxford University Press, 2001) 5–6; and R Cotterrell, 'Sociological Interpretations of Legal Development' (1995) 2 *European Journal of Law and Economics* 352.

[19] See D Kairys, 'Introduction' in D Kairys (ed), *The Politics of Law: a Progressive Critique* (3rd edn, New York, Basic Books, 1998) 5, 14–15; A Ross, *On Law and Justice* (London, Stevens & Sons, 1958) 334–9; and J Raz, 'Rights and Individual Well-Being' in J Raz, Ethics in the Public Domain: Essays in the Morality of Law and Politics (Oxford, Clarendon Press, 1994) 37–40. See also Justice R Jackson, *The Supreme Court in the American System of Government* (Cambridge, Harvard University Press, 1955) 20–2, 51–4. Against, *West Virginia State Board of Education v Barnette*, 319 U.S. 642 (1973).

whatever human beings hold to as the underpinning reasons behind more immediate reasons for acting, for approving action, and for preferring certain ways of acting and states of affairs to others. They are as such themselves not necessarily backed by further or ulterior reasons.[20]

Political order is the complex of actors, both in their institutionalised forms and in the looser form of interest groups, and their relationships interrelating in the production of politics, ie of values then to be implemented into the community using the law-making. This order is characterised, in Weberian terminology, as having the primary criterion of action, the 'striving for a share of power or for influence on the distribution of power'.[21]

Political material is both the conceptual and ideological data shaped by the political actors (eg in political party programmes) but also those created and used by scholars in order to understand, explain and criticise the values chosen and the processes that have led to their selection (eg political scientists, moral philosophers, studies in economic policy).

In conclusion, it is necessary to note that hereafter, 'politics', 'politics of law' and 'legal politics' are used synonymously and, if nothing otherwise is specified, they all refer to the different aspects of the political phenomenon as seen from the perspective of the legal actors. Moreover, in particular when speaking of 'law-politics relations', the term 'politics' sometimes is used as synonymous to political phenomenon in general, ie also encompassing that which here has been defined as political order and political material.

---

[20] MacCormick, *H.L.A. Hart* (n 12 above) 48.
[21] M Weber, 'The Profession and Vocation of Politics' in P Lassman and R Speirs (eds), *Max Weber: Political Writings* (Cambridge, Cambridge University Press, 1994) 311. Power in this definition simply refers to the concrete capacity of forcing people do things that they otherwise are not willing to do. See M Weber, *The Theory of Social and Economic Organization* (T Parsons (ed), Glencoe, The Free Press, 1964) 152.

1

Law and Politics in Contemporary Legal Theory

A COUPLE OF years ago, Duxbury pointed out that 'the political nature of law represents a fundamental—if not the fundamental—problem of modern jurisprudence'.[1] As the legal theoretical interest in the issue of the relations between law and politics is so intense, this work examines from a legal theoretical perspective one specific moment of these relations. However, it is natural to first start from the very beginning: how do contemporary legal theories answer the question of how much politics there is in law.

After a brief clarification of the methodology used for tackling and systematising these positions, the approaches of the different legal theoretical streams are classified in three ideal-typical models. For the 'autonomous model' (legal positivism and analytical jurisprudence), the relations between law and politics are characterised as between two connected but still autonomous phenomena. The 'embedded model' (critical legal studies, law and economics, and John Finnis' natural law theory) depicts instead the law-politics relations as law embedded in politics. Finally, the American and Scandinavian legal realisms are presented as representatives of a third ideal-typical model, designated as 'intersecting', for within these theories, law and politics are two intersecting phenomena.

The chapter ends with a brief discussion as to how all three models, and the legal theories encompassed therein, share a common terrain. Each mirrors the peculiar situation of modern law: law and politics tend to keep the features of being two different phenomena as well as of presenting regions of interaction, although with differences as to extent and intensity.

I. LAW AND POLITICS DEBATE: DIFFERENT DIRECTIONS, SAME STARTING LINE

Before entering into the methodology of classifying the various legal theories as to their answer to the issue of the relations between law and

[1] N Duxbury, 'The Theory and History of American Law and Politics' (1993) 13 *OJLS* 270.

politics, one could probably question whether there is 'the' issue of law and politics. In other words, one could point out the fact that the contemporary legal theories, when facing the issue, tend to position themselves in different directions of discussion, ending then in discussing different things, somehow overlapping with each other but nevertheless pretty much recognisible as distinct.

One could easily argue, for example, that in the ninteenth century's codifications' debates which affected both Europe and the United States, the debate turned on the belief that 'the law'—meaning the common law, properly understood—somehow reflected something that was above mere politics. The 'correct' common law either reflected the spirit of a nation at a particular stage of development, the customs of the people, or perhaps even an ideal of rationality. By contrast, legislation, or in other terms the 'politician's law', was the importation of inappropriate foreign ideas or the mere reflection of temporary alliances of particular pressure groups. This idea of 'law vs. politics' thus turned on a fairly strong idea of the autonomy of law and legal reasoning, combined with doubts about the legitimacy or value of the 'politician's law' or legislation.[2]

Much more recently, on the other hand, critical legal studies (CLS) theorists stated that the basic starting point in order to understand the law is the recognition that 'law is politics'. This is largely a denial of the autonomy of legal reasoning, as it will be seen in this chapter, but where autonomy is understood in a less substantial way. Here the autonomy of legal reasoning (rebutted by CLS) would simply mean the understanding that judges can and should reach results that are independent of what the judges might subjectively prefer.[3] Even further, according to Scalia the issue of law and politics would mean simply that judges should not allow their decisions to be unconstrained by clear textual meaning or the American founding fathers' intentions; otherwise their decisions could be nothing other than their own political preferences.[4]

It is then true that most legal theories, even if they all speak of the 'law and politics' issue, in the end they speak of different directions or aspects of the issue. However, this chapter aims at pointing out that, though different legal theories discuss in different directions about whether and how politics and law relates, still they all have to ground their discussion

---

[2] See eg, FC Savigny (von), *System of the Modern Roman Law* (Westport, Hyperion Press, 1979) 31–40 (reprint 1867); and JC Carter, 'The Ideal and the Actual in the Law' (1890) 24 *American Law Review* 756, 772–5. See also M Reiman, 'The Historical School against Codification: Savigny, Carter, and the Defeat of the New York Civil Code' (1989) 37 *American Journal of Comparative Law* 97.

[3] See eg, RL Abel, 'Ideology and Community in the First Wave of Critical Legal Studies by Richard W. Bauman' (2003) 30 *Journal of Law and Society* 605 (book review).

[4] See eg, A Scalia, 'The Rule of Law as a Law of Rules' (1989) 56 *University of Chicago Law Review* 1184.

on 'groups' or 'ideal-typical ways' of considering law, law-making and legal discipline as having (or not) a political nature. In other words, the central point of this part of the work is exactly the one of bringing down the different legal theories from their different direction of debates and grouping them on a common starting line, ie common basic ways of perceiving law, law-making and legal discipline in relation to the political world.

For example, it is true that, when talking about the issue of law and politics, Hans Kelsen (and a good many other legal positivists) aims mainly to focus in the direction of what it will be soon defined as the epistemological aspect of the question, namely the possibility or not of investigating the law as separate from the political or moral discourse. Instead, CLS, as pointed out, move their attention mostly into the discussion of the 'dynamic' aspects of the issue, namely whether the black letter of a statute, a precedent or Constitution plays a role or not in the process leading to law-making judicial decisions or statutes 'implementing' the ideals of a Constitution.

Despite these different directions or level of debate, both Kelsen and CLS in the end need to ground their discussion on some ideas of how much of the political there is in law, law-making and legal discipline. For example, CLS focus on the politicisation of judicial activity as a starting point in an idea of law which is per se open to political influences. Conversely, Kelsen, stressing the fact that what he is aiming at is a 'pure' theory of law, starts from an idea of more or less ontological separation between what is law and what is politics.[5]

II. LAW, POLITICS AND LEGAL THEORY: A WAY TO TACKLE THE QUESTIONS

Modern law is subject to a system of forces towing it in opposite directions, affecting the very nature of the legal phenomenon. The very fact that these contemporary tensions stretch the law towards and, at the same time, away from politics, cannot leave the work of legal scholars unaffected.

Traces of these forces as operating on modern Western legal systems can then be detected in the positions taken by contemporary legal theories as to the issue of law and politics. On one side, contemporary legal scholars are inclined to be attracted into a dyadic way of solving the law and politics dilemma. Contemporary legal theories tend to depict the legal phenomenon either as being shaped by political powers or as dominated by its

---

[5] See eg, D Kairys, 'Law and Politics' (1984) 52 *George Washington Law Review* 245; and H Kelsen, 'On the Pure Theory of Law' (1966) 1 *Israel Law Review* 1.

internal rationality. On the other side, because of the commensurate strength of the forces pulling the law towards and away from politics, this dichotomy law-as-politics vs. law-or-politics remains a tendency. Contemporary legal theories then are stretched on a quantitatively and qualitatively broad spectrum of intermediary positions, where law is depicted as a mixture of political shaping and internal rationality.[6]

As these positions are so complicated and diffuse, the methodology of investigation and systematisation of contemporary legal theories and their positions on law and politics relations has been constructed on two major platforms: answers provided to fundamental issues as to the relations between law and politics; as well as a grouping in major ideal-typical models.

A. Fundamental Issues as to the Relations between Law and Politics

The perspective investigated in establishing the divisive line among the different theories primarily takes into consideration how legal scholars think law is related to politics.[7] The differences among the different theories have been drawn based more on how the schools and legal scholars define their positions on the law-politics issues than on how they have been categorised by their critics. This work focuses on whether such theories explicitly embrace the idea that law and politics have to be studied as two different phenomena, as two similar phenomena or as two intersecting phenomena. Once this perspective for the investigation of the contemporary legal theories is chosen, the second step is to summarise three aspects, the static, dynamic and epistemological, as to the major issues taken into consideration in the debate about the relations between law and politics.

(i) Static Aspect: What Distinguishes Law from Politics?

Only a few exceptions can be found among legal scholars claiming that the content of the law is either completely independent from or completely dependent upon politics, particularly after the growth of the nation state. As to this first aspect, the content of the law cannot be viewed as

---

[6] See R Cotterrell, *Law's Community: Legal Theory in Sociological Perspective* (Oxford, Clarendon Press, 1995) 165–66, 277–8. See also J Raz, 'On the Functions of Law' in AWB Simpson (ed), *Oxford Essays in Jurisprudence (Second Series)* (Oxford, Clarendon Press, 1973) 280–8.

[7] The question of *why* legal scholars think in terms of law and politics, namely what are their sociological, political or moral backgrounds, is then not addressed here. See eg, R Nobles and D Schiff, *A Sociology of Jurisprudence* (Oxford, Hart Publishing, 2006) 1–18; or R Cotterrell, *The Politics of Jurisprudence: A Critical Introduction to Legal Philosophy* (2nd edn, London, Lexis Nexis, 2003) 13–19.

completely independent from politics because the organisational political form of the nation state is characterised, in part, by the very fact that the law is a tool available to political actors in order to effectuate programmes within a certain community.

On the other hand, the content of the law does not usually completely disappear into politics. The nation state has brought with it the principle of the separation of powers. From an institutional point of view, this implies that the actors legislating a statute are not the same as those applying it. Moreover, the increasing specialisation and sophistication of legal categories and concepts have made it almost obligatory for politicians to employ persons educated in the specific art of drafting laws.

As this is the environment in which most contemporary legal scholars live and work, it is then almost natural that the vast majority of scholars claim that the content of the law is separate from or identified with politics only to a certain extent. In spite of this common ground, it is possible, in particular among the major schools, to find a dividing line based on the issue of whether the political substance or message the law always carries also affects the structures and forms of the law itself.[8]

The divisive question then becomes whether the law is flexible by nature, ie whether it tends to adapt its forms and nature according to the political substances it carries; or, alternatively, whether the law is rigid, ie whether it tends to keep the same forms and nature regardless of political content. The central question is whether the law, as perceived by legal actors, changes its shape and manner of functioning in accordance with the values the political actors are aiming to implement in a community.[9]

(ii) Dynamic Aspect: How Does Law-making Interrelate with the Political Order?

Moving to the second dynamic aspect of the relationship between law and politics, the legal schools address the functioning of law-making here as an alternative or dependent process with respect to the political order and its processes. This is particularly true when the aim of politics is to control the entire life of a community, all its social, economic and cultural aspects. This aim is typical of the nation state, taken to its extreme by the welfare state and, although in very different forms, by totalitarian regimes such as the Nazi and the Soviet ones. Law-making in its functioning appears to be more and more an integral part of the political machinery. The process of

---

[8] See eg, the famous debate between HLA Hart, 'Positivism and the Separation of Law and Morals' (1958) 71 *Harvard Law Review* 615 and L Fuller, 'Positivism and Fidelity to Law:A Reply to Professor Hart' (1958) 71 *Harvard Law Review* 648.

[9] See A Aarnio, *Reason and Authority: A Treatise on the Dynamic Paradigm of Legal Dogmatics* (Cambridge, Harvard University Press, 1997) 20–25.

the creation of new legal norms, categories and concepts is viewed as strongly affected by the political environment.

On the other hand, there is a tendency towards an increasing specialisation of the legal world, making it more difficult for the political order to interfere with the work of the courts, lawyers and legal scholars. Moreover, the growing establishment of the rule of law has generally taken away any complete freedom of action from the political sphere, limiting the political influences inside the legal world and the law-making mechanisms to certain specific areas and through specific modalities of action.[10]

These diverging tendencies, affecting relations between the law-making and the political order, also impact legal theory. A line of demarcation can be drawn between the theories according to the solutions presented as to the question of whether law-making operates by its own rules and mechanisms, ie the idea of a closed law-making, or whether it simply is integrated into the larger political order, ie the idea of an open law-making.[11]

(iii) Epistemological Aspect: to What Degree does the Legal Discipline take into Consideration the Political Material?

The assembling of the different contemporary legal theories into an ideal-type model has also been done according to the answers given to a third question: to what extent does the legal discipline take into consideration the political material in its work, ie the epistemological aspect of the relationship between law and politics. This issue is a typical, although not exclusive, province of contemporary legal theories. With the growth of politics as an autonomous object of investigation, and with the rise of political science faculties in various Western universities, legal scholars began to focus on whether and to what extent their discipline was influenced by categories and concepts developed in non-legal academic environments.

The environment surrounding universities and research institutions complicates this epistemological question. On one side, there is a socio-political reality always pushing towards the integration of the law into a broader political context and encouraging a more political approach to the study of law, an approach more oriented towards the goals of the law that are external to the legal system itself. On the other side, there is also the tendency towards an increasing specialisation of both the legal profession and the legal conceptual apparatus, a tendency urging the constitution of

---

[10] See H Berman, *Law and Revolution: the Formation of the Western Legal Tradition* (Cambridge, Harvard University Press, 1983) 9–10; and P Stein and J Shand, *Legal Values in Western Society* (Edinburgh, Edinburgh University Press, 1974) 32–4.

[11] *See* Aarnio, *Reason and Authority* (n 9 above) 53–4.

disciplines focusing only on purely legal technical matters, addressing only the language of the law and leaving politics to the politicians.

This tension has led to two different approaches toward the issue of the purity of that which is considered within the legal discipline. The first is the pure approach to legal studies, embracing all those theories claiming the necessity of a legal discipline not contaminated by political categories and concepts such as 'democracy' or 'legitimisation'. The second is the mixed approach to legal studies, maintained by those scholars asserting the necessity of integrating into the legal discipline categories and concepts not specifically belonging to the legal language, but still relevant in order to fully understand current legal phenomenon.

B. Ideal-Type as a Heuristic Device

By examining the positions taken by contemporary legal theories with respect to these three aspects, an ideal-typology of three models is presented: an autonomous model, an embedded model and an intersecting model. Similarly to the utility of Weber's ideal-types when applied to the complexity of social reality, these models are intended to be a heuristic device helpful for mapping out the complex world of contemporary legal theories. Moreover, they assist in revealing certain similar fundamental ways of understanding the relation of law and politics, similarities among legal movements otherwise treated as very distinct from each other (eg between CLS and law and economics).[12]

Naturally, there are limitations with respect to the use of the ideal-typologies as heuristic devices in order to classify the positions of the different legal schools in the models as to these aspects. In particular, a limitation arises from the fact that the classification according to the typologies used here is loosely based on the ideal-type methodology of Weber.[13] Subsequently, when it comes to the single scholar or even less to a legal philosophical movement, it is not possible in reality to sharply distinguish between the theories or the legal scholars falling within the 'pure' embedded model or the 'pure' autonomous model. On the contrary, as the models are ideal-types, most legal theories and legal scholars would actually never fit in one model or another. It is more likely that they would be placed in-between, as contemporary legal scholars tend to embrace a certain model, but almost always with one or more features from the

---

[12] For a similar use of ideal-types in order to map out different legal theoretical positions about the issue of law and society, see R Gordon, 'Critical Legal Histories' (1984) 36 *Stanford Law Review* 59.
[13] See M Weber, *The Methodology of the Social Sciences* (E Shils and H Finch (eds), New York, Free Press, 1949) 99–100. See also A Ross, *Why Democracy?* (Cambridge, Harvard University Press, 1952) 87.

others. The manifest presence in modern societies of multiple and often conflicting tendencies softens the positions of even the more radical individual scholars. For example, a recently developed mitigated version of legal positivistic incorporationism has no problem in stating 'a moral principle can be a necessary condition for the status of a norm as a legal norm'.[14]

Although accepting the substantial validity of such possible methodological objections, one should also keep in mind that in this work, the ideal-type models are used in accordance with Weber as heuristic devices, ie as tools and not aims for the investigation. The models presented here therefore cannot be considered photographs, faithfully representing the reality of how contemporary legal theories consider law and politics relations. Instead, they more resemble surrealistic paintings used in order to begin a process of interpretation and evaluation of such a reality.

Each ideal-type model epitomises in its pure form certain features of how legal scholars depict the relationship between law and politics. In this way, although not fully ascribable specifically to one theory or one legal scholar, the models nevertheless can be helpful in revealing certain fundamental streams or tendencies that link or differentiate the various contemporary legal theories and their representative scholars.[15]

The analysis of the different contemporary legal theories and their positions as to the relation between the legal and the political phenomenon can now begin, supported by this methodology.

III. EITHER LAW OR POLITICS: THE AUTONOMOUS MODEL

One of the tasks most often pursued by legal scholars beginning in the second half of the nineteenth and throughout the entirety of the twentieth century has been that of trying to categorise the legal phenomenon as a specific phenomenon. In this pursuit, many scholars have embraced that which can be portrayed as an autonomous model when viewing the relationship between law and politics. The relationship is one between two autonomous phenomena, processes of creation and exploratory disciplines. Embracing the autonomous model means that despite acknowledging the presence of contacts between law and politics, the inner nature of the law and its functioning and consequently also its analysis can only be described in terms and categories particular and specific to the law itself, with sparse relations to non-legal systems, in particular the political system. Included

---

[14]   M Kramer, *Where Law and Morality Meet* (Oxford, Oxford University Press, 2004) 17.
[15]   See eg, *ibid* 42–3. See also *ibid* 230.

among the schools adopting such an ideal-type model for describing the relationship between the law and politics are legal positivism and analytical jurisprudence.

It is true, as pointed out by Bix, that legal positivism and analytical jurisprudence stress their idea of a separation between the study of law and the study of politics.[16] However, the purpose of this part consists of showing how this clear separation between two kinds of disciplines or studies ultimately is based on or presupposes the very idea of actual separation between the two objects of those studies: between the very law and the very politics.[17]

Recent developments within legal positivism, in particular in the inclusive and incorporationist directions, do not significantly affect the idea embraced here, that legal positivism in general can be seen as tendentiously depicting an image of autonomy of the legal phenomenon from the political one. When it comes to the issue of the relationship between law and politics, both the inclusive, incorporationist and exclusive legal positivisms appear to remain anchored in the general legal positivistic idea that the law is something per se different from the political phenomenon and the kind of moral, economic or cultural values that the latter expresses.[18]

Although not examined in this work, it is worth mentioning that another important legal school embraces the autonomous model: Luhmann's autopoietic approach to the law, and in particular its full development inside the legal world as argued by Teubner.[19] Kelsen, Hart, the autopoietic approach, and even the most recent developments of legal positivism converge therefore towards a similar position where they all 'emphasize the closed character and autonomy of a legal system impermeable to extralegal principles'.[20]

A. The Rigidity of Law from Politics

A common point of departure for each of these schools and scholars is the fact that the law is considered, more or less, as structurally rigid against

---

[16] See B Bix, *Jurisprudence: Theory and Context* (3rd edn, London, Sweet & Maxwell, 2003) 33–4. See also R Posner, *The Problems of Jurisprudence* (Cambridge, Harvard University Press, 1990) 24.

[17] See Cotterrell, *The Politics of Jurisprudence* (n 7 above) 106–7.

[18] See J Raz, 'The Problem about the Nature of Law' in J Raz, *Ethics in the Public Domain: Essays in the Morality of Law and Politics* (Oxford, Clarendon Press, 1994) 192; Kramer, *Where Law and Morality Meet* (n 14 above) 223–44; W Waluchow, 'Authority and the Practical Difference Thesis: a Defense of Inclusive Legal Positivism' (2000) 6 *Legal Theory* 80.

[19] See N Luhmann, 'Law as Social System' (1989) 83 *Northwestern University Law Review* 136; and G Teubner, 'Introduction to Autopoietic Law' in G Teubner (ed), *Autopoietic Law: a New Approach to Law and Society* (Berlin, Walter de Gruyter, 1988) 1–2. See also Cotterrell, *Law's Community* (n 6 above) 105–8.

[20] J Habermas, *Between Facts and Norms: Contributions to a Discourse Theory of Law and Democracy* (Cambridge, The MIT Press, 1998) 202.

politics. The rigidity of the law entails that the law is based, in its definition, on forms and structures that tend to remain constant regardless of the political content given to them or the political environment in which they operate. The law does not lose its nature simply because it is filled with inhuman content, for example the orders of a dictator instead of decisions taken by a democratically elected Parliament. The law is the law for the very reason that its most characteristic feature, its normativity, can be properly derived only from an internal, legal perspective. In the end, for legal positivism and analytical jurisprudence, the law certainly is open to receiving contributions to its content from the surrounding political world in terms of values; the structures of the law (either in terms of *Sollen* or of legal language), however, still tend to be rigid, ie to remain the same no matter the values that enter.[21]

For example, Kelsen recognises that both the law and politics try to make people do something, the law being 'a social order, that is to say an order regulating the mutual behavior of human beings'.[22] Further, law and politics both have the same characteristic in that they try to establish a bridge by means of the law of imputation (if someone performs an abortion, then he or she must/ought to be imprisoned) between two elements (abortion and imprisonment) not connected by any cause-effect relation in the natural world.[23]

For Kelsen, the essence of the law as distinct from politics is traceable instead to the distinction between a subjective and an objective meaning of legal statements. The fundamental difference is the fact that the ultimate constituting elements of the political dimension of the law are the subjective meanings of the law itself, ie the meanings attached to the legal statement by the actor creating it in terms of commands or requests. The political dimension of the law consists in the feelings expressed in subjective meaning ('abortion must be punished') addressed to the community. Political statements are statements advertising the values one wishes to implement into the community through the use of legal tools.[24]

The law, in contrast to politics, is constituted of a system of norms, 'a person who commits an abortion ought to be punished with x years imprisonment'. This complex of norms has objective meanings not given to them by the subjective intent of the enactor but by the location of such

---

[21] See eg, J Gardner, 'Legal Positivism: 5 ½ Myths' (2001) 46 *American Journal of Jurisprudence* 201.

[22] H Kelsen, 'Law, State, and Justice in the Pure Theory of Law' in H Kelsen, *What is Justice? Justice, Law, and Politics in the Mirror of Science* (Berkeley, University of California Press, 1957) 289.

[23] See H Kelsen, *The Pure Theory of Law* (Berkeley, University of California Press, 1970) 89–91.

[24] See *ibid* 2–3. See also H Kelsen, *Allgemeine Staatslehre* (Berlin, Julius Springer, 1925) 28.

norms in a wider and hierarchical construction of other legal norms (*Stufenbau*). The meanings of legal norms are objective as they can only be derived from a construction situated outside the subjective perspectives of the legislator, judge, scholar or politician: the normative reality of Ought, the reality of the legal system.[25]

The Kelsenian separation of law from politics occurs at the structural level, not at the material level. Kelsen is well aware that the content of the law depends upon political considerations. However, he recognises this dependency only as to the content of the objective meanings constituting the system of norms, not to their nature. In the end, law is structurally separated from politics because a characteristic of the law is that it is formed by a specific and distinctive type of means (the legal norms), keeping its internal structure regardless of the varying political messages it is charged with during its formation or its application to concrete cases.[26]

Although analytical jurisprudence is often considered a part of the more general movement of legal positivism, its patterns of approaching the question of how the law relates to politics differ considerably. Hart openly acknowledges that the legal system belongs to a wider social reality and that legal rules are a specific kind of social rules grounded upon social practices.[27]

Hart's recognition of the fact that the values arising from the social environment fill the legal system with a certain content does not, however, imply that he considers such values as having a constitutive role in the nature and structure of the legal system as built upon these very values. Basing his investigation of the legal system and its constitutive parts on an analysis of the legal language, Hart focuses on the features present in certain legal concepts, that is in logical-linguistic unities of different legal rules.[28] Considering the legal language from an internal perspective, Hart arrives at the conclusion that it still is possible to identify the constitutive features of the system of legal rules as not derived, at least directly, from the value-world, either as politics or as morals. Such features peculiar to the legal system, namely its generality, persistency and the general habit of

[25] See Kelsen, *The Pure Theory of Law* (n 23 above) 3–5. Although beginning with different patterns, Waldron more or less arrives at the same conclusion. See J Waldron, *Law and Disagreement* (Oxford, Oxford University Press, 1999) 144.

[26] See Kelsen, 'On the Pure Theory of Law' (n 5 above) 5. See also T Honoré, 'The Basic Norm of a Society' in SL Paulson and B Litschewski Paulson (eds), *Normativity and Norms: Critical Perspectives on Kelsenian Themes* (Oxford, Clarendon Press, 1998) 94.

[27] See HLA Hart, *The Concept of Law* (Oxford, Clarendon Press, 1961) 80; and HLA Hart, 'Postscript' in HLA Hart, *The Concept of Law* (PA Bulloch and J Raz (eds), 2nd edn, Oxford, Clarendon Press, 1994) 240, 255.

[28] See HLA Hart, 'Problems of the Philosophy of Law' in HLA Hart, *Essays in Jurisprudence and Philosophy* (Oxford, Clarendon Press, 1983) 90. See also J Coleman, 'Second Thoughts and Other First Impressions' in B Bix (ed), *Analyzing Law: New Essays in Legal Theory* (Oxford, Clarendon Press, 1998) 258.

obedience, remain the same, characterising the legal phenomenon regardless of the moral or political values (and the issues attached to them), which the rules are loaded with or built upon. The law in the end is a linguistic tool whose essence then tends to be grounded upon, but still autonomous from, all of the values for whose implementation into the community the tool is being used.[29]

It is true that Hart stresses as a characteristic aspect of legal concepts the fact that they have a core of established meanings surrounded by a penumbra of uncertain meanings. It then can be argued that political criteria actually should come into the depiction of law as given by Hart when it comes to deciding cases falling into the penumbral meaning of a certain legal concept. Hart himself is well aware of the possibility of such criticism and counters it by restating that vagueness and ambiguity do not mean that the concepts are, in this penumbral area, politicised. Even this penumbra, Hart argues, usually does not allow political concepts and categories to come into the area reserved to the legal concepts. This area of uncertainty as to legal concepts and categories does not belong to politics; it is an integral part of Hart's idea of law as it is an expression of linguistic or conceptual problems.[30]

According to Hart, continuity exists between the core and penumbra of a certain legal concept, consisting of the fact that legal language, as many other languages, tends to have an open texture. The introduction of non-legal linguistic criteria (such as the evaluation of social policy in a decision by a judge) breaks it (ie one goes outside the text into a reality different from the linguistic one), not allowing us to see that there is a legal rationality, specific to the world of legal language, behind the many apparently discrepant uses of the same term.[31]

B. Closing the Law-Making to the Political Order

This rigidity of the law, as intended by the theories within the autonomous model, tends to be translated into a closedness of law-making towards other orders in general and the political order in particular. The closedness of law-making in the autonomous model results from the view by legal

---

[29] See Hart, *The Concept of Law* (n 27 above) 21–3, 49—50, 73; and HLA Hart, 'Commands and Authoritative Legal Reasons' in HLA Hart, *Essays on Bentham: Jurisprudence and Political Theory* (Oxford, Clarendon Press, 1982) 254–5. Compare J Coleman, *The Practice of Principle: In Defence of a Pragmatist Approach to Legal Theory* (Oxford, Oxford University Press 2003) 81–3.

[30] See Hart, 'Positivism and the Separation of Law and Morals' (n 8 above) 607–8. See also B Bix, *Law, Language, and Legal Determinacy* (Oxford, Clarendon Press, 1993) 35.

[31] See Hart, 'Positivism and the Separation of Law and Morals' (n 8 above) 614–15; and HLA Hart, 'Analytical Jurisprudence in Mid-Twentieth Century: a Reply to Professor Bodenheimer' (1957) 105 *University of Pennsylvania Law Review* 956, 963 fn 20, 968.

positivists and analytical legal philosophers that law-making receives inputs from the political order (eg in form of legislative propositions) but once these inputs arrive into the law-making, their treatment is purely according to the rationality and parameters offered by the legal order itself. The workings of law-making and its results (eg enacted statutes, judicial opinions, scholarly works) are influenced by the battles and victorious parties in the political arena only before they are translated into legal categories and concepts, that is only before the political instances are converted into law.

The political order is seen by these theories mainly as the arena in which the goals law-making is to fulfil are evaluated and decided. Law-making, on the other side, is perceived as a politically neutral machine in that it tends to be detached in its way of functioning, producing and creatively applying the law, from the political processes and the various value-contents the different political actors wish to give to their use of the legal machinery.[32] The legal system is influenced in its operational aspects only by an extremely limited (and mostly at the highest constitutional level) number of inputs coming from the political discourse.

The answers produced by legal positivism and analytical jurisprudence are similar. They both try to save the closedness of law-making and legal application mechanisms by referring to a highest binding legal norm. Most of the time, this is implicit in a national legal system and establishes the fundamental normative criteria used in order to separate that which belongs to the legal system (the valid law) from that which belongs to the political system (a political statement).

According to Kelsen, from a dynamic perspective the legal system can be seen as a hierarchical system in which the legal validity of certain norms, ie their being the carrier of an objective meaning, is ensured by the fact that a higher norm has given this objective quality to certain subjects and their declarations, when expressed according to certain forms and procedure. In its turn, the higher valid norm takes its own objective meaning from an even higher norm, for example, a constitutional norm establishing the procedure and competence of a Parliament when enacting a statute.[33]

The result, after all the steps are taken, is that the foundation of the validity of the entire legal system is based completely on that which Kelsen calls the Basic Norm. It is the Basic Norm that decides which subjective

---

[32] See eg, Kelsen, *The Pure Theory of Law* (n 23 above) 63. See also J Waldron, 'Legislation, Authority, and Voting' (1996) 84 *Georgetwon Law Journal* 2189.

[33] See H Kelsen, *General Theory of Law and State* (Cambridge, Harvard University Press, 1949) 128–35; and Kelsen, *The Pure Theory of Law* (n 23 above) 8–10, 233–6. See also J Raz, 'Kelsen's Theory of the Basic Norm' in Paulson and Litschewski Paulson (eds), *Normativity and Norms* (n 26 above) 50. But see C Santiago Nino, 'Confusions surrounding Kelsen's Concept of Validity' in Paulson and Litschewski Paulson (eds), *Normativity and Norms* (n 26 above) 256–8.

instances, eg political statements, are allowed to enter, at the various steps of the hierarchical system (*Stufenbau*), into the legal system and then acquire an objective meaning, becoming valid law. The Basic Norm is important then in the interrelationship between the political and legal systems for its transcendental-logical function throughout the entire law-making. It is the key passage presupposed by the legal actors for determining that which remains within the subjective meaning of politics, and that which can acquire the objective meaning of law.[34]

However, consistent with his legal positivistic premises, Kelsen clearly emphasises the lack of interest of the legal system as to the content of the Basic Norm. That which is relevant within law-making is that the Basic Norm performs the function of transforming non-legal instances (or values) into valid law. The choice of the types of instances the Basic Norm determines as legally relevant is not interesting to the legal actors, whether it is the political value of obeying the first constitution or the value of obedience to the Fuehrer. The Kelsenian law-making is then a complex of mechanisms, procedures and actors which tend to work in the same way (and according to their own criterion of legal validity), unaffected by the processes and the results happening in the political order.[35]

Hart also feels the need, as did Kelsen, to identify a normative turning point, a crossroad that allows and controls when and how the inputs coming from the political order can enter into the legal one. Hart's closure of the procedures and mechanisms of creation and implementation of the law is evidenced by the fact that the turning point transforming political inputs into legal categories or rules is a presupposed valid secondary rule (Rule of Recognition), ie 'a rule for conclusive identification of the primary rules of obligation'.[36] The transformation of political statements into law is regulated inside the legal order with the use of legal categories such as competence or validity, and not from the political order, with the use of political categories such as 'social justice' or 'democracy'. Hart's legal theory thus portrays the law as tending to be a self-regulating system of rules, whose way of working in the acceptance or rejection of political instances is based on the norms themselves.[37]

It is true that for Hart, the Rule of Recognition is of an empirical nature in the sense that it can only be revealed by looking at how the legal actors

---

[34] See Kelsen, *The Pure Theory of Law* (n 23 above) 193–5; and Kelsen, *General Theory of Law and State* (n 33 above) 116–17.

[35] See Kelsen, *The Pure Theory of Law* (n 23 above) 217–18. See also J Raz, *The Concept of a Legal System: An Introduction to the Theory of Legal System* (2nd edn, Oxford, Clarendon Press, 1980) 100; and JW Harris, 'When and Why Does the Grundnorm Change?' (1971) 29 *CLJ* 116.

[36] Hart, *The Concept of Law* (n 27 above) 92.

[37] See Cotterrell, *The Politics of Jurisprudence* (n 7 above) 94–5; and J Coleman, 'Rules and Social Facts' (1991) 14 *Harvard Journal of Law and Public Policy* 707.

actually think; therefore the social context is the ultimate foundation of the validity of the legal system.[38] However, that which is most relevant for Hartian law-making is not how such empirical evidence of the ultimate foundation of the validity of the legal system (eg the general social approval of the latter as 'just'), although fundamental for its existence and working, objectively appears, in other words, its external perspective. Instead, it is how such empirical data is perceived inside the legal order itself, rather its internal, or normative, perspective.[39]

For example, this normative feature of the Rule of Recognition, relevant for law-making, is confirmed by one of the essential aspects for the existence of a legal order itself, that is its continuity. For Hart, the more radical upheavals in a political order (eg, a revolution) do not affect the manner in which law-making functions in a society. The latter always has as a point of departure for its functioning an Ought-statement, a rule internally perceived by legal actors, prescribing that the new law-giver has the right to enact new legal norms. The 'Rule of Recognition ... [is the] first step from the pre-legal to the legal', but not as a political product of a revolution, but as 'the acknowledgement of reference to the writing or inscription as authoritative, i.e. as the proper way of disposing of doubts as to the existence of the rule'.[40]

C. A Legal Discipline Purified of Political Material

Moving to the issue of how the legal discipline should relate itself and its investigations in general to politics and political material, the theories within the autonomous model usually deny any need for the presence of political elements within the legal analysis. The legal discipline, as with natural or social sciences, is defined as an autonomous branch of knowledge precisely due to its autonomous working space, the law. As the law is described in a rigid terminology, ie making use only of strictly legal terms

---

[38] *See* Hart, *The Concept of Law* (n 27 above) 92. By basing the Rule of Recognition upon the social context, certain of Hart's commentators refer to a 'social thesis' as implicitly endorsed in his idea of law. See W Waluchow, 'The Weak Social Thesis' (1989) 9 *OJLS* 26; and J Raz, 'Legal Positivism and the Sources of Law' in J Raz, *The Authority of Law: Essays on Law and Morality* (Oxford, Oxford University Press, 1979) 37.

[39] See Hart, 'Postscript' (n 27 above) 255–7. See also Coleman, *The Practice of Principle* (n 29 above) 77–83. Compare the critique in L Murphy, 'The Political Question of the Concept of Law' in J Coleman (ed), *Hart's Postscript: Essays on the Postscript to the Concept of Law* (Oxford, Oxford University Press, 2001) 372, who in the end is forced to identify the Rule of Recognition with a legal entity ('constitutional provision').

[40] Hart, *The Concept of Law* (n 27 above) 92. See also R Sartorius, 'Hart's Concept of Law' in R Summers (ed), *More Essays in Legal Philosophy* (Oxford, Basil Blackwell, 1971) 157. Through a slightly different pattern, the inclusive legal positivism reaches the same conclusion as Hart does. See eg, W Waluchow, *Inclusive Legal Positivism* (Oxford, Clarendon Press, 1994) 39.

and qualities, it seems almost natural for the theories falling within the autonomous model to promote a 'pure' idea of the legal discipline. The legal phenomenon is to be purified of any political dust, or in other words, of the categories and concepts typical for other scientific branches, such as political science or sociology.[41]

As seen above, the legal scholars within the autonomous model rarely claim that the phenomenon the legal scholar is to investigate (ie the object of the pure legal science) lacks any connection whatsoever with other systems, such as political or social ones. However, in order to discover the basic structures of the law, legal scholars have to pass through the empirical dust surrounding the legal phenomenon, through the different subjective meanings attached to the law (as in Kelsen) or the political usage of the legal language (as in Hart). They have to go deep into the core of the law and fulfil the primary goal of the legal discipline: to identify, describe and investigate the positive law as it objectively is expressed in legal norms.[42]

For example, Kelsen starts by directly pointing out how legal politics and legal science are different from the psychological and sociological approaches to the legal phenomenon for the very ontology of the object of investigation. Within psychology, for example, an object of investigation is the human will, intended as an empirical manifestation of a bio-psychological being living in the space-time reality. In contrast, legal politics and legal science focus on the personal will, that is an expression in the world of Ought, coming from an entity existing only as far as the ethical and legal systems recognise it.[43]

However, in the famous *incipit* of Kelsen's *The Pure Theory of Law*, legal politics is in its turn clearly distinguished from legal science. The political approach to the legal phenomenon is characterised by the fact that the central point of the investigation is not the reality of the law (law as it is), but the interests and conflicts behind the law (how the law ought to be or be produced).[44]

In contrast, legal work, in order to be defined as scientific, has to rationally explain the reality of the law. The law, at least for those parts

---

[41] See H Kelsen, *Introduction to the Problems of Legal Theory* (Oxford, Clarendon Press, 1996) 18–19.

[42] See eg, HLA Hart, 'Definition and Theory in Jurisprudence' in Hart, *Essays in Jurisprudence and Philosophy* (n 28 above) 47; Kelsen, *The Pure Theory of Law* (n 23 above) 70; Waluchow, *Inclusive Legal Positivism* (n 40 above) 15–30; or G Postema, 'The Normativity of Law' in R Gavinson (ed), *Issues in Contemporary Legal Philosophy: the Influence of H.L.A. Hart* (Oxford, Clarendon Press, 1987) 85.

[43] See H Kelsen, *Über Grenzen zwischen juristischer und soziologischer Methode* (1970) 52–5.

[44] See Kelsen, *The Pure Theory of Law* (n 23 above) 1. As to the ambiguity of the term 'legal science' in the Kelsenian writings, see S Paulson, 'Appendix I: Supplementary Notes' in H Kelsen, *Introduction to the Problems of Legal Theory* (n 41 above) 127–31.

dealt with by the legal discipline, does not consist of either interests or conflicts, but of a system of norms. Legal scientists then should not be interested in the type of values that are or should be transformed into law, as their content is irrelevant for the functioning and the very existence (validity) of the legal system. That which matters to the legal scholar is finding out whether the norms under investigation are valid law, ie whether they are part of a valid legal system or, in other words, can be derived from an existing Basic Norm.[45]

Despite the slide into the world of empirical reality through the idea that valid law is derived from an existing Basic Norm, ie observable in the concrete behaviours of the majority of a community, it still remains clear that according to Kelsen, the legal scholar, in order to study the legal machinery and its way of working, does not need to know either who the driver behind the wheel is or the direction the car will be driven. For him, the tools of investigation have to be compatible with the object of investigation, the legal order; therefore, using concepts such as 'justice' or 'democracy' misleads the entire investigation, since the focus then no longer is on the objective legal machinery but on the subjective choice of goals, for whose fulfilment such machinery is used. On the contrary, pure concepts such as validity, competence and legal persons are welcome in the Kelsenian construction, as their origins and ends are entirely inside the legal world, ie inside the legal machinery, and therefore entirely Ought-statements.[46]

The same ideal of a pure legal discipline is present in Hart's analysis, although he starts from a point quite distant from Kelsen's. While Kelsen focuses his attention on the clear distinction between subjective and objective meanings attached to the law, the major concern for Hart is pointing out that the peculiar features of the legal phenomenon (eg generality, continuity, etc) are given to it by the fact that specific words and concepts are used in a specific context. It is pointless for the legal discipline to define single words such as 'right' and 'corporation' outside the linguistic context. The legal discipline, on the contrary, has to move in two specific directions, internal and external to the legal order. Both directions tend to be normatively pure, as they both take as their point of departure how the concepts are conceived and used inside the legal order by the legal actors, or in Hartian terminology, their internal aspect. The declared

---

[45] See H Kelsen, 'The Pure Theory of Law and Analytical Jurisprudence' (1941) 55 *Harvard Law Review* 49; and Kelsen, *The Pure Theory of Law* (n 23 above) 86–7, 210. See also Raz, 'The Problem about the Nature of Law' (n 18 above) 185.

[46] See Kelsen, 'The Pure Theory of Law and Analytical Jurisprudence' (n 45 above) 51; and Kelsen, *The Pure Theory of Law* (n 23 above) 73–5. See for critiques J Raz, 'The Purity of the Pure Theory' in R Tur and W Twining (eds), *Essays on Kelsen* (Oxford, Clarendon Press, 1986) 82; and HLA Hart, 'Kelsen Visited' in Paulson and Litschewski Paulson (eds), *Normativity and Norms* (n 26 above) 70–6.

internal task of the legal discipline, however, is quite traditional and shared with the other legal theories. It consists of putting the different legal concepts on the map of legal thinking. The legal discipline has to properly construct the conceptual apparatus used in its work.[47]

The external task—and here comes the original contribution—is founded on Hart's basic idea that the law is characterised by using words in a particular manner. This particularity is given to them by the legal context in which such words and concepts operate. This must be done in order to clarify the specific meanings such concepts and categories acquire, as well as to distinguish them from the use such concepts can have in ordinary everyday or political language. The task of the legal discipline is 'the elucidation of the use of [legal] words in characteristic legal contexts'.[48]

With the help of the linguistic scrutiny offered by analytical jurisprudence, the legal discipline can draw a clear line between the normative uses of terms such as 'corporation' or 'rights', and other uses by sciences studying law as a psychological, social, moral or political phenomenon. In this manner, Hart excludes from the materials available to the legal discipline sociological investigations of how certain legal concepts are perceived in society and the political science investigations as to the type of uses a certain political actor has of certain legal categories.

Hart does not deny that some general benefits can be derived from knowing that which is going on with respect, for example, to the frontiers of moral philosophy, political sciences or sociology.[49] However, and this is repeatedly stressed by Hart, this can only be an activity complementary to the fundamental normative core of legal science. Similarly to Kelsen, Hart then promotes a legal discipline which cannot gain any essential advantage from other non-purely normative materials and methodologies because of both the peculiarity of its object of investigation and the fact that 'legal notions ... can be elucidated by *methods properly adapted* to their special character', ie analytical methods[50] (emphasis added).

---

[47] See Hart, 'Analytical Jurisprudence in Mid-Twentieth Century' (n 31 above) 972. See also Murphy, 'The Political Question of the Concept of Law' (n 39 above) 380; and S Perry, 'Hart's Methodological Positivism' in Coleman (ed), *Hart's Postscript* (n 39 above) 342–7.

[48] Hart, 'Analytical Jurisprudence in Mid-Twentieth Century' (n 31 above) 961–2. See also Hart, *The Concept of Law* (n 27 above) chs II, IV; and N MacCormick, *H.L.A. Hart* (Stanford, Stanford University Press, 1981) 29.

[49] See eg, HLA Hart, 'Abortion Law Reform: the English Experience' (1972) 8 *Melbourne University Law Review* 394, 400–8. See also Coleman, *The Practice of Principle* (n 29 above) 199–201.

[50] Hart, 'Definition and Theory in Jurisprudence' (n 42 above) 21. See also Raz, 'The Purity of the Pure Theory' (n 46 above) 96–7; and Coleman, 'Rules and Social Facts' (n 37 above) 715–17. Compare F Schauer, 'Constitutional Positivism' (1993) 25 *Connecticut Law Review* 800.

IV. LAW IS POLITICS: THE EMBEDDED MODEL

The slogan 'law is politics' summarises, although in a quite rudimentary manner, the central perspective adopted by the theories and scholars ascribed as the embedded model with respect to the relationship between law and politics. To state that the law is embedded within politics, according to this model, means that the legal phenomenon is nested within the political phenomenon.[51]

This embedded relationship between law and politics is viewed as a two-systems relation in which the legal system is embedded within the wider context of the political order. In this model, the interrelationships and exchanges between the two phenomena are frequent, eg, from the drafting of statutes to the legal reasoning of judges, as well as disseminated within all the levels, from the structures and nature of the law to the manner in which the legal discipline is portrayed. This frequency of exchange often renders it very difficult to identify distinctive features within the legal phenomenon.

The embedded model unites under its flag several and, as to certain aspects, quite contrasting legal theories: contemporary natural law theories, CLS and the school of law and economics. Though they are not investigated in this part of the work, public choice theory, and the movement of law and society can be considered as also endorsing a view of law as embedded in the political phenomenon.[52]

A. The Flexibility of the Law towards Politics

For this heterogeneous group of theories, the law becomes an integral part of a wider context, the political and moral environment in which statutes, judgments and other legal production take place. A certain norm or category becomes fully legal, ie truly binding for the community, only if it fulfils certain requirements determined by this external environment. These can be requirements such as 'goodness' or 'justice', and also those of 'efficiency' or 'fidelity'.

The theories covered by the embedded model can generally be distinguished from those of the autonomous model for considering as a constitutive part of the law the economic, moral or *stricto sensu* political

---

[51] See A Hunt, 'The Politics of Law and the Law of Politics' in K Tuori *et al* (eds), *Law and Power: Critical and Socio-Legal Essays* (Liverpool, Deborah Charles Publications, 1997) 51–3. As to the concept of embeddedness, see M Granovetter, 'Economic Action and Social Structure: the Problem of Embeddedness' (1985) 91 *American Journal of Sociology* 485.

[52] See eg, L Friedman, *The Limits of Law: a Critique and a Proposal* (Siegen, Center for Studies on Changing Norms and Mobility, 1986) 8, 13; and D Farber and P Frickey, *Law and Public Choice: a Critical Introduction* (Chicago, University of Chicago Press, 1999) 55–62.

ends, for whose implementation in the community the legal phenomenon is used. In other words, law is certainly considered by natural law theory, CLS and law and economics as an authoritative tool in the hands of the political actors, but the label 'law' is assigned on the basis of which moral, political or economic value the tool is going to promote in the community.

Naturally, this does not mean that the uniqueness of the legal phenomenon according to the embedded model disappears. The theories produced within the embedded model remain normative theories. The law, in the fulfilment of non-legal values, plays a central role due to its very authoritative and obligatory nature. It is the Ought nature of the value that distinguishes legal norms and the legal system from other kinds of regulative instruments as used by the political system in order to gain a result.

However, characteristic for the theories placed within this embedded model is a definition of the nature and structures of law as flexible. In contrast with the autonomous model, these theories claim that some of the fundamental features constitutive of the legal phenomenon have to be found outside the legal world, therefore rendering the internal structures of the law themselves necessarily flexible to the changes occurring at the political and moral levels. Consequently, the answer to the question of what the law is necessarily has to pass by and pay tribute to the political or moral environment, for example in terms of statements such as 'just and therefore valid law'.

One of the most prominent representatives of the embedded model is certainly contemporary natural law theory, in particular in the version presented by John Finnis. In contrast with classical natural law, contemporary natural law scholars particularly stress the fact that the law cannot be explained merely in political or moral terms. The law, although incorporated in a wider moral and political context, occupies a characteristic space distinct from both. Just as for Kelsen and Hart, the distinction results, with respect to politics, in a depiction of the law by modern natural law scholars as consisting of specific authoritative statements, and not general assessments of the goals to be pursued by the authoritative apparatus.[53]

Despite this shift from traditional natural law theory towards positions closer to legal positivism, when it comes to the issue of what the law is, Finnis' law remains political in its nature. According to Finnis, law is a

---

[53] See J Finnis, 'The Truth in Legal Positivism' in RP George (ed), *The Autonomy of Law: Essays on Legal Positivism* (Oxford, Oxford University Press, 1996) 204–5; PE Soper, 'Some Natural Confusions about Natural Law' (1992) 90 *Michigan Law Review* 2394; and B Bix, 'Natural Law Theory' in D Patterson (ed), *A Companion to the Philosophy of Law and Legal Theory* (Oxford, Blackwell Press, 1996) 223–40.

complex of rules 'directed to *reasonably* resolving any of the community co-ordination problems ... for the *common good* of [the] community'[54] (emphasis added).

This definition directly foresees political evaluations, evaluations taking place concerning the choice of the values to be implemented via the law within a community: the political value of the 'reasonability' of the law produced, ie the choice of appropriate legal means in order to satisfy certain goals; and the political value of a common good of a community as the guiding light for the work of the legal apparatus, ie the fulfilment of the ideal of justice.[55]

For Finnis such a community, in particular in modern territorial states, is entirely identical with the political community. It is not a coincidence that Finnis, in explaining what is meant by political community, uses as an example in addition to the contemporary territorial state, the other historical form where such embracement of the law in a wider political environment is most distinctive: the Greek *polis*.[56]

Finnis perceives the law as then tending towards an ontology of structural flexibility to the surrounding political environment, as it is characterised both by being constituted by value-choices criteria and by being directed at implementing such values into a group of persons primarily identified by their belonging to a community which has been primarily defined from a political standpoint.

If the law for natural law scholars still retains certain specific qualities regardless of the surrounding political environment, eg its forms as authoritative statements vs mere political propaganda, for the CLS movement the law seems so flexible towards politics that it disappears completely into the sea of ideologies, categories and value-conflicts forming the political world. Also on this same path are those schools that are considered, more or less, derived from the critical approach to the legal phenomenon, in particular, feminist legal theories, critical race theory and the postmodern approach to the law.[57]

The resulting disappearance of law into the political ocean for CLS and its spin-off schools is derived by focusing on the function and mechanisms

---

[54] J Finnis, *Natural Law and Natural Rights* (Oxford, Clarendon Press, 1980) 276.

[55] See *ibid* 267; and J Finnis, 'On the Incoherence of Legal Positivism' (2000) 75 *Notre Dame Law Review* 1610. See also B Bix, 'On the Dividing Line between Natural Law Theory and Legal Positivism' (2000) 75 *Notre Dame Law Review* 1622.

[56] See Finnis, *Natural Law and Natural Rights* (n 54 above) 148–9. See also N MacCormick, 'Natural Law Reconsidered' (1981) 1 *OJLS* 105.

[57] See MDA Freeman, *Lloyd's Introduction to Jurisprudence* (7th edn, London, Sweet & Maxwell, 2001) 1041; and Bix, *Jurisprudence* (n 16 above) 221.

of law rather than on clearly framing the law itself, by focusing rather on the politicisation of the interpretation of the law than simply on the politicisation of the law.[58]

Similar to natural law legal theorists, CLS scholars define the law as embracing political and economic features, as for them the apparatus of legal concepts and categories tends to encompass competing ideals and politics by means of judicial and doctrinal interpretation. The discord one finds in the different and often contradictory interpretations of concepts and legal categories is simply the reflection of the discord between the different political values.

The law is not simply the tool of the dominating elites, as it is for most contemporary Marxist legal theories. According to CLS, the law tends to be more pluralistic, absorbing and expressing at the legal level almost simultaneously the wide spectrum of conflicting values and ideologies vying with each other within the political order.[59] That which is important in order to understand what the law is, is the complex and fragmented historical, social and political contingency in which the interpretation of the law takes place: who is in charge, for what purpose and how the process of filling the empty bottles of legal concepts and categories with their political content occurs.[60]

If one shifts to the approach of the school of law and economics, and in particular the Chicago School of Posner, as to the issue of the relationship between law and politics, one observes here an opening of the law towards the political phenomenon, and in particular, towards economic values.

According to law and economics' scholarship, the law is political because it is an open-ended set of concepts characterised by their being derived from a series of social actions by legislators, judges and lawyers: 'How could legal ideas be "uncoloured by anything outside the law", when … the law is—and should be—shaped by social needs and interests?'.[61]

The inner structure (or logic) of the complex of social actions going under the name of law tends therefore to reflect the needs and interests of the economic and political environments in which such social actions take

---

[58] See eg, R Mangabeira Unger, 'The Critical Legal Studies Movement' (1982) 96 *Harvard Law Review* 568, 582; or D Kennedy, 'Form and Substance in Private Law Adjudication' (1976) 89 *Harvard Law Review* 1685.

[59] See Unger, 'The Critical Legal Studies Movement' (n 58 above) 570–8; D Kennedy, 'The Structure of Blackstone's Commentaries' (1979) 28 *Buffalo Law Review* 211; and A Altman, 'Legal Realism, Critical Legal Studies, and Dworkin' (1986) 15 *Philosophy and Public Affairs* 222. Compare L Althusser, *Sur la reproduction* (Paris, Presses Universitaires de France, 1995) ch XI.

[60] See Note, 'Round and Round the Bramble Bush: from Legal Realism to Critical Legal Scholarship' (1982) 95 *Harvard Law Review* 1678; and P Gabel and J Feinman, 'Contract Law as Ideology' in D Kairys (ed), *The Politics of Law: a Progressive Critique* (3rd edn, New York, Basic Books, 1998) 497–8, 504–9.

[61] Posner, *The Problems of Jurisprudence* (n 16 above) 243. See also *ibid* 225–6.

place. Consequently, Posner explicitly states that the logic of the law cannot be fully explained by making reference to a purely legal kind of relationship, and that the logic of the law has a source external to the legal world. Claiming, as Posner does, that '[t]he logic of the law is really economics', is a way of making the ontology of law flexible to and dependent on politics, as the law then is an activity produced according to the non-legal values of 'efficiency' or of 'welfare maximisation' living in a certain community.[62] In the case of the modern capitalist society, for example, the need for efficiency in markets is translated into an efficiency criterion inspiring the logic of income tax law.[63]

B. Making Law or Making Politics?

When it comes to the moment of analysis as to the relationship between law-making and the political system, the theorists falling within the embedded model adopt a clear position of an openness of the first towards the latter. Similar to the theories falling within the autonomous model, those within the embedded model maintain that the political inputs coming from the political system have to be transformed into a final legal product by a specific group of persons, working according to specific criteria, using specific categories and concepts. For example, the will of a certain party as to distributing the risks of certain economic activities within the national community has to be transformed by members of a parliamentary committee, according to the parliamentary procedures concerning legislative propositions, through a use of the legal tool called strict liability.

Within the embedded model, however, the law-making is open to the political order in the sense that there is no clear distinction between the formation and the process of selection of certain values inside the political order, and the formation and selection of certain corresponding legal categories inside the law-making procedures. In contrast to the closure of law-making within the autonomous model, the law-making here is open to the political order in the sense that the rationality and the parameters supervising the working of a legal system tend to be directly imported by the political order. For example, in drafting legislation, the legislature, according to the theories falling within the embedded model, is entitled to expressly motivate the adoption of strict liability as it improves the value of economic solidarity among the members of the national community. The working of the law-making and its results (eg in the form of statutes or

---

[62] R Posner, 'The Economic Approach to Law' (1975) 53 *Texas Law Review* 764. See also P Rubin, 'Why is Common Law Efficient?' (1977) VI *Journal of Legal Studies* 53.
[63] See eg, L Kaplow and S Shavell, 'Why the Legal System is Less Efficient than the Income Tax in Redistributing Income' (1994) XXII *Journal of Legal Studies* 667.

judicial decisions) are continuously influenced by the confrontations occurring at the political level. The influence of the political order as to the
working of the law-making occurs before, during and after the transformation of certain political values into legal categories. The embracers of the
embedded model consider the law-making as a mechanism whose manner
of working and results are predominately determined by the battles taking
place within the political arena.[64]

It is very difficult for the scholars falling within the embedded model to
distinguish the point at which the transformation of political statements
into legally valid statements occurs. To solve this problem, most scholars
make reference to factual criteria, such as the opinion of the majority of
judges in the law and economics school, or to moral criteria for the natural
law scholars. The issue then becomes how to identify the extra-legal
criteria that permit the political order to open the law-making, allowing its
own concepts and ideas to travel freely in the space occupied by the legal
discourse, without the necessity of being transformed into purely legal
concepts and categories.[65]

This openness towards the political order is fairly clear in natural law
theory's representation of what the law-making processes are and how they
work. As discussed previously, the legal system according to Finnis is not
simply a set of rules but counts among its constitutive elements parameters
and criteria (such as the common good) that can also be found in the
surrounding social and political environment. In particular, the values
existing in these 'other' environments get into the legal system through a
process defined by Finnis as *determinatio*.[66]

Determinatio is the mechanism of transformation of the general principles of politics into law. It occurs through a practical reasoning (following
one of the 'intermediate principles' described by Finnis), a reasoning
directed at fulfilling one of the basic goods the legal system is to promote.[67]
In this implanting into the legal system the values formed and expressed in
the political order, the *determinatio* is not simply a deductive process
produced by law-makers such as legislators or judges.

---

[64]   See eg, Posner, *The Problems of Jurisprudence* (n 16 above) 442: 'Law and economics
and critical legal studies resemble each other ... in looking outside law for its springs and
lifeblood.'

[65]   See eg, Kairys, 'Law and Politics' (n 5 above) 247. In this section, extra-legal criteria
simply mean that such criteria are not entirely originated by the internal (formal) logic of a
law-making process. See eg, M Weber, *Economy and Society* (G Roth and C Wittich (eds),
Berkeley, University of California Press, 1978) 657; and Hart, *The Concept of Law* (n 27
above) 94. Against E Mensch, 'The History of Mainstream Legal Thought' in Kairys (ed), *The
Politics of Law* (n 60 above) 38–9.

[66]   See Finnis, *Natural Law and Natural Rights* (n 54 above) 282. See also *ibid* 271; and J
Finnis, 'On "The Critical Legal Studies Movement"' (1985) 30 *American Journal of
Jurisprudence* 35.

[67]   See Finnis, *Natural Law and Natural Rights* (n 54 above) 86–9, 100–26.

Finnis stresses that the *determinatio* does not work as a type of mathematical formula but as a social mechanism of authoritative adjudication and, therefore, it requires an active intervention and selection by law-makers according to the intermediate principles of the 'best' legal principles for the realisation of the common goods. The political order is introduced into the dynamical aspects of the legal system, not only at the level of choosing the values to implement, but also in choosing the legal instruments which best fit the purpose of implementing these basic goods into a certain community.[68]

The dynamic aspects of the legal phenomenon for Finnis are then largely dominated by the fact that the law-making tends to be open to the political system. The legal actors have to operate inside and consequently adapt their work to a larger political framework, a complex of goods and procedures designed and chosen by the political order, its reasoning and its values.

If one shifts attention to CLS and their 'law is politics' premise, it is difficult there even to distinguish between the system producing law and the system producing politics. Law is politics does not simply mean that the structure of law tends to reflect the political struggle going on in the political world. It also means that the law-making is considered by CLS as one of the primary enforcing mechanisms through which political values are introduced under the guise of an objective and 'natural' legal form into the everyday life of a certain community.[69]

This embedding of the law-making within the political order then occurs at two levels. First, the law-making is completely open to the political order at a macro-level. Politics affects the law when the legislator (both in the legislative and judicial form) has to construct those rationalised schemes through which to resolve social and economic conflicts. The law-making is totally open to the political order and almost totally dependent upon the battles occurring within when it comes to the macro-level of choosing the type of fundamental legal categories upon which the legal system is to be based.[70]

The second stage at which the law-making opens its borders to the political system, according to CLS, is more at a micro-level, that is at the moment when judges choose to apply a certain rationalisation, namely principles and categories formalised in the traditional legal sources, to the concrete case. The different principles and categories have been rationalised at the macro-level by legislation or previous judicial decisions and they

---

[68] *See* J Finnis, 'The Authority of Law in the Predicament of Contemporary Social Theory' (1984) 1 *Notre Dame Journal of Law, Ethics and Public Policy* 133.
[69] See R Gordon, 'Law and Ideology' in Freeman, *Lloyd's Introduction to Jurisprudence* (n 57 above) 1057.
[70] See eg, Unger, 'The Critical Legal Studies Movement' (n 58 above) 568 fn 59, 593–7.

are all applicable to the same case because of their vagueness and the per se indeterminacy of the legal language. The choice made by the judge among the principles and categories formalised in the traditional legal sources is then rooted in the political and social environments in which the judge operates.[71]

In contrast to CLS, the relationship between the law-making and the political order as envisioned by the school of law and economics is not as clearly in the direction of an openness of the first towards the second. At first blush, it can appear that the school of law and economics considers law-making a neutral system where both the actors and processes tend to follow their own economic logic of efficiency, a logic which does not leave any space for concepts such as 'morality' or 'democracy'.[72]

Law and economics scholars, however, embrace a model of a relationship between law and politics that in the end includes an idea of openness of the law-making towards the political order. It is true that the focus of the scholarship has been devoted to the relationship between the legal and economic systems. Nevertheless, the political order keeps a centrality in their analysis of the legal phenomenon. The political order is the key system through which economic approaches to the law can enter into the economy and society through law-making. In particular, this happens when Posner states that wealth maximisation, a value assumed as per se good, has been and still is the basic belief shaping the common law-making.[73]

Law and economics depicts law-making as a system of processes and actors lacking a relevant degree of autonomy both in their acting and in their resulting choices of new laws. The space given to the law-making is squeezed, on one side, by the construction of certain policies by the political actors. On the other side, the action of the law-makers is dependent upon the evaluation of the impacts such policies have, mainly on the economic system. In both cases, the primary criteria the law-making and its actors have to look to in their functioning are mainly non-legal principles of a political or economic nature respectively. Law-making, in particular in its judicial form, then becomes a sort of ceramic crucible between two iron pots where respect for the 'soundness of the solutions as

---

[71] See eg, P Gabel and P Harris, 'Building Power and Breaking Images: Critical Legal Theory and the Practice of Law' (1983) 11 *New York University Review of Law and Social Change* 383.

[72] For example, Posner claims the possibility of more or less excluding moral or *stricto sensu* political values from the judicial law-making of freedom of speech and religion. See R Posner, 'The Law and Economics Movement' (1987) 77 *American Economic Review* 5.

[73] See R Posner, *Frontiers of Legal Theory* (Cambridge, Harvard University Press, 2001) 100–1, 110–15.

a matter of public policy' and the 'best promotion of the goals of society'
become the guiding lights in the work of the judges.[74]

C. A Mixed Legal Discipline for a Mixed Law

The issue as to how the legal discipline should handle materials of political
origin is, for the theories falling within the embedded model, heavily
affected by their ideas of the law and law-making. As the nature of the law
and the functioning of the law-making are strongly interconnected with
politics and the political order, it is consequential for these theories to
stress and promote the use by the legal discipline of both the materials and
the methodologies developed in the various branches of knowledge dealing
with the political world. The theories subsumed within the embedded
model neither solely nor primarily refer to the queen of the sciences
investigating the political world, ie political science. They also take into
consideration other branches of human knowledge, those which, albeit
perhaps not primarily, have a specific perspective and approach to politics,
such as economics, sociology and moral philosophy.

Of course, this does not result in the disappearance of the legal discipline
as an autonomous branch of investigation.[75] However, since the legal
phenomenon is embedded within the political environment and is malle-
able to the political order, the legal discipline does not need to refrain from
looking around in order to obtain from the same environment better tools
and methods for understanding and teaching the law. The result is that the
legal discipline is configured as mixed, composed both of normative
components (such as the use of the doctrinal concepts of competence and
jurisdiction) and more political categories (such as the possibility of
declaring a law invalid as it is 'undemocratic').

The schools falling within the embedded model impose an interdisciplinary approach as the only way to strip the legal phenomenon down to its
stricto sensu political, economic or moral roots. They find an inadequacy
within a purely normative legal analysis for truly penetrating the constituting elements of the law. As the latter's ontology is something more than a
purely normative statement, the embedded model's theories conclude that
the investigation of the legal phenomenon has to occur with the help of

---

[74] See *ibid* 155, 163, 166 fn 42; Posner, *The Problems of Jurisprudence* (n 16 above)
232–4; and R Posner, 'Pragmatic Adjudication' (1996) 18 *Cardozo Law Review* 4.

[75] Even in the Nazi and Soviet regimes, where the embedding of law into politics was
taken to its extreme, faculties of law and legal doctrine as such never ceased to exist. See eg,
A Vyschinsky, 'The Fundamental Tasks of the Science of Soviet Socialist Law' in J Hazard
(ed), *Soviet Legal Philosophy* (Cambridge, Harvard University Press, 1951) 317–21; and I
Ward, *Law, Philosophy and National Socialism: Heidegger, Schmitt and Radbruch in Context*
(Frankfurt am Main, Peter Lang, 1992) 11–13.

those disciplines whose object of analysis co-exists with the normative aspects at the core of the law, from moral philosophy to cost-benefit analysis.

This mixed character of the legal discipline is explicitly adopted by Finnis, for whom the introduction of moral and political features into the study of law occurs at three levels. First, Finnis' idea of the law is based on the assumption that the legal phenomenon, in order to be fully normative, has to be placed in a wider legitimising environment of a moral nature. This also directly affects his view of the legal discipline. Legal scholars must pass through the purely legal dimension to reach to its moral and political ground and somehow even to share such a moral inner truth of the law to the point that 'it is quite possible to draft the entire legal system without using normative vocabulary at all'.[76]

The mixed character of the legal discipline is also reflected in the methodology used in order to produce such penetration through the legal phenomenon. Since the law is derived by the values expressed within the political community with the use of the method of *determinatio* and since *determinatio* is a general heuristic tool of a more political and moral nature, the legal discipline then has to be familiar with ways of reasoning primarily of a moral and political character, in particular practical reasoning, instead of those of a more purely legal nature (such as reasoning by analogy).[77]

Finally, the legal discipline is considered by Finnis as mixed in relation to the political material because it ultimately has the duty of generating a value-charged result. According to Finnis, the ultimate goal of legal knowledge is to determine whether a legal system works well, that is whether the law-makers have produced norms, principles and categories adherent to the fundamental moral and political values on which a valid legal system has to be based.[78]

Even though CLS also embraces an idea of a mixed nature of the legal discipline, they reject the natural law theory's idea of a complex of values as the driving and guiding force of the legal discipline. For them, the engine of development in legal studies neither lies in legal positivism's introspective work nor in the values and traditions 'naturally' attached to the

---

[76] Finnis, *Natural Law and Natural Rights* (n 54 above) 282. See also *ibid* 3–13; J Finnis, 'The Authority of Law in the Predicament of Contemporary Social Theory' (n 68 above) 115–16; M Moore, *Educating Oneself in Public: Critical Essays in Jurisprudence* (Oxford, Oxford University Press, 2000) 342; and J Goldsworthy, 'Fact and Value in the New Natural Law Theory' (1996) 41 *American Journal of Jurisprudence* 22.

[77] See RP George, 'Human Flourishing as a Criterion of Morality: a Critique of Perry's Naturalism' (1989) 16 *Tulane Law Review* 1462.

[78] See eg, J Finnis, 'Public Reason, Abortion, and Cloning' (1998) 32 *Valparaiso University Law Review* 377. See also Bix, *Jurisprudence* (n 16 above) 72–3.

surrounding environment.[79] The legal discipline instead finds the source and energy of its work and progress according to CLS in the political and, to some extent, economic struggle. From this source, legal scholars have to proceed and fulfil two basic goals of the legal discipline: depth of insight and, through it, political utility. These double entrances of the political environment into the legal discipline as invoked by CLS can also be defined as inquiry (theoretical speculation) and social experimentation (practical activity).[80]

Starting with the entrance of the political environment into the legal discipline's inquiries, if law is politics and much law is created in the common law through the judiciary, then the primary goal of legal knowledge according to CLS is to expose the 'hidden motive' of the law, in particular in the decisions of judges. Legal scholars have to go through the formal logic of legal reasoning and legal language and break into the reign of politics, into the area of values the law-makers intended to promote when enacting a statute or writing a judicial decision. It then becomes almost natural that CLS stresses the necessity for the legal discipline to expand both their investigative task and their theoretical apparatus towards materials and theories proper to these political underpinnings of the law.[81]

The necessity of such a mixture of legal and political material is functional to the fulfilment of the other basic goals of the legal discipline, 'political utility', or social experimentation. The study of the law is also a mixed discipline when it comes to the moment of contemplating the result of this hopefully deep insight. According to CLS, the legal discipline has the specific goal of helping society to free itself from the false idea that legal reasoning is grounded on an objective basis, and that by dissecting legal construction, it is possible to find in it a rational foundation for the adjudication of value-conflicts. In this way, CLS aims to directly integrate the legal discipline into the social processes of selecting values to realise into a community through the law.[82]

While CLS has always from the very beginning openly recognised the political character of the methodology and the results of the legal discipline

---

[79] See R Mangabeira Unger, 'Legal Analysis as Institutional Imagination' in R Rawlings (ed), *Law, Society and Economy: Centenary Essays for the London School of Economics and Political Science 1895–1995* (Oxford, Clarendon Press, 1996) 179.

[80] See Note, 'Round and Round the Bramble Bush' (n 60 above) 1686. See eg, Kennedy, 'Form and Substance in Private Law Adjudication' (n 58 above) 1687.

[81] See Unger, 'The Critical Legal Studies Movement' (n 58 above) 570–7. It should be noted that CLS scholars have, however, a sceptical attitude towards empirical research produced by the social sciences. See Gordon, 'Critical Legal Histories' (n 12 above) 101–2. Against Note, 'Round and Round the Bramble Bush' (n 60 above) 1682.

[82] See *ibid* 1689; and Unger, 'The Critical Legal Studies Movement' (n 58 above) 583. See also JW Singer, 'The Player and the Cards: Nihilism and Legal Theory' (1984) 94 *Yale Law Journal* 25.

as promoted by them, the path followed by law and economics to the recognition of the mixed character of the legal discipline has been more convoluted. Law and economics started with the claim of proposing a scientific approach to the legal phenomenon, an approach detached from values of a *stricto sensu* political nature.[83] This detachment, however, did not free the legal discipline from the necessity of finding categories and principles outside the legal world. This dependency of the legal discipline on non-legal categories was derived from the fact that law and economics stressed the centrality of purely economic criteria, such as efficiency, as the driving force of both the law-applying and law-making processes. As a consequence, legal scholars were forced to adopt the conceptual apparatus produced by the economic sciences and in particular micro-economics. The early stage of law and economics was then in favour of a scientific approach to the law, not of a legal science.[84]

Beginning in the 1970s, this mixed character of the legal discipline (legal rules and economic material) has been further emphasised by the shift of law and economics towards a more political consideration of the legal discipline. This shift occurred mostly due to the fact that, with time and criticism, law and economics scholars came to realise that efficiency, in its turn, is not an independent and stable factor, but a function depending upon a particular distribution or, in other words, on an economic-political environment.[85]

Once law and economics introduces as the goal of the legal phenomenon criteria such as welfare maximisation or social wealth, it forces legal scholars to think and reason in political terms, terms of values assumed as 'right' for a community. Moreover, the legal discipline is then opened to the theoretical debate occurring in the world where the ideas of welfare and social wealth have their origin: political theories and political philosophies. Posner himself explicitly recognises that law and economics, together with CLS in particular, has forced legal actors to abandon a strict adherence to principles such as logic, analogy or stare decisis and instead look at the law

---

[83] A classical example in this direction is the article founding the school of law and economics by RH Coase, 'The Problem of Social Cost' (1960) 3 *Journal of Law and Economics* 41.

[84] See G Calabresi, 'The New Economic Analysis of Law: Scholarship, Sophistry, or Self-Indulgence? Maccabaean Lecture in Jurisprudence' (1982) LXVII *Proceedings of the British Academy* 86.

[85] *See* R Posner, 'Some Uses and Abuses of Economics in Law' (1979) 46 *University of Chicago Law Review* 288; and Calabresi, 'The New Economic Analysis of Law' (n 84 above) 87–91. But see JR Hackney, 'Law and Neoclassical Economics: Science, Politics, and the Reconfiguration of American Tort Law Theory' (1997) 15 *Law and History Review* 277, 307–22.

'from the outside, from perspectives shaped by other fields of scholarly inquiry, such as economics ... [or] political theory'.[86]

In the softer version of law and economics as elaborated by Guido Calabresi, there is even space for the concept of justice, a classical concept of the schools within the embedded model. In Calabresi's construction, this is a value that must be used by the legal discipline in order to limit any aberrations a pure application of other political principles, such as the utilitarian wealth maximisation, might entail.[87]

V. LAW AND POLITICS: THE INTERSECTING MODEL

The typology of autonomous vs embedded models condenses that which in reality is a more complex phenomenon: the universe of differing answers given by contemporary legal theories as to the central question of how the law relates to politics. Despite this generalisation, typical of investigations using models, it can be maintained that this typology covers the vast majority of contemporary legal theories. The typology, however, is incomplete, since it does not address the answers given by two movements appearing in the Western legal culture in the first half of the twentieth century and which have had a vast impact, both on legal thinking and on legal practice: the American and Scandinavian legal realisms.[88]

Before starting the analysis of this group of legal theories, one clarification, however, is required. As already seen above, it is quite difficult in general to speak of a movement or a stream of legal thought. In the case of the legal realists, this is even more challenging because of their tendency, in particular in the United States, to encompass a wide range of legal-theoretical positions. Moreover, it is often difficult to find common elements between the American and the Scandinavian legal realisms. They differ both in their theoretical premises (pragmatism in the United States, the moral philosophy of the Swede Axel Hägerström) and in the focus of their investigations (the work of the courts in the United States, the

---

[86] R Posner, 'Legal Scholarship Today' (2002) 115 *Harvard Law Review* 1316. See also Posner, 'The Law and Economics Movement' (n 72 above) 4. Compare M Horwitz, 'Law and Economics: Science or Politics?' (1980) 8 *Hofstra Law Review* 912.

[87] See G Calabresi, 'An Exchange about Law and Economics: a Letter to Ronald Dworkin' (1980) 8 *Hofstra Law Review* 559. See also G Calabresi and P Bobbit, *Tragic Choices* (New York, Norton, 1978) 83–7. But see R Posner, *Economic Analysis of Law* (4th edn, Boston, Little, Brown & Company, 1992) 27.

[88] See W Twining, *Karl Llewellyn and the Realist Movement* (London, Weidenfeld & Nicolson, 1973) 382; and H-H Vogel, *Der skandinavischer Rechtsrealismus* (Frankfurt am Main, Metzner Verlag, 1972) 9. Against T Grey, 'Judicial Review and Legal Pragmatism' (2003) 38 *Wake Forest Law Review* 492, 507–10; and L Kelman, *Legal Realism at Yale 1927–1960* (Chapel Hill, University of North Carolina Press, 1986) 229.

statutory texts in Scandinavia). These differences have led some authors even to state that the only thing these two movements have in common is the label 'legal realism'.[89]

Despite their positions taken with respect to this problem, the goal of this section is the very demonstration that the American and Scandinavian legal realists' attitudes concerning the issue of law and politics bring them to the same path: the proposal of an intersecting model, within which law and politics are portrayed as two intersecting phenomena. This third way of viewing law and politics is typical of legal theories of recent formation and mirrors the phenomena typical of the contemporary age. Though the philosophical roots of the American and Scandinavian legal realisms stretch back to the end of the nineteenth and beginning of the twentieth centuries, the theories covered by the intersecting model directly face the core of the twentieth century.[90] In their own basic features, the legal realisms embrace and attempt to resolve the basic dilemma faced by legal theories today: a law which is under a duality of forces, centripetal and centrifugal, in its relation to the political mass.

Facing this specific reality, the legal theories encompassed by the intersecting model offer a new approach to the law and legal issues. The legal realists' approach to the issue of the relationships between law and politics is intended to be alternative to the traditional legal theoretical streams represented by legal positivism and natural law theories, based on the fundamental idea of law as a phenomenon partially distinct from the political one.

In the intersecting model, in contrast to the embedded one, the law only partially collides with politics and is not totally embedded into the political mass; the law keeps a certain degree of separation. Law is distinct from politics because the law has a true normative core, an area which can be defined, worked and investigated using only a specific theoretical apparatus produced by and inside the legal world. A distinction exists between law and politics since, at least historically, they have diverged as two different ways of forcing or convincing people onto paths they otherwise may not have followed. Over time, the law has acquired a certain degree of

---

[89] See W Friedmann, *Legal Theory* (5th edn, New York, Columbia University Press, 1967) 304–5; H McCoubrey and N White, *Textbook on Jurisprudence* (3rd edn, London, Blackstone Press, 1999) 178; and W Twining, 'Talk about Realism' (1985) 60 *New York University Law Review* 361. See also G Alexander, 'Comparing the Two Legal Realisms, American and Scandinavian' (2002) 50 *American Journal of Comparative Law* 132; and N Duxbury, *Patterns of American Jurisprudence* (Oxford, Clarendon Press, 1995) 68–71.
[90] See M Martin, *Legal Realism: American and Scandinavian* (Bern, Peter Lang, 1997) 2; and A Ross, *On Law and Justice* (London, Stevens & Sons, 1958) x.

autonomous legitimacy, ie a legitimacy built more on the specific ways a certain rule is enacted and implemented (its normative features) than on its content (its political goals).[91]

However, the intersecting model differs from the autonomous model to the extent that this separation of law from politics is only partial. The law, in order to be fully seen in all its constitutive parts, has to be placed in a position that somewhat coincides with the area occupied by politics. This is because the theories covered by the intersecting model perceive the law as written words, that is as the bearers of the values of the writers, the goals they possess when they write or implement them. For this reason, the legal phenomenon in the intersecting model is also considered to a certain extent as having a political nature.

A. Law and Politics in the Legal Realisms

When it comes to law and its relations to politics, the legal theories within the intersecting model favour a partial rigidity of the legal concepts and categories. They see the law as a phenomenon whose essence eventually consists of being a specific normative phenomenon, ie in terms stressing the separation and rigidity of the legal structure towards the political world. In the intersecting model, law is seen as instrumental to politics, but is still considered a neutral tool that can be used in order to implement radically different values into society. As in the autonomous model, law is conceived as a technology, with its own space and its own rules, a main reason why legal realisms are sometimes treated as a particular version or a spin-off of legal positivism.[92]

However, in contrast to legal positivism and analytical jurisprudence, the intersecting model's theories also constantly stress the fact that the law is more than a logical and closed system of rules written on paper, more than the law-in-books. The legal realists begin their construction from the assessment that the law is an empirical phenomenon, constituted by a

---

[91] See eg, K Llewellyn, 'On Reading and Using the Newer Jurisprudence' (1940) 40 *Columbia Law Review* 589; and A Ross, *Towards a Realistic Jurisprudence: A Criticism of the Dualism in Law* (Copenhagen, Ejnar Munksgaard, 1947) 72. See also N MacCormick, *Legal Reasoning and Legal Theory* (Oxford, Clarendon Press, 1997) 188.

[92] See R Summers, 'On Identifying and Reconstructing a General Legal Theory: Some Thoughts Prompted by Professor Moore's Critique' (1984) 69 *Cornell Law Review* 1017; and J Bjarup, 'Law and Legal Knowledge from a Realistic Perspective' in M Atienza *et al* (eds), *Theorie des Rechts und der Gesellschaft. Festschrift für Werner Krawietz zum 70. Geburtstag* (Berlin, Duncker & Humblot, 2003) 459–83. Against Freeman, *Lloyd's Introduction to Jurisprudence* (n 57 above) 810–11; A Sebok, 'Misunderstanding Positivism' (1995) 93 *Michigan Law Review* 2094; Hart, *The Concept of Law* (n 27 above) 132–44; and R Summers, *Instrumentalism and American Legal Theory* (Ithaca, Cornell University Press, 1982) 21.

combination of human behaviours and prevalent ideas as to what consti-
tutes the law. The law is primarily the law-in-action.[93]

The intersecting model's theories then open the door to the empirical
aspects of the legal phenomenon as constitutive elements of the very nature
of law, an opening both to the concrete behaviours of human beings and to
their socio-psychological underpinnings. As a consequence, the legal categories and concepts directly pay the price of this enlargement of the
nature of the law. The legal conceptual apparatus is forced to allow to a
certain extent the entrance of categories and concepts of social and
political natures. For this very reason, the theories covered by the intersecting model can generally be seen as having the idea of a partial rigidity of
the law in relation to politics.[94]

This multifaceted relation of law towards politics is present in American
legal realism where the complexity of the nature of law originates in the
very fundamental features of the legal phenomenon, which they understand as a mixed construction of normative elements (decisions of the
courts) and socio-psychological elements (judicial behaviours).

According to American legal realists, the rigidity of the law towards
politics exists in their basic assumption that the law is predominantly the
result of the work of the courts and their decisions in concrete cases. This
identification of the law with the decisions of the courts leads to the
rejection of any ontology of the legal phenomenon trying to establish the
law's grounds elsewhere, in particular in the value world. On the path
established by Holmes, the Ought-statements forming the judicial decisions
are labelled 'legal' regardless of whether they are directed at fulfilling value
'f' or the opposite value 'e', since the ambiguity of legal language and legal
categories allows for the possibility that the same category can fulfil
different values.[95]

---

[93]   See K Llewellyn, 'Some Realism about Realism' (1931) 44 *Harvard Law Review* 1237,
points 5 and 6. See also R Pound, 'Law in Books and Law in Action' (1910) 44 *American
Law Review* 35. The possibility of having an idea of law as normative and, at the same time,
as empirical phenomenon is made possible for the legal realists by disconnecting the idea of
the normativity of the law from the formalistic idea of law. See B Leiter, 'Is There an
'American' Jurisprudence?' (1997) 17 *OJLS* 374; and Bix, *Jurisprudence* (n 16 above)
179–80. Against Duxbury, *Patterns of American Jurisprudence* (n 89 above) 64.
[94]   See eg, Ross, *Towards a Realistic Jurisprudence* (n 91 above) 11–13, 49; and, in a more
indirect form, Llewellyn, 'On Reading and Using the Newer Jurisprudence' (n 91 above)
586–9.
[95]   See F Cohen, 'The Ethical Basis of Legal Criticism' (1931) 41 *Yale Law Journal* 204. See
eg, K Llewellyn, *The Common Law Tradition: Deciding Appeals* (Boston, Little, Brown &
Company, 1960) 189. See also OW Holmes, 'The Path of the Law' (1897) 10 *Harvard Law
Review* 459; J Murphy and J Coleman, *The Philosophy of Law: an Introduction to
Jurisprudence* (Totowa, Rowman & Allanheld, 1984) 39; and W Rumble, *American Legal
Realism: Skepticism, Reform, and the Judicial Process* (Ithaca, Cornell University Press, 1968)
55–63.

However, the idea of the indeterminacy of the legal language does not necessarily imply, as it does for CLS, a flexible idea of the law towards politics, ie an idea that the determinacy of the legal language has to be found referring to values produced outside the legal world. Just the opposite, one of the central themes for all American realists is improving as much as possible the predictability of judicial decisions. This has to be done looking primarily into the same legal world's categories and concepts, into the judicial decisions and their legal language. Rules, technique and officials are the constitutive elements of the 'real' law and, more importantly, in the end judges choose among different legal constructions, ie among different normative categories and not among different values.[96]

This choice among different legal categories, however, is the point at which American legal realists begin to open the structures of law. They make the law more flexible, or better, only partially rigid towards the political world. In fact, this very act of choosing among the different legal-conceptual structures that are law, is the moment when judges are most heavily influenced by the values-environment in which they are educated, live and work. The American legal realists introduce here the socio-psychological element of judicial behaviours as a component of the law, a law always seen as the concrete rules produced by the judiciary. It is this very idea that the law is what judges produce, and not what is in the books, that makes the American realist point out how the social and political environments in which judges operate have to be taken into consideration when dealing with the issue of what the law is. Only after that can one really understand how and why a certain rule, concept or category has been created or chosen in a judicial decision to become law.[97]

Although coming from a different theoretical background as well as premises, the Scandinavian legal realists follow their American colleagues in that the Scandinavians also tend to embrace an idea of a partial rigidity in the law's nature and structure towards politics. By directly focusing on the different concepts and categories that constitute the essence of the law (such as rights, duties, property and damages), the Scandinavian realists draw two concurring ideas of the nature of the law.

---

[96] See Llewellyn, *The Common Law Tradition* (n 95 above) 12 n 1; and Llewellyn, 'Some Realism about Realism' (n 93 above) 1252. See also Twining, *Karl Llewellyn and the Realist Movement* (n 88 above) 490–1; Summers, *Instrumentalism and American Legal Theory* (n 92 above) ch 4; and B Leiter, 'Legal Realism, Hard Positivism, and the Limits of Conceptual Analysis' in Coleman (ed), *Hart's Postscript* (n 39 above) 278.

[97] See Llewellyn, *The Common Law Tradition* (n 95 above) 201; K Llewellyn, 'A Realistic Jurisprudence:The Next Step' (1930) 30 *Columbia Law Review* 453; W Cook, 'Facts and Statements of Fact' (1937) 4 *University of Chicago Law Review* 233; and J Frank, *Law and the Modern Mind* (London, Stevens & Sons, 1949) 23. See also B Leiter, 'Legal Realism and Legal Positivism Reconsidered' (2001) 111 *Ethics* 285.

First, legal concepts and categories are per se detached from any system of moral, religious or political values; the concepts of rights or duties are as attached to moral or political values as much as is the expression *tû-tû*.[98] The law is a complex of linguistic or symbolic signals enacted with the purpose of provoking a certain behaviour or non-behaviour in the address-ees; they are 'directives' showing the paths the community or the judges ought to follow. These signals, regardless of the values they bear, always work as stimuli (with words or symbols) in order to gain responses (with behaviours) from the members of the community. A norm is legal, and therefore binding to the community, even if it is highly unjust or economi-cally inefficient. That which is fundamental when speaking of a legal concept or category is that it works in reality as a stimulus to make people follow certain patterns of behaviours.[99]

The fact, however, that concepts and norms have 'to work in reality' to be considered legal, introduces the second feature in the Scandinavian realists' depiction of the nature of law. This empirical aspect of the legal realists' idea of the nature of law renders the legal phenomenon, similarly to American realism, only partially rigid towards the political world.

According to the Scandinavian legal realists, the law has the quality of binding a certain community or certain legal actors to certain patterns of behaviours, as long as the law is valid. The source of validity, however, has to be found outside the law, namely within the space-time co-ordinates of the empirical reality. A legal norm or concept is considered valid, and therefore transformed by the mere declaration of the intention to binding statements, as soon as it is 'in force' or, in other words, as soon as the majority of the community of addressees observes it and considers it 'socially binding'.[100]

Accordingly, although it does not make any sense to introduce as constitutive elements of law concepts such as 'democratic' or 'just', they still are of fundamental importance for having a binding law, ie a 'real' law. The legal categories and concepts in general reflect the values spread in a

---

[98]   See A Ross, 'Tû-tû' (1957) 70 *Harvard Law Review* 818.

[99]   See Ross, *On Law and Justice* (n 90 above) 8; K Olivecrona, *Law as Fact* (2nd edn, London, Stevens & Sons, 1971) 128–34; and V Lundstedt, *Legal Thinking Revised: My Views on Law* (Stockholm, Almqvist & Wiksell, 1956) ch 1. This separation of values and the law brought Olivecrona to publicly support the full validity of the Nazi regime as a legal order. See generally K Olivecrona, *England oder Deutschland?* (Lübeck, Reichskontor der Nordischen Gesellschaft/W. Limpert Verlagshaus, 1941).

[100]   See Ross, *On Law and Justice* (n 90 above) 34–8, 55; and Olivecrona, *Law as Fact* (n 99 above) 112–14. See, for criticism of Ross' idea of validity, HLA Hart, 'Scandinavian Realism' (1959) 1959 *CLJ* 238; and Ross' defense in 'The Concept of Law by H.L.A. Hart' (1962) 71 *Yale Law Journal* 1186 (book review).

certain community and/or among certain legal actors. Only in this way will the law be followed by the majority of people and perceived as binding by the community of addressees.[101]

B. The Legal Realists Open the Law-Making

Moving to the relationships between the processes of production of new legal categories and concepts and the political order, the theories covered by the intersecting model designate the law-making as open to political processes. In particular, the law-making process is structurally open to choices made in the political arena, of values to be implemented into a community through the law.

As in the embedded model, both American and Scandinavian legal realists claim that the procedures and directions taken in the political order directly influence the workings of the law-making processes. Legal actors are human beings, educated by and operating inside a larger community and a larger political system of production and selection of values. If the focus is on the law-in-action or on the law as fact, then the environment in which the actions or the facts take place becomes of primary importance for the creation of those very actions and facts.[102]

It has to be pointed out that the open character of the law-making does not specifically characterise the theoretical proposals made by the legal realisms. All legal theories, more or less, admit that the functioning of the political order interferes with the functioning of the legal order. The innovative contribution of the openness proposed by the theories covered by the intersecting model (and also by the embedded model), is that the political stimuli and processes of production of those stimuli have to be treated as an integral part of the law-making procedures. The progressive environment of a law faculty where a judge has been educated then has to be considered an integral part of the legal process through which he or she recognises the idea of 'diffuse interests' as legally relevant for the promotion of a civil action against a corporation by an NGO.

This feature of law-making as being open to that occurring inside the political order is particularly evident with the American legal realists. They designate the law-making procedures as open to the political order in one fundamental moment of the process: during the interpretation of statutes and precedents by the judges.

---

[101] See eg, Lundstedt, *Legal Thinking Revised* (n 99 above) 150; and Olivecrona, *Law as Fact* (n 99 above) 111, 272.

[102] '[T]he Realist hero is the social engineer who masterfully wields law as an instrument of policy.' Gordon, 'Critical Legal Histories' (n 12 above) 67.

In investigating the work of judges, legal realists point out how, during the interpretative process regarding precedents and statutes, judges often face a normative dilemma. Because of the vagueness and obscurity of both statutes and judicial precedents, judges can easily justify two or more contrasting legal solutions to the same concrete case.[103] According to American realists, it is in this very choosing by the judges that the law-making opens itself to the political order.

This choice of one legal path over another is indeed taken with reference also (but not only) to the procedures and choices occurring in the political arena. During the selection process as to which normative solution should be reached, the judge is strongly influenced both by the values the chosen solution is to implement into the society, and by the environment the judge has been educated and is living within.[104]

Actually, it is possible to distinguish within American legal realism two lines of interpretation as to the way the law-making processes operate as a means of the values produced in the political arena.[105] The first line roughly corresponds to the supporters of fact-scepticism. Values enter into the law-making processes, and influence their way of operating, mainly through the fact that the legal actors ultimately are human beings and therefore carriers in their work of their own private values, values in and with which the legal actors have grown. In other words, because of the indeterminacy of the legal language, the judges directly make use of their own private value systems in order to establish a normative meaning of the categories and concepts of such language and, on those bases, decide a case.[106]

The second line roughly corresponds to the adherents of the rule-scepticism stream. For them, the political order influences the production activities of the legal system mainly through the fact that the legal actors actually tend, during the interpretative process of statutes and precedents, to consider the values expressed by the political arena more than their own

---

[103] See K Llewellyn, *Bramble Bush: On Our Law and its Study* (Dobbs Ferry, Oceana Publications, 1996) 2, 74. See eg, K Llewellyn, 'Remarks on the Theory of Appellate Decision and the Rules or Canons about How Statutes are to be Constructed' (1950) 3 *Vanderbilt Law Review* 395. See also W Rumble, 'American Legal Realism and the Reduction of Uncertainty' (1964) 13 *Journal of Public Law* 51.

[104] See Llewellyn, 'A Realistic Jurisprudence' (n 97 above) 442–7; and F Cohen, 'The Ethical Basis of Legal Criticism' (1931) 41 *Yale Law Journal* 219. See also Summers, *Instrumentalism and American Legal Theory* (n 92 above) 209.

[105] This distinction is a specific application in the law-making area of Leiter's division between an 'Idiosyncrasy Wing' and a 'Sociological Wing' in American legal realism. See B Leiter, 'Positivism, Formalism, Realism: Legal Positivism in American Jurisprudence by Anthony Sebok' (1999) 99 *Columbia Law Review* 1148 (book review).

[106] See F Cohen, 'Transcendental Nonsense and the Functional Approach' (1935) 35 *Columbia Law Review* 845; and Frank, *Law and the Modern Mind* (n 97 above) 104, 111. See also B Leiter, 'Legal Realism' in Patterson (ed), *A Companion to the Philosophy of Law and Legal Theory* (n 53 above) 271.

private value system. Though the private values of judges also play a very important role, the judiciary still tends to decide to implement the best among the values as given by the political actors.[107]

An explanation for the combination, in American legal realist theories, of a rigid character of the law with an open design of the law-making process can be traced back to their programme. The target audience of their theories are professional lawyers and judges. As a consequence, legal realists have to keep a partially rigid distinction between legal and political concepts in order to preserve the specificity of such legal professions. Nevertheless, since for lawyers and judges, the most important goal is to resolve a case, then it is quite expected that legal realists open the law-making processes in order to give lawyers a broader set of interpretative and creative tools to support their legal reasoning, by admitting, for instance, the use of criminological reasoning in a criminal case.[108]

Scandinavian realism also portrays the law-making processes and procedures as open towards the political world. The opening of the law-making has its starting point in the Scandinavian realist's idea of law-making as the processes producing valid legal concepts and categories. As discussed previously, the latter are considered valid, and therefore binding, when they are followed by the majority of the addressees. The law-making, in order to remain a system of processes directed at producing valid law, has to set in motion processes and procedures that produce statutes and judicial decisions that embrace and realise the values shared by, or at least not contrary to, the feelings of the majority of the addressees.[109]

For Scandinavian legal realists, in particular, a central element of the processes and procedure for the making of the law is the legal language. The language is the primary means through which legal rules are produced by a legal order and addressed to the community. The legal language is considered by the Scandinavian realists as having primarily a directive function of influencing human behaviours.[110]

---

[107] See Llewellyn, *The Common Law Tradition* (n 95 above) 24–5. See eg, K Llewellyn, 'American Common Law Tradition, and American Democracy' in K Llewellyn, *Jurisprudence: Realism in Theory and Practice* (Chicago, University of Chicago Press, 1971) 287–99. See also Rumble, *American Legal Realism* (n 95 above) 191.

[108] See eg, Llewellyn, 'Some Realism about Realism' (n 93 above) 1236, points 1–3. See also Rumble, *American Legal Realism* (n 95 above) 194–5; Murphy and Coleman, *The Philosophy of Law* (n 95 above) 40; and HLA Hart, 'American Jurisprudence through English Eyes: the Nightmare and the Noble Dream' in Hart, *Essays in Jurisprudence and Philosophy* (n 28 above) 127–8.

[109] See Lundstedt, *Legal Thinking Revised* (n 99 above) 149; Ross, *Why Democracy?* (n 13 above) 231–43; and Olivecrona, *Law as Fact* (n 99 above) 189–90.

[110] See Ross, *On Law and Justice* (n 90 above) 158–60; and K Olivecrona, 'The Imperative Element in the Law' (1964) 18 *Rutgers Law Review* 800. See also F Schmidt, 'The Uppsala School of Legal Thinking' (1978) 22 *Scandinavian Studies in Law* 171.

This influence occurs, as seen above, through a process based on a linguistic or sometimes symbolic stimuli-response reaction. Therefore, it is of vital importance for the legal order that it send out the 'right' linguistic stimuli in order to get the strived for reactions. The correctness of the stimuli, in its turn, depends upon the socio-psychological environment in which the legal language is used. The traditional constitutive elements of the legal language, such as the concepts of rights and duties, are per se meaningless, but they acquire their authoritative status simply because and from the moment they are inserted in a certain social and political framework. It is this framework, and the values it carries, that then heavily influence the law-making through determining, as Ross would say, the semantic reference of concepts and categories that otherwise would be a mere *tû-tû*. The law-making is then open because it tends to mirror in its production the changes and conflicts among the dominant values occurring in the political order. The legal order otherwise runs the risk of becoming 'not-in-force-anymore' and therefore no longer a valid system.[111]

C. The Realists' Legal Discipline and the Political Material

The considerations of the nature and the role played by the legal discipline occupy a crucial position in the theories covered by the intersecting model. This centrality is mainly due to the fact that the legal realists try to combine two elements that, during the history of legal analysis, have always seemed to be irreconcilable: a (partially) rigid nature of the law towards politics and, at the same time, a law-making open to the influences and to the processes occurring in the political order.[112]

Basing their analysis on these two apparently repelling poles, the theories covered by the intersecting model try to find a point of convergence in the construction of a new typology of legal discipline. On one side, they open the law-making of the legal system to the influences of the processes occurring in the political world. A scientific investigation of legal phenomenon is an investigation aimed at finding out what the law really is. Law is one of the most powerful tools in the hands of the political establishment, used to get their goals implemented into the society. Legal scholars

---

[111] *See* Olivecrona, *Law as Fact* (n 99 above) 297–303, 371–7; Ross, *On Law and Justice* (n 90 above) 352–3; and Lundstedt, *Legal Thinking Revised* (n 99 above) 16–17.

[112] It has to be stressed that this historical incompatibility is not of an absolute character. See eg, D Brink, 'Legal Positivism and Natural Law Reconsidered' (1985) 68 *The Monist* 369. But see Bix, 'On the Dividing Line between Natural Law Theory and Legal Positivism' (n 55 above) 1618–24; and J Coleman and B Leiter, 'Determinacy, Objectivity, and Authority' (1993) 142 *University of Pennsylvania Law Review* 554.

therefore have to take into consideration that which is happening in the political world as relevant for that which is to happen in the legal world during the creation of new laws.

The legal discipline needs to focus on those parts or elements of a legal phenomenon that are politically charged in order to discover and bring into the light of day the political that is still in the reality of law. The intersecting model's theories then unlock the doors of the legal discipline to categories such as 'welfare' or 'policy', categories produced by disciplines typical of the political arena such as political science or political philosophy.

On the other side, this mixed nature of the legal discipline is of a partial character. The theories covered by the intersecting model claim that the legal discipline, in order to receive the label of a 'scientific' discipline, has to stress the specific nature of its object of investigation, the law. The political material tends to flow freely between different value options but when it is introduced into the legal world, it is often subjected to legal limitations and constraints either of doctrinal, judicial or legislative production. The legal discipline, in order to be viewed as a scientific form of knowledge, therefore has to also take into consideration the (partial) rigidity of principles and doctrines constitutive of the law.[113]

American legal realism certainly goes in this direction of considering the nature of the legal discipline towards the political material as partially mixed. Because of the open character of the law-making processes towards external influences coming from the political world, the main path leads in the direction of a mixed nature of legal studies. According to the realist vision, the goal of legal scholars is to investigate the law as it really is. The legal inquiry must go further than the law-in-books, the written rules and principles, and look into the real law: the regularities of the behaviours of legal officials and in particular of judges.[114]

Judicial behaviours are not produced in a vacuum of rules and principles but are strongly affected by the value system in which judges live and work. Legal scholars therefore must venture into a wider landscape than merely the law-in-books. They must go into a field where human beings, their lives and their actions together play a central role. The legal discipline cannot avoid taking into consideration the results provided by non-legal

---

[113] See A Kronman, 'Jurisprudential Responses to Legal Realism' (1988) 73 *Cornell Law Review* 337. As to the 'unclear' character of legal realists' ideas of the legal discipline, see eg, A Scalia, 'The Rule of Law as a Law of Rules' (1989) 56 *University of Chicago Law Review* 1182; and J Sundberg, 'Scandinavian Unrealism: Co-report on Scandinavian Legal Philosophy' (1986) 9 *Rechtstheorie* 311.

[114] See eg, Llewellyn, 'A Realistic Jurisprudence' (n 97 above) 444. See also Summers, *Instrumentalism and American Legal Theory* (n 92 above) 154–5; and B Leiter, 'Rethinking Legal Realism: Toward a Naturalized Jurisprudence' (1997) 76 *Texas Law Review* 285, 298–300.

disciplines, such as sociology, political science, statistics, criminology and economics. As Llewellyn states, '[t]o right, to left, in front, are materials crying out for use'.[115] Only by using those materials external to the traditional legal field can the legal discipline then have a comprehensive view of the legal phenomenon and its place and functions in society.

At the same time as the American realists present the mixed nature of legal studies, they also try to follow another path. In order to preserve their idea of the partial rigidity of the law towards the political world, the legal realists affirm the necessity of the legal discipline itself constituting a scientific approach to the law. It is a secondary track pulling towards an idea of a discipline more autonomous from the world of values or, in other words, only partially mixed.

After rejecting the formalistic vision of the legal discipline as a study of law-in-books, American realists still claim the existence of a specific space in which the legal discipline plays a central role: the space of the law-in-action. In particular, the legal realists bring to the surface the necessity of separating the analysis of what law actually is in-action from what the law ought to be in-action. That is, they stress the necessity for investigators to treat the law as it appears in the judges' behaviours, not as it ought to appear according to judicial or other value systems. This necessity of separating within legal inquiries the law from its political or moral aspects is functional to the legal realists' aim of offering, to a certain extent, a normative legal discipline, that is a discipline that can provide legal actors with an inventory of clarified legal concepts and categories.[116]

The Scandinavian legal realists also propose a legal discipline that is mixed in its relation to the political material as they stress the necessity for legal scholars to make use, in their investigations, not only of the traditional legal analysis, but also of material produced by political science, social science, anthropology and, to some extent, statistics. The legal discipline, in order to be included in the world of science, has to analyse the law as an empirical phenomenon, eg looking to the ideas of what the law is among members of a community or among judges. Legal scholars must analyse how the law and its elements manifest themselves in the space-time dimensions.[117]

In particular, the Scandinavian legal realists stress the importance for legal scholars of deeply investigating the main means used by law to come

---

[115] K Llewellyn, 'On What is Wrong with So-called Legal Education' (1935) 35 *Columbia Law Review* 678. See eg, K Llewellyn, 'Law and the Social Sciences: Especially Sociology' (1949) 62 *Harvard Law Review* 1294.

[116] See Llewellyn, 'Some Realism about Realism' (n 93 above) 1235; and K Llewellyn, 'My Philosophy of Law' in *My Philosophy of Law: Credos of Sixteen American Scholars* (Boston, Boston Law Book, 1941) 195. See eg, K Llewellyn, 'The Theory of Legal "Science"' (1941) 20 *North Carolina Law Review* 22; or Llewellyn, *Bramble Bush* (n 103 above) 4–5.

[117] See eg, Lundstedt, *Legal Thinking Revised* (n 99 above) 18.

into reality: the legal language. This inquiry cannot be concluded using only traditional analytical tools (eg investigating the logical coherence of legal concepts within different statutes enacted in the course of time). Legal scholars must use material coming from history, political science, social science, psychology, socio-linguistics and anthropology. This has to be done in order to place the different legal concepts and categories into a wider value context in which these concepts and categories originated or have been used.[118] For example, this enlargement of the materials available to the legal discipline implies the necessity of redefining the traditional sources of legally relevant materials to which legal scholars look in order to find the solution to a legal question. In particular, the legal discipline needs to start from the empirical reality of the debate occurring inside the political arena and decide in favour not of the solution that is the best according to the legal order, but of the solution that best fits in a certain community.[119]

This mixed nature of the legal discipline, however, is conceived by the Scandinavian realists as being partial. The Scandinavian legal realists repeatedly stress the fact that the legal discipline is constituted by and deals with ideas of law and, therefore, the legal discipline cannot neglect to take into consideration these ideas of law as the community or judges conceive them: as if they were pure from the political dust. Legal scholars, although working with other materials, must also allow for those aspects of the legal phenomenon that traditionally characterise it among the people; in particular, the operation of the law according to logical reasoning and by means of specific concepts.[120]

The reasoning behind the production of political material tends always to take into consideration simultaneously differing interests or values, developing categories such as 'social justice', in order to integrate opposing solutions and values, eg by compromising individual and collective justice. In contrast, in the reasoning put forward by the legal discipline, the *tertium* is often *non datum*; that is, the choice is only between two opposite poles, for instance either validity or invalidity, and a compromising solution is thus not at stake. The choice is to be made between a correct statement

---

[118] See K Olivecrona, 'Legal Language and Reality' in RA Newman (ed), *Essays in Jurisprudence in Honor of Roscoe Pound* (Indianapolis, Bobbs-Merrill Hill, 1962) 177–85.

[119] See eg, PO Ekelöf, 'Teleological Construction of Statutes' (1958) 2 *Scandinavian Studies in Law* 84; or Lundstedt, *Legal Thinking Revised* (n 99 above) 69, 267–8. See also J Bjarup, *Skandinavischer Realismus: Hägerström – Lundstedt – Olivecrona – Ross* (Munich, Karl Albert Freiburg, 1978) 85.

[120] See eg, Ross, *On Law and Justice* (n 90 above) ch 2; Olivecrona, *Law as Fact* (n 99 above) 184–5; and Lundstedt, *Legal Thinking Revised* (n 99 above) 8–9. See also V Aubert, 'The Structure of Legal Thinking' in A Andneæs (ed), *Legal Essays: a Tribute to Frede Castberg on the Occasion of his 70th Birthday* (Oslo, Universitetsforlaget, 1963) 61–2.

reflecting the law in force and an incorrect statement dealing with norms that actually are not in force and therefore are not valid.[121]

VI. COMMON POINTS OF THE THREE MODELS

Combining the conclusions drawn in Parts II and III with the intersecting model presented in the last part, it is possible to draw a table representing the models relating law to politics (see Table 1.1). It can be clearly seen from Table 1.1 that the results for each model are unique, each having its own particular way of viewing how and to what extent the legal phenomenon relates to the political one. The theories covered by the autonomous model tend to see the law and its system of production as relatively closed to that which happens in the political world. In contrast, scholars of both the embedded and the intersecting models tend to open the legal phenomenon to the world in which the values to be implemented in a community are produced and selected.

Table 1.1: Politics and law in the autonomous, embedded and intersecting models

	Relationship of law to politics (static aspect)	*Relationship between law-making and political order (dynamic aspect)*	*Relationship of legal discipline to political material (epistemological aspect)*
Autonomous model (Legal positivism, analytical jurisprudence)	*Rigidity* of law	*Closed* law-making	*Pure* legal discipline
Embedded model (Natural law theory, CLS, law and economics)	*Flexibility* of law	*Open* law-making	*Mixed* legal discipline
Intersecting model (American and Scandinavian legal realisms)	*Partial rigidity* of law	*Open* law-making	*Partially mixed* legal discipline

---

[121] See Ross, *On Law and Justice* (n 90 above) 38–50, 321; and Olivecrona, *Law as Fact* (n 99 above) 261–7.

However, the legal movements covered by the intersecting model distinguish themselves from the positions taken, for example, by CLS and natural law scholars. It is true that legal realists consider law-making as open to the influences coming from the political world and that this openness is reflected in a mixed nature of legal discipline, ie in its being open to the use of material produced in the political arena. Nevertheless, this opening of the legal discipline is only partial since the theories covered by the intersecting model still retain a certain degree of autonomy with respect to the legal concepts and categories as towards the conceptual political apparatus.[122]

Despite these distinctions, it is still possible to find at least two common points of discussion among the different models, even if their answers differ. This is due to the fact that most of the contemporary legal theories, regardless of the model in which they fall, tend to reflect the historical situation in which they operate.

First, as seen in the introductory chapter, one force pulls in the direction of concentrating the law into the hands of politicians, therefore requiring a law more structurally obedient to reasons of politics than, for example, to those of systematic legal development. Each of the theories covered by the three models then begins their analysis from the fact that law and politics relate to each other. That which actually characterises their approaches, and distinguishes the models, is the degree of intensity in the interrelationship between law and politics, not the dilemma of its presence or absence.

The degree of intensity is extreme in the embedded model. Here the norms are considered law only when they adapt themselves to certain values produced inside the political arena; the law-making is widely open to that which is happening inside the political world and the legal discipline is actually of a mixed nature, largely making use of material and categories produced inside the political arena. It is a model in which one phenomenon (law) is surrounded entirely by the other (politics).

The relationship between law and politics can also be less obvious, as in the intersecting model. The legal realist theories covered by this model posit the openness of both the processes leading to the creation of the law, and to a certain degree, the legal discipline, towards the political phenomenon. However, they still try to keep the law as a partially rigid concept, for whose nature only a limited amount of political concepts and categories are required as constitutive elements. In this model, the two phenomena of law and politics overlap, while keeping a certain degree of an autonomous hard core, whose nature can be fully explained making a limited use of the other's categories and concepts. For example, the

---

[122] See eg, Cohen, 'Transcendental Nonsense and the Functional Approach' (n 106 above) 845. See also Note, 'Round and Round the Bramble Bush' (n 60 above) 1669.

American realist idea of law then leaves relevant spaces (although inside a framework maintaining a rigidity of the law) to the political conceptual apparatus. The orientation by the judiciary in favour of giving normative status to one concept instead of the other is mostly determined by non-normative elements; *in primis*, the social environment and the political ideology of the judges.[123]

In the third model, law and politics are considered as two autonomous phenomena. Both the nature of the law and law-making processes of the legal order do not directly require any reference to the political world; moreover, the legal discipline avoids any contact with the political material and conceptual apparatus. Although this model stresses the central and monopolising role played by the legal world in deciding how and when the values are transferred into the legal world, the autonomous model also still recognises that there actually is a transfer of values from the political world to the world of law. Neither Kelsen nor Hart deny the fact that law, in particular in this contemporary age, is mostly produced by political actors, ie by institutional subjects whose primary goal is to see their values implemented into a community. That which is typical of legal positivism and analytical jurisprudence is not that they deny such spaces of contacts between law and politics, but the fact that they reduce their extent and frequency as much as possible.[124]

The second common point of discussion starts from the ascertainment that the increasing complexity and number of areas the political world recognises as its domain, and therefore regulates by law, in their turn cause a force pulling the law in the opposite direction. This increasing politicisation of community life encourages a development of the idea of law as rigid to the outside reality, with its own rules as monopolised by a group of legal professionals. The different models then start from the fact that law and politics, regardless of the intensity of their relations, actually identify two phenomena that cannot be fully assimilated within each other.

This separation between law and politics is transparent for the theories within the autonomous and intersecting models, in particular because of their idea of a hard core of the law with a normative nature. Even one of the most temperate versions of the current legal positivistic movement, the institutional theory, begins with the assumption of structural diversity between the law and the world of values. MacCormick clearly states that

---

[123] See Cohen, 'Transcendental Nonsense and the Functional Approach' (n 106 above) 839. See also Leiter, 'Legal Realism' (n 106 above) 270; and OW Holmes, *The Common Law* (New York, Dover Publications, 1991) 41.

[124] See J Raz, 'On the Autonomy of Legal Reasoning' in Raz, *Ethics in the Public Domain* (n 18 above) 314–15; and Waluchow, *Inclusive Legal Positivism* (n 40 above) 80–1. See also N Luhmann, 'Closure and Openness: On Reality in the World of Law' in Teubner (ed), *Autopoietic Law* (n 19 above) 335–48; and Coleman, *The Practice of Principle* (n 29 above) 4–5 n 4.

'politics is not law, nor law politics, despite occasional assertions to the contrary from the ramparts of Critical Legal Studies'.[125]

This division becomes opaque when speaking of the embedded model. This model is characterised, indeed, by the law being implanted inside the political phenomenon, and for its existence and procreation being dependent upon that which is happening inside the political world. Nevertheless, embeddedness does not mean the dissolution of law into politics.

First, all the theories covered by the embedded model still speak of two different phenomena, one called law, the other, politics. Stressing the dependency of the first to the second does not imply that they are simply two words identifying one phenomenon. It is true, in particular within CLS, that 'law is politics', but this statement simply points to the fact that the law tends to become incorporated into the political world and its conflicts. Still, the law is not assimilated into politics and there is always a difference between the two phenomena.[126]

For example, according to Finnis, there is still a difference between a political order and the operational aspects of the legal system embedded within it. The political order is characterised as producing 'unstable' outputs such as political statements or propaganda. On the contrary, the very purpose of the law-making process is to give to such outputs a certain degree of rigidity by incorporating political statements, for instance, into a formal statute enacted by Parliament.[127] Similarly, according to law and economics, a line, very thin but still present, can be drawn separating the legal system from politics. In particular, the existence of this line is based on the fact that the legal system usually presents a certain degree of path dependence, that is rigidity or inertia towards legal innovation.[128]

Secondly, each of the theories covered by the embedded model are designed for the very purpose of rousing lawyers and judges. Law and economics followers, natural law scholars and CLS want to create a consciousness of their central positions in the wider political environment, and also of the possibility of operating as legal actors, influencing both what happens inside their legal world as well as what happens outside in the surrounding political world.

---

[125] N MacCormick, 'Institutional Normative Order: a Conception of Law' (1997) 82 *Cornell Law Review* 1062. See also Ross, *On Law and Justice* (n 90 above) 326–9.

[126] See Hunt, 'The Politics of Law and the Law of Politics' (n 51 above) 51–6. See eg, D Lyons, 'Justification and Judicial Responsibility' (1984) 72 *CLR* 188; and Posner, *The Problems of Jurisprudence* (n 16 above) 153–4.

[127] See Finnis, 'On "The Critical Legal Studies Movement"' (n 66 above) 38; and Finnis, 'The Authority of Law in the Predicament of Contemporary Social Theory' (n 68 above) 136.

[128] See Posner, *Frontiers of Legal Theory* (n 73 above) 153–4, 158–9. See eg, M Bussani *et al*, 'Liability for Pure Financial Loss in Europe: an Economic Restatement' (2003) 51 *American Journal of Comparative Law* 125.

This influencing of the surrounding world can naturally take various directions, according to the values or politics whose protection or implementation the different theories tend to prioritise. For example, law and economics privileges the influence of the political world in a laissez-faire direction as to economic questions. In contrast, natural law theories tend to be more concerned with using lawyers and judges in order to mark the extreme borders the political power can never transgress if it still wants to make use of the tool of coercion called law.

Even if 'law is politics', with the right type of legal education and training, legal actors can still play a part in the political world, a role not as politicians but as politically-oriented judges or lawyers. The fact that the vast majority of representatives of the theories covered by the embedded model have produced a large bulk of the legal writings stressing the need to reform the law, not abolish it, is then not a coincidence. This is a clear indication of the fact that for those within the embedded model, the law is also a vital component of the political phenomenon that cannot be substituted by other types of coercive procedures or mechanisms.[129]

In summary, the fact that the law is subjugated to this system of two strong simultaneously opposing and pulling forces, in turn affects the manner by which contemporary legal theories perceive the law: law and politics always tend to be depicted as two (more or less) different phenomena, which however (with a higher or lower degree of frequency) communicate with each other. Central to the investigation of the relationships between law and politics then is the analysis of one of the links through which the communication and transmission between law and politics take place. This link is one of the moments when politics touches the law and, more specifically, deals with the mechanism through which the values constituted in the world of politics are transferred into the legal world.

VII. CONCLUSION

This chapter has mapped out the positions of certain contemporary legal theories on an issue that is fundamental in this modern age: the relationships between law and politics. The centrality of this issue is demonstrated by the fact that all the major legal-theoretical streams have addressed it in one way or another. The goal of this chapter has been to look to some of

---

[129] See R Gordon, '"Of Law and the River", and of Nihilism and Academic Freedom' (1985) 35 *Journal of Legal Education* 14. See also eg, Kennedy, 'Form and Substance in Private Law Adjudication' (n 58 above) 1777.

these major contemporary legal theories and build a typology under which certain of these ways of dealing with the relations of law to politics can be assembled.

After briefly defining the methodological grounds the typology is built upon, the first ideal-type has been labelled as autonomous according to the answers given to three questions: the static issue, the nature of law; the dynamic issue, the production of law; and the epistemological issue, the character of the legal discipline. This model unites those theories that argue for a sharp distinction between the legal phenomenon and the world of politics.

In particular, the focus here has been on how the relations between law and politics have been portrayed by legal positivism, namely by Kelsen, and by analytical jurisprudence, as espoused by Hart. These legal theoretical movements, although explicitly recognising the factual necessity of relations between the legal and the political worlds, tend to keep the two separate by arguing the rigidity of the law's structures towards the complex of values, as well as the processes through which such values are chosen. Moreover, Kelsen and Hart stress the feature of autonomy of the legal phenomenon by portraying law-making and the legal discipline as tendentially closed and pure, towards the political order and the material produced by and within it respectively.

A second way of approaching the question of how the law relates to politics has also been identified, portraying the legal phenomenon as embedded and, to some extent, blended with the processes and values of the political phenomenon. In particular, modern natural law theory as represented by Finnis, CLS and law and economics portray the law as embraced by politics because of its flexible nature towards the values and their production in the political world, because the law-making is open towards the value-conflicts taking place inside the political order, and finally because the legal discipline is considered to be mixed with legal and political material.

A third way of approaching the question of how the law relates to politics is also identified: the legal realists' model of the law intersecting politics. In this way, both legal realisms want to save the specificity of the legal phenomenon, which remains partially rigid in its relations to the political conceptual apparatus. At the same time, its dependency relation towards the political actors is stressed by portraying the law-making as open to the mechanisms and influences coming from the political order; resulting in a partially mixed legal scholarship, where legal scholars in their reasoning can use materials produced in the political arena within certain structural limitations.

Finally, the intersecting, autonomous and embedded models have a common field, from which their different perspectives all commence: law and politics are two different objects that interact with each other, this common field produced by the specific and somehow contradictory characters of the relations between legal and political phenomena in our times. This opens the possibility for focusing attention in chapter two on whether and how the legal theories embracing such different models have treated a central moment of the relations between law and politics, namely the moment in which the value-dimensions of the legal phenomenon interact with the law and law-making processes.

2

Law, Politics and the Grey Box

CHAPTER ONE PRESENTED the relations between law and politics for selected contemporary legal theories in terms of three models: the autonomous model, the embedded model and the intersecting model. Law and politics can be seen either as two autonomous entities, as law embedded in politics, or as intersecting each other. In all three models, law and politics keep the feature of being two different phenomena, while presenting at the same time regions of interaction, though differing in extent and intensity.

This chapter analyses one of those areas in which law and politics meet, namely the zone here temporarily referred to as the 'transformational moment'. This is the moment at which the values produced inside the political arena are transformed into legal categories and concepts, a crucial function in the relations between law and politics as portrayed by contemporary legal theories. Despite this central position of these images of law in the relations to the political world, most of the legal theoretical movements, for different reasons, have somehow left such a transformational moment at the periphery of their investigations.

I. THE GREY BOX: THE TRANSFORMATIONAL MOMENT IN CONTEMPORARY LEGAL THEORIES

The vast majority of contemporary legal theories usually reserve, as shown in chapter one, a certain space in their theoretical debates as to investigating the relations between law and politics. Moreover, as seen, the legal theories disagree not only as to the degree of distinction between law and politics, but also as to the nature of the relations between the two phenomena. For example, on one extreme CLS considers law and politics as almost sharing the same nature, law being an integral part of the political process. On the other extreme, there exists in the Kelsenian depiction an almost ontological gap that separates law and politics, the two being located on different dimensions of reality (the normative reality for the law and the value reality for politics).[1]

Despite such differences, the vast majority of contemporary legal theories recognise, in one way or another, that the legal and political phenomena have spaces where they touch upon each other. The spaces where law touches politics can be broad and frequent, as for the theories covered by the embedded model, or to a more limited extent and less frequently, as in the legal realisms. Even for the theories covered by the autonomous model, law necessarily is linked to politics, although the relations tend to be reduced to a minimum level. In any case, for none of the theories covered by the three models is the law a product emerging *sua sponte* or operating in a vacuum. An essential role is always played by the surrounding political environment, ie the non-legal environment producing, combining and selecting the values to be implemented into a community by means of the law.

It is true that the nature of such values and the processes of their production and/or selection can vary considerably according to the legal theories. The values can be of a moral nature (eg the right to live), of an economic nature (eg the protection of commercial transactions) or of a political nature *stricto sensu* (eg the freedom of expression). In a similar way, the processes of production and selection of such values also can be of a moral nature (eg by using principles of reasonableness), an economic nature (eg by striving for the efficiency of an economic system), or a political nature *stricto sensu* (eg by mirroring the wishes of the ruling elite). Despite these differences, in all the legal theories the political environment always plays a key role both in the production and in the selection of the 'values-wannabe-law'. When viewed from the inside of the legal world or, in other words, whether and when they become relevant for the legal system, these values and the processes formation and/or selection acquire, in the eyes of the different legal theories, the same quality in relation to the law. They are ideal models of behaviour that an individual or a group of individuals (political actors) aim to impose upon a community by invoking the coercive properties of the law.[2]

---

[1]   See eg, L Kornhauser and L Sager, 'Unpacking the Court' (1986) 96 *Yale Law Journal* 85, 95; and H Kelsen, 'The Pure Theory of Law and Analytical Jurisprudence' (1941) 55 *Harvard Law Review* 45.

[2]   See eg, M Van Hoecke, *Law as Communication* (Oxford, Hart Publishing, 2002) 64; or W Waluchow, *Inclusive Legal Positivism* (Oxford, Clarendon Press, 1994) 43. But see a possible distinction from the normative perspective between political values and moral values in N MacCormick, 'Institutional Normative Order: A Conception of Law' (1997) 82 *Cornell Law Review* 1062. For a general consideration on the instrumental relations between values and norms, see A Giddens, *Introduction to Sociology* (2nd edn, New York, WW Norton & Company, 1996) 58.

In addition to this political contextualisation of the legal phenomenon, contemporary legal theories also keep as their lowest common denominator the fact that law and politics are two different phenomena. To a lesser or greater extent, as in the embedded and autonomous models respectively, the legal world is considered as something special in relation to politics, something different. This is particularly true in light of the previous analysis, where it is evident that most of the contemporary legal theories do claim a certain (low or high) degree of autonomy of law from politics, regardless of whether the latter are considered autonomous, embedded or intersecting. Even for the theories most loyal to the embedded model, the law-making, although embedded in a political environment and therefore highly charged by the political atmosphere, still keeps a certain degree of separation from the propaganda and persuasive statements characterising the processes occurring in, and the results coming from, the political world.[3]

In summary, contemporary legal theories then portray the law as being somehow different from the political phenomenon and, at the same time, as having points of contacts with it, although varying in intensity and quality according to the legal theories under investigation. Among the several points of contact the legal phenomenon has with the political phenomenon, one in particular is present in all the theories described in the previous chapters: the *transformational moment*. This refers to the moment when the law-making and its actors transform the values expressed inside the political arena into legal categories and concepts. In other words, this is the moment in the law-making process when certain legal concepts and categories are used (or invented) because of their being the legal tools most suited (according to the most different criteria and parameters) for transforming certain values into law.[4]

For example, it is the moment when the value of an interventionist attitude of the state with respect to the economy (in order to protect the public) is transformed into several legal limitations or counter-principles as to the general legal principle of freedom of contract.[5] Alternatively, it can be the moment when the legislator decides to use the legal concept of strict liability for damages arising from the negligence of a nuclear-power station operator. This decision can be taken, on one hand, in order to increase the general value of securing a certain community (at least economically) from

---

[3] See eg, K Klare, 'The Politics of Duncan Kennedy's Critique' (2001) 22 *Cardozo Law Review* 1078.

[4] The necessity of a transformation when moving from a political discourse to a legal discourse is also pointed out by J Habermas, *Between Facts and Norms: Contributions to a Discourse Theory of Law and Democracy* (Cambridge, The MIT Press, 1998) 255.

[5] See eg, the Sherman Act of 1890, 15 USC §§ 1–7 (2000). See also GC Cheshire et al, *Cheshire, Fifoot, and Furmston's Law of Contract* (13th edn, London, Butterworths, 1996) 352–3.

nuclear incidents. On the other hand, the legislator, in using a strict liability concept, also aims at keeping alive (in particular through limitations in the damages that can be awarded) the value of not bringing certain economic activities, dangerous but vital for the economic system, to a complete standstill.

As the following shows, the centrality of this transformational moment for all three models in terms of the relations between law and politics is evident. It is the moment that designates the border (more or less clearly) at which the political phenomenon leaves space to the legal phenomenon. It is the box which is inserted into the picture of the boundaries between the political world and the legal phenomenon as drawn by the vast majority of contemporary legal theories, allowing politics and law to touch upon each other and, at the same time, to keep their distinct characters.

Despite placing this key moment at the centre of the working of their ideas of law in relation to politics, contemporary legal theories seem, generally speaking, to have paid relatively little attention to this important moment (as with the embedded and autonomous models) or to have investigated it from a unilateral perspective (as for the intersecting model).

The box in which values become law is certainly not completely ignored or unexplored by contemporary legal theories; legal scholars do not portray the transformational moment as a black box where values become law. It is more that legal scholars simply leave this moment in a grey world, either as an underestimated or not adequately analysed moment of the law-making processes. What it is or how it works tends to be either left outside the major concerns of legal scholars (as for Kelsen) or is simply assumed as unnecessary, the moment's content and way of working almost self-evident (as for CLS).

This very problem, ie the one of giving a central position to the transformational moment in the idea of what the law is and how the law-making processes work, while somehow leaving its investigation in the background, affects most contemporary legal theories. Although the reasons behind this choice of different legal theories for leaving the transformational moment in the grey area of their interests are various, a common background can be traced to the fact that the issue of the relationships between law and politics has often been approached from the perspective of the legal actors. This has caused the vanishing of the question of law and politics into the wider ocean as represented by the issue of the definition of what is and is not law, as well as what legal actors should or should not consider as their domain. The issue of whether and to what extent the law interrelates with politics has often been absorbed into the general questions of what a valid law is and, consequently, how a legal actor can distinguish a valid law from an invalid one. These questions are those which have preoccupied the minds of the most prominent of the past century's legal scholars as soon as the issue of the relation of values and law came into the spotlight of the theoretical discussion.[6]

II. THE TRANSFORMATIONAL MOMENT AND THE AUTONOMOUS MODEL

Starting with the autonomous model, the moment of transformation of values into law plays a central role in the law and law-making as described by legal positivists and by Hart's analytical jurisprudence. A crucial position in this model is attributed to the transformational moment by the very features through which Kelsen and Hart characterise law and law-making in general.

For both Kelsen and Hart, the nature of the law and its functioning can only be described, at least from a legal perspective, in terms and categories particular and specific to the law itself. They both state that law and law-making are normative phenomena. The law and law-making are phenomena whose existence and operational results (eg statutes or judicial decisions) have their ontological and epistemological dimensions only by using parameters and criteria built by the law and law-making themselves (eg the criterion of legal validity).

In particular, Hart refers to the legal culture shared by the actors operating inside the legal world (the internal point of view) as the only perspective capable of penetrating the essence of the law. Hart focuses on the distinction between internal and external perspectives in order to point out that legal actors, when they operate as such, see and use the law as an autonomous entity. This autonomy is ensured by making reference to the Rule of Recognition as its ultimate foundation. The Rule of Recognition is a normative justification of the legal order, ie a justification based on its being a rule (eg 'whatever Rex I enacts is law') and not on its expressing certain values (eg 'whatever virtuous Rex I enacts is law').[7]

Kelsen also aims at giving an autonomous normative essence to the law and law-making, ie a foundation internal to them. As seen in chapter one,

---

[6] See eg, HLA Hart, 'Positivism and the Separation of Law and Morals' (1958) 71 *Harvard Law Review* 622; L Fuller, 'Positivism and Fidelity to Law: A Reply to Professor Hart' (1958) 71 *Harvard Law Review* 644; R Dworkin, 'The Model of Rules' (1967) 35 *University of Chicago Law Review* 22; and J Raz, 'Legal Principles and the Limits of Law' (1972) 81 *Yale Law Journal* 842. See also J Waldron, 'Legal and Political Philosophy' in J Coleman and S Shapiro (eds), *The Oxford Handbook of Jurisprudence and Philosophy of Law* (Oxford, Oxford University Press, 2002) 361–8. As to the socio-political reasons behind this propensity, see R Cotterrell, *The Politics of Jurisprudence: a Critical Introduction to Legal Philosophy* (2nd edn, London, Lexis Nexis, 2003) 11–13.

[7] See HLA Hart, *The Concept of Law* (Oxford, Clarendon Press, 1961) 55–60. See also J Coleman, 'Incorporationism, Conventionality, and the Practical Difference Thesis' in J Coleman (ed), *Hart's Postscript: Essays on the Postscript to the Concept of Law* (Oxford, Oxford University Press, 2001) 120.

he then focuses on the objective meaning as the true essence of the law and law-making, a meaning given to a statute or a judicial decision by their positions at a particular step in a long stairway, namely the *Stufenbau*. The law and law-making are normative not only because they are constructed by norms, but also because they are ultimately grounded on a norm, the Basic Norm.[8]

Because of these very normative features of the law and law-making, the transformational moment becomes a central process in the autonomous model of relating law and politics. In fact, for both Kelsen and Hart, the political environment affects the legal actors. Hart does not have any problem stating:

> It is of crucial importance that cases for decision do not arise in a vacuum but in the course of the operation of a working body of rules, an operation in which a multiplicity of diverse considerations are continuously recognised as good reasons for a decision. These include a wide variety of individual and social interests, social and political aims, and standards of morality and justice.[9]

For example, when deciding a case in contract law between a multinational corporation and an individual consumer, the judge cannot avoid taking into consideration the moral or the political *stricto sensu* environment in which the dispute is taking place.

However, for both Kelsen and Hart, only the values produced inside the political world that have been recognised by the legal order through a process of statutory or judicial law-making, ie that have become valid law, can have space as law in a judicial courtroom or in a faculty of law. For example, the political value of 'protecting the weaker part of society' should not, according to either Kelsen or Hart, have any legal relevancy and therefore should not bind, at least as a legally binding norm, either the judge or the population. This is true unless the political value is transformed into legal categories, such as the protection of consumers through mandatory provisions, to be inserted *ex lege* in certain types of contracts (eg insurance contracts) regardless of the different agreement made by the parties.

The entrance into the legal world (as legally binding rules) and into legal discussions (as a matter for the legal discipline) is permitted only to those political instances and values that have become legally relevant, ie that

---

[8]   See H Kelsen, *The Pure Theory of Law* (Berkeley, University of California Press, 1970) 221–4; H Kelsen, 'Value Judgments in the Science of Law' in H Kelsen, *What is Justice? Justice, Law, and Politics in the Mirror of Science* (Berkeley, University of California Press, 1957) 213–18; and H Kelsen, 'The Function of a Constitution' in R Tur and W Twining (eds), *Essays on Kelsen* (Oxford, Clarendon Press, 1986) 118–19.

[9]   HLA Hart, 'Problems of the Philosophy of Law' in HLA Hart, *Essays in Jurisprudence and Philosophy* (Oxford, Clarendon Press, 1983) 107. See also Kelsen, 'The Pure Theory of Law and Analytical Jurisprudence' (n 1 above) 54; and T Campbell, 'The Point of Legal Positivism' (1998) 9 *King's College Law Journal* 66.

have gone through the transformational box and have taken the shape of legal categories and concepts. This box transforming values into law can be positioned at a higher level of the legal system, such as in the Kelsenian Basic Norm or in the Hartian Rule of Recognition. Kelsen states the role of the Basic Norm as transferring the meaning of the statements from a subjective dimension expressing the personal value of the legislator or judge, to an objective one defined according to its position in the legal system.[10] In a similar way, Hart's Rule of Recognition 'sets criteria against which other rules [eg moral or political *stricto sensu*] can be tested' and, in case of a positive response, admitted into the world of the law.[11]

The transformational process can also take place at a lower level, such as in the judicial decisional process. Kelsen stresses, for example, the importance of the judicial moment as the moment of creation of either individual norms or, for common- aw countries, of norms of a statutory level through the doctrine of precedent.[12] In replying to Dworkin's criticisms, Hart also points out the limited law-creating power of judges, a limited but nevertheless existent power.[13]

The theories covered by the autonomous model then recognise this moment of the transformation of values into legal categories and concepts as a crucial moment. During it, that which will affect the community as law is separated from that which is to operate as political statements, ie as statements lacking the essential feature of being considered binding by the legal actors. The Kelsenian and Hartian general ideas of law and law-making then require the positioning of the transformational moment in a crucial location: when the valid law is created out of non-legally relevant instances, for example, when a statute binding a judge is created from political statements in the national assembly. The transformational moment is the box that determines the ontological border of what belongs (and what does not) to the law and the epistemological border of what is the object of legal studies.

It is true that legal positivism and analytical jurisprudence tend to consider the transformational processes as taking place in a finite moment.

---

[10] See Kelsen, *The Pure Theory of Law* (n 8 above) 201–5; and Kelsen, 'The Function of a Constitution' (n 8 above) 112–15. See also N Bobbio, 'Kelsen and Legal Power' in SL Paulson and B Litschewski Paulson (eds), *Normativity and Norms: Critical Perspectives on Kelsenian Themes* (Oxford, Clarendon Press, 1998) 438; and A Carrino, 'Reflections on Legal Science, Law, and Power' in Paulson and Litschewski Paulson (eds), *ibid* 517.

[11] N MacCormick, *H.L.A. Hart* (Stanford, Stanford University Press, 1981) 109. See also HLA Hart, 'Postscript' in HLA Hart, *The Concept of Law* (PA Bulloch and J Raz (eds), 2nd edn, Oxford, Clarendon Press, 1994) 258; and J Coleman, 'Negative and Positive Positivism' (1982) XI *Journal of Legal Studies* 162.

[12] See Kelsen, *The Pure Theory of Law* (n 8 above) 238–9; and H Kelsen, *General Theory of Law and State* (Cambridge, Harvard University Press, 1949) 272.

[13] See Hart, 'Postscript' (n 11 above) 272–6. See also Hart, *The Concept of Law* (n 7 above) 130–2.

When the transformation from values into legal concepts and categories occurs, either at the highest level (eg in the Kelsenian first constitution) or at a lower level (eg in the Hartian judicial reasoning), the legal actors convert, in the twinkling of an eye, the values expressed in the political arena into legal categories and concepts. For example, according to the theories grouped under the autonomous model, legislators drafting a constitution or judges deciding a case simply find in the legal category of 'due compensation' for land expropriated by public authorities, the best balance of private and public interests or, in other words, the middle-value between the values of the sacredness of private property and the submission of the individual to the interests of the community.[14]

However, although occupying a limited space in their designs of law and law-making, the transformational moment for both legal positivism and analytical jurisprudence retains a crucial position. It is the narrow and short bridge that connects the two autonomous worlds of law and politics, allowing politics to transfer its values into law, after the values are transformed into structures of legal concepts and categories. It is the box that the values expressed in the political world have to pass through in order to have a space, as valid law, in the working and reasoning taking place in the legal world.

A. The Transformational Moment at the Periphery of the Autonomous Model's Investigation

Kelsen and Hart have an idea of a legal investigation that only considers the law as its object. Even if for different philosophical reasons, it is important for both Kelsen and Hart to clearly demarcate the legal field before commencing any scientific investigation of it.[15] The law is constituted of legal rules articulated in legal categories and concepts, ie by patterns of behaviours articulated in categories and concepts accepted into the legal world (via the Basic Norm or the Rule of Recognition). Hence this moment of transformation plays the fundamental role of distinguishing what can be the object of a legal investigation from what it has to leave to the other branches of knowledge, such as political science or moral philosophy.

One of the first tasks of a legal positivistic or analytical jurisprudential investigation then should be the analysis of the transformational process, ie

---

[14]   See R Cotterrell, *Law's Community: Legal Theory in Sociological Perspective* (Oxford, Clarendon Press, 1995) 97.

[15]   As to the different philosophical roots for such an epistemological premise, see SL Paulson, 'The Neo-Kantian Dimension of Kelsen's Pure Theory of Law' (1992) 12 *OJLS* 324; and HLA Hart, 'Introduction' in HLA Hart, *Essays in Jurisprudence and Philosophy* (Oxford, Clarendon Press, 1983) 1–4.

the process that results in drawing the sharp line of the autonomous model where politics ends and the law begins. This task should be pursued in particular in light of the fact that both legal positivism and analytical jurisprudence have as a fundamental task of their investigations the urgency of the separation of legal statements from value-charged statements.[16] In other words, one expects the centrality of the transformational box in the portrayals of the law and law-making as proposed by legal positivism and analytical jurisprudence to also seep into their legal inquiries.

Instead, Kelsen and Hart propose a narrowing of the lens through which the legal investigator should look at the relations between law and politics, a restriction that, in the end, excludes most of the transformational moment. They somehow leave the box where values are transformed into law in the twilight of legal investigation.[17] For Kelsen, this pushing of the analysis of the transformational moments into a grey zone is due to his claim that values are not a subject matter for scientific cognition, that is to say there cannot be a normative science of values. Values cannot be investigated in terms of a normative account or Ought-propositions but only in terms of descriptive or Is-propositions. This, as seen before, implies an ontological and epistemological shift from the legal world and the legal investigation to the space-time reality and the socio-political studies respectively.[18]

Kelsen admits that the law-making process cannot be completely separated from politics. However, when it comes to legal investigation, why and how values have been transformed into law is outside the sphere of the competence of the legal scholar.[19] On the contrary, Hart leaves the door open to a normative investigation of values. He introduces as one of the fundamental features of legal language its open character, and the idea of a penumbra of meanings surrounding legal concepts and categories (eg in the definition of due process). Using this area of uncertainty, the judge in particular can play a more political role, ie a role of transforming and inserting values into the penumbral areas of meaning of a legal concept. More generally, Hart recognises that:

the further ways in which law mirrors morality are myriad, and still insufficiently studied ... No 'positivist' could deny that these [mirrorings] are facts, or

---

[16] See HLA Hart, 'Analytical Jurisprudence in Mid-Twentieth Century: a Reply to Professor Bodenheimer' (1957) 105 *University of Pennsylvania Law Review* 972; and Kelsen, *General Theory of Law and State* (n 12 above) 437–9.

[17] See Cotterrell, *The Politics of Jurisprudence* (n 6 above) 143.

[18] See Kelsen, 'Value Judgments in the Science of Law' (n 8 above) 227–30.

[19] See H Kelsen, 'Science and Politics' in Kelsen, *What is Justice?* (n 8 above) 365.

that the stability of legal orders depends in part upon such types of correspondence with morals. If this is what is meant by the necessary connection of law and morals, its existence should be conceded.[20]

However, Hart himself seems to hold the possibility of conducting a legal analysis of this connection in low estimate. For example, he positions the transformational process of the judge under the umbrella of traditional legal judicial interpretative processes by stating that the question of whether the judge plays a legislative role and inserts certain values by making use of the penumbra of the law is not important.[21] What really is important for a legal scholar is focusing on the judicial activity directed at expanding the space occupied by the clarified legal concepts at the expense of the penumbral area, an expansion without involving value-reasoning. In this way, Hart is able to admit, on the one hand, a normative investigation of the values, while on the other keeping it separate from the descriptive or conceptual inquiry of the law, ie the inquiry for which the legal scholar must aim.[22]

Although for different reasons, Kelsen's and Hart's attention is not then focused on how and why values get transformed into law, but mostly on the day-after such transformations occur, ie when it is a question of deciding which values produced in the political arena are in or out of the legal world, which values came out of the transformational box. Questions as to how the process of transformation occurs and why certain legal categories and concepts have been chosen (or newly created) as better corresponding to the values the political actors wish to implement in the community, tend to be left deliberately in the grey area of their investigating spotlights by the theories covered by the autonomous model.[23] These legal theories do not address, for example, the issue of how and why 'due compensation' in the case of expropriation for the construction of the public infrastructure is considered by the legislator drafting the constitution, or by a judge, as the most faithful legal translation of the value of balancing the collective interest in seizure and the individual interest in being secure in ownership.

---

[20]   See Hart, *The Concept of Law* (n 7 above) 199–200. See also Hart, 'Positivism and the Separation of Law and Morals' (n 6 above) 606–15.

[21]   *Ibid* 612. This negative attitude towards the legal investigation of the connecting points between law and morals does not hinder Hart from attempting other kinds of non-legally relevant investigations of such points, eg investigations of a more traditional moral nature. See eg, HLA Hart, *Law, Liberty, and Morality* (Stanford, Stanford University Press, 1965) 34–8.

[22]   See Hart, 'Positivism and the Separation of Law and Morals' (n 6 above) 615; and Hart, 'Problems of the Philosophy of Law' (n 9 above) 110.

[23]   This lack of interest with respect to the transformational moment can be ascribed to a more general lack of interest of legal positivists as to providing a predictive theory of the law-making processes in favour of a mere description of already existing results coming out of such processes. See eg, S Perry, 'Hart's Methodological Positivism' in Coleman (ed), *Hart's Postscript* (n 7 above) 326–8.

It is true that Hart and Kelsen admit a value-panorama in which the transformation has to take place, a panorama that both the legislator and the judge should take into consideration when they want to transform values into valid law. In particular, the transformation has to be made by legal actors either according to a Rule of Recognition as the 'rule of the group to be supported by the social pressure' (Hart) or into 'by and large effective' legal concepts and categories (Kelsen).[24] However, this panorama of social and political values that the process of transformation has to take into account remains in the horizon for both Hart and Kelsen. When it comes to the investigation of the transformational processes, both Kelsen and Hart arrive at the same conclusion: both legal positivists and followers of analytical jurisprudence explicitly (as Kelsen) or factually (as Hart) deny any interest, at least from the legal studies' perspective, in the processes and modes of working of the transformational moment, restricting the area of legal inquiry to the valid, or positive, law.[25]

What happens to the values before they become fully valid law cannot be given a space in legal studies as this passage concerns something not fully valid law (yet). Kelsen and Hart deliberately leave outside or at the borders of the legal inquiry the study of how the box connecting law and politics makes particular political events law, while other political events remain outside the legal field. For example, under the autonomous model, a legal analysis of the introduction of a system of strict liability should not go beyond that stated in the statutes, in the judicial decisions, or (at least for Hart) considered to be legally relevant by the legal community. The theories covered by the autonomous model do not require any investigation of the types of values for which strict liability is the legal version. They do not require an answer from a legal scholar to the questions of whether strict liability is the transformation into law of moral or economic values, of the protection of the safety of the community or of the competing value of encouraging economic activities in dangerous areas through establishing their terms of liability clearly.[26]

Much criticism has been directed at the effects of these choices, of either ignoring (Kelsen) or not fully developing (Hart) an analysis of one basic element in their theoretical houses: the passage from the political field to

---

[24] Hart, *The Concept of Law* (n 7 above) 92 and Kelsen, *The Pure Theory of Law* (n 8 above) 212. See also Hart, 'Analytical Jurisprudence in Mid-Twentieth Century' (n 16 above) 955; and Kelsen, 'Value Judgments in the Science of Law' (n 8 above) 225.

[25] See eg, Hart, *The Concept of Law* (n 7 above) 206; or H Kelsen, *Allgemeine Staatslehre* (Berlin, Julius Springer, 1925) 321.

[26] See eg, Hart, *The Concept of Law* (n 7 above) 168–76. Compare M Kramer, *Where Law and Morality Meet* (Oxford, Oxford University Press, 2004) 249–74. For a criticism as to some of the effects of Hart's silence concerning the transformational moment, see MacCormick, *H.L.A. Hart* (n 11 above) 133.

the legal one. The critique has often been based on stressing the consequences of Kelsen's ignoring the actual political nature of his box (eg the Basic Norm) or Hart's not fully developing the socio-political underpinnings of his Rule of Recognition and its role of demarcating the pre-legal from the legal.[27] As pointed out by Raz, Kelsen leaves unresolved, for example, a basic dilemma by failing to investigate the transformational moment. On one hand, he admits the influences of the political environment on the judicial law-making and, consequently, on the law. On the other hand, in order to save the purity of his legal theory, Kelsen simply excludes such influences from his investigation of what the law is, as if they did not exist legally.[28]

III. THE TRANSFORMATIONAL MOMENT AND THE EMBEDDED MODEL

The moment of transformation is central in the functioning of the law and law-making as portrayed by the autonomous model because it is the place where law and politics are distinguished from each other. Within the embedded model, the moment of transforming values into legal categories and concepts is also crucial, but for the opposite reason: this moment is the place where politics begins its embedding process of the law and its law-making. The transformational moment represents only the first step in a wider process at the end of which the law is embedded into the political surroundings.

As seen in chapter one, the legal phenomenon according to the embedded model is constantly and widely open to influences coming from the political arena. The values produced in the political arena affect the law through its entire life, from its formation to its interpretation to its application. They almost do not find any barriers to the entrance of such values into the legal world. Legal concepts and categories parallel that taking place inside the political world, both in terms of processes (mirroring conflicts between different values) and of final results (the prevalence of one group of values over others). For example, Unger states that the 'current content of public and private law fails to present a single,

---

[27] See eg, A Ross, *On Law and Justice* (London, Stevens & Sons, 1958) 69–70; J Stone, *Legal System and Lawyers' Reasonings* (Stanford, Stanford University Press, 1968) 127–31; J Cohen, 'The Political Element in Legal Theory: a Look at Kelsen's Pure Theory' (1978) 88 *Yale Law Journal* 13; Cotterrell, *The Politics of Jurisprudence* (n 6 above) 90–2; and K Greenawalt, 'The Rule of Recognition and the Constitution' (1987) 85 *Michigan Law Review* 630. As to Hart and the possibility of the existence in reality of several rules of recognition inside a legal order, see J Raz, 'The Identity of Legal Systems' (1971) 59 *California Law Review* 810.

[28] See J Raz, 'The Problem about the Nature of Law' in J Raz, *Ethics in the Public Domain: Essays in the Morality of Law and Politics* (Oxford, Clarendon Press, 1994) 186.

unequivocal version of the democracy and the market. On the contrary, it contains in confused and undeveloped form the elements of different versions.'[29]

The transformational moment in the embedded model plays a fundamental function in relating the law to the surrounding political environment. It is the first step in the life of a statute or a judicial decision, at least from the legal actors' perspective, in which the legal phenomenon acquires its embedded nature. More explicitly than legal positivists and analytical jurisprudence scholars, the legal theories covered by the embedded model state the existence and the central position occupied in their design of law and law-making by the process of transforming values into legal categories and concepts.[30]

The crucial role of the transformational moment in the embedded model is given by the fact that it indicates the very moment when the legal concepts are constructed and/or adopted by judges or legislators for the reason that such concepts are able to properly introduce into the legal world the instances of the surrounding political environment. Such instances can be the basic forms of human good, the political values of the ruling elite, or the efficiency of a capitalistic economic system. Regardless of their content, the different theories covered by the embedded model have the fact in common that it is *in primis* due to the nature of this transformational moment that the legal phenomenon ends up incorporated into politics: there is an open passage of values (and value-conflicts) from politics to law.

In Unger's famous article, 'The Critical Legal Studies Movement', the basic idea shared by the embedded model's theories, that the openness of the transformational moment makes both the law flexible to that which happens in the surrounding political context and the law-making open to the processes occurring in the political arena, is traceable to one example. Unger suggests that the 'destabilisation rights' could be the best legal version of the American value of equal protection. These rights (legal categories) are indeed 'the results from the interaction between a social idea and beliefs about the actual working of a society', ie they are a product of the interaction of values.[31]

---

[29] R Mangabeira Unger, 'The Critical Legal Studies Movement' (1982) 96 *Harvard Law Review* 570. See also R Posner, 'The Ethical and Political Basis of the Efficiency Norm in Common Law Adjudication' (1980) 8 *Hofstra Law Review* 495; and J Finnis, 'On "Positivism" and "Legal Rational Authority"' (1985) 5 *OJLS* 84, 87–8.

[30] See eg, I Ehrlich and R Posner, 'An Economic Analysis of Legal Rulemaking' (1974) III *Journal of Legal Studies* 260. As to the different commencements of the process of the embodiment of the law into politics for political actors, see R Dworkin, *Law's Empire* (Cambridge, Harvard University Press, 1997) 190–5.

[31] See Unger, 'The Critical Legal Studies Movement' (n 29 above) 612.

Similar to the autonomous model, the theories covered by the embedded model also recognise that political instances have to be transformed in order to be loaded into the tracks of the legal machinery. The values have to take the shape of legal concepts and categories.[32] What primarily characterises the theories covered by the embedded model, however, is their concept of this transformational moment. In contrast to the autonomous model, the transformational moment is perceived here as having a fluid nature. It is not a finite moment but covers and inserts itself in every aspect both of the law and the working of the law-making.

This moment of transformation is generally spread along the entire law-making process, from the value-charged messages of the Constitution to the political underpinning of administrative decisions, and among its different actors, from the drafters of a constitution to the public servants working in a local administrative office.[33] This insertion of political values into the embedded legal world takes different forms according to the different legal theories covered by the embedded model: as a logical-deductive process for natural legal scholars, as a socio-linguistic phenomenon for CLS adherents, or as judicial reasoning for law and economics followers.

In Finnis' legal theory, the insertion of non-legal concepts and categories into the legal arena occurs through the process of *determinatio*, a process of deriving legal rules from moral values. Finnis points out in particular how legal concepts as adopted or created by judges or by legislators are most of the time second-degree *determinationes*. The legal concepts and categories can be derived by any legal actor enjoying a creative role in accordance with the principle of practical reasonableness, with the final goal of promoting the general requirement of favouring continuity in human affairs. This continuity in its turn is functional to the general good of humankind.[34]

CLS scholars also acknowledge the crucial position played by the processes of the transformation of values into law, but they find the operation of the processes of transformation in the indeterminate nature of the legal language. For CLS, the transformation occurs through the interpretations made by legal actors (either the legislator, judge or public

---

[32] See eg, J Finnis, 'On the Incoherence of Legal Positivism' (2000) 75 *Notre Dame Law Review* 1604. See also R Mangabeira Unger, *What Should Legal Analysis Become?* (London, Verso 1996) 139–42; J Finnis, *Natural Law and Natural Rights* (Oxford, Clarendon Press, 1980) 169–73; and R Posner, 'Wealth Maximization Revisited' (1985) 2 *Notre Dame Journal of Law, Ethics and Public Policy* 94, where Posner admits the necessity of a preliminary assignment of property rights in order to have wealth maximisation as a guiding value.

[33] See eg, M Moore, *Educating Oneself in Public: Critical Essays in Jurisprudence* (Oxford, Oxford University Press, 2000) 300, 330–2; or M Kelman, 'Trashing' (1984) 36 *Stanford Law Review* 337.

[34] See Finnis, *Natural Law and Natural Rights* (n 32 above) 286–8.

servant) of the vaguely expressed legal concepts and categories drawn, for example, from the Constitution or a statute. The legal actors, in their turn, are the direct product of a particular political value-environment, constantly tending to mould the vague legal language with interpretative propositions built up around such values. The legal actors give rise to a 'manipulation of the legal materials to provide the illusionfor themselves and for the others—that the law supports or requires what they do'.[35]

In the same way as the other legal theories covered by the embedded model, the school of law and economics places the transformational moment in a central position in its depiction of the relations between the legal world and the world of politics. Both in the descriptive and in the prescriptive modes of analysis developed inside the school of law and economics, the transformational process is the moment when 'instances' in the case of the prescriptive version or 'objective economic values' in the descriptive version, such as free trade or property rights, are transformed and introduced into the law-making.[36]

The transformational process takes the form of legal reasoning and it is within the legal reasoning, for both judges and legislative bodies, that one can detect the transfer of an economic view from the political environment to the legal world through the creation of efficient judicial solutions. For example, the transformational moment is presented by the law and economics movement in the form of the judicial economic reasoning behind the binding interpretation of the First Amendment of the US Constitution (production of legal category) as encouraging the value of 'free market in two particular "goods"—ideas, and religion'.[37]

It is this very omnipresence and constant working of the transformational moment that gives their main features to the theories belonging to the embedded model. These features are the opening of the law-making towards the political world, and the rendering of law flexible towards the values produced inside this world. The transformational moment also plays another function, a function similar to the one performed in the

---

[35] D Kairys, 'Introduction' in D Kairys (ed), *The Politics of Law: a Progressive Critique* (3rd edn, New York, Basic Books, 1998) 14. See also D Kennedy, 'Legal Education as Training for Hierarchy' in *ibid* 60–2; K Klare, 'Labor Law as Ideology: Toward a New Historiography of Collective Bargaining Law' (1981) 4 *Industrial Relations Law Journal* 469; and D Trubek, 'Where the Action is: Critical Legal Studies and Empiricism' (1984) 36 *Stanford Law Review* 603.

[36] See eg, Posner, 'Wealth Maximization Revisited' (n 32 above) 104. See also D Brion, 'Norms and Values in Law and Economics' in B Bouckaert and G De Geest (eds), *Encyclopedia of Law and Economics* vol I (Celtenham, Edward Elgar Publishing, 2000) 1042–8.

[37] R Posner, 'The Law and Economics Movement' (1987) 77 *American Economic Review* 12. See also Ehrlich and Posner, 'An Economic Analysis of Legal Rulemaking' (n 30 above) 278; and R Posner, 'The Problematics of Moral and Legal Theory' (1998) 111 *Harvard Law Review* 1700 and App.

autonomous model. It works as a dividing line between law and politics. It is the transformational moment that ensures that the law, although embedded in (and therefore strongly influenced by) the political environment, retains certain unique features differentiating it from politics and preventing the legal phenomenon from disappearing into the surrounding political ocean.

As already seen in chapter one, the theories covered by the embedded model still maintain despite their vision of the law-making as open towards the political order, a (thin) line separating the legal phenomenon and the surrounding value-environment. For natural law theories, CLS and law and economics, the law, despite everything, is a product of a specific group of persons, working according to specific criteria and using specific categories and concepts. All elements (persons, procedures and concepts) are heavily moulded and influenced by the political environment in which they operate, but they do not evaporate within it.[38]

The theories covered by the embedded model propose, in the end, an idea of the law as flexible towards politics, not as an evaporating law. They expose an idea of law and law-making that, when it comes into contact with the political arena and its value outputs, does not vanish into thin air but adapts itself flexibly to such outputs. Legal categories and concepts adapt themselves to politics while still circling around a hard-core centre of a specific legal nature (eg the use of a certain kind of language, legal language, and not political propaganda's language). For the followers of the embedded model, generally speaking, law *is not* politics, but rather law *expresses* (often in a contradictory way) that which happens inside politics.[39]

Law tends to keep a certain degree of (limited) autonomy since all political messages for which the law is the dutiful carrier nevertheless have to be transformed by a certain group of actors (usually also identified by the legal order itself, eg in the Constitution) into legal categories and concepts in order to have space in a judicial decision or in a statute. Politics has to become (to some extent) law (or at least legal language) in order, thereafter, to give a strong political imprinting to the law itself. In this fashion, the transformational moment then plays the very important role

[38] See eg, J Finnis, 'The Authority of Law in the Predicament of Contemporary Social Theory' (1984) 1 *Notre Dame Journal of Law, Ethics and Public Policy* 118. See also B Bix, 'Law as an Autonomous Discipline' in P Cane and M Tushnet (eds), *The Oxford Handbook of Legal Studies* (Oxford, Oxford University Press, 2003) 977.

[39] *See* R Posner, *The Problems of Jurisprudence* (Cambridge, Harvard University Press, 1990) 243. See also Finnis, *Natural Law and Natural Rights* (n 32 above) 260–4; Unger, 'The Critical Legal Studies Movement' (n 29 above) 564; and P Gabel and P Harris, 'Building Power and Breaking Images: Critical Legal Theory and the Practice of Law' (1983) 11 *New York University Review of Law and Social Change* 369.

of constituting the thin line allowing the law to have its own (although embedded) nature and function inside the mass of the political arena.

A. Self-Evidence of the Transformational Moment

From this explicit recognition of the centrality of the transformational moment in the relations between law and politics, it does not, however, follow that it is given a central position in the investigations produced by the scholars of natural law, CLS or law and economics. On the contrary, the study of the transformational moment in the end is left by such schools at the periphery of their investigations of the legal phenomenon. In fact, within the embedded model, every legal act by every legal actor becomes so deeply rooted in the political messages they carry that the transformational process becomes a sort of self-evident and automatic path. It is almost naturally driven by the rules of the fundamental nature of human beings (as in natural law theories), the structural linguistic indeterminacy of law (as in CLS), or the inner goal of economic efficiency driving the work of the judges (as in law and economics).[40]

It is almost self-evident for CLS scholars, for example, that a conservative judge will be less favourable to punitive damages as pleaded by an individual against a large corporation.[41] As history has shown, however, a conservative judicial establishment can sometimes decide otherwise. This can occur because the same establishment can embrace other moral or political values, values that the legal category of punitive damages could promote (eg the protection of individual rights against abuses by large organisations). Moreover, judicial sympathy towards individual claims can be explained by the presence of a formalistic ideology of 'their duty being one of applying the law' which is deeply rooted in the judicial legal culture. As a consequence, the judges feel obliged (despite their personal value systems) to apply a liberal interpretation to a statute in terms of punitive damages.[42]

---

[40] See eg, D Kennedy, 'Freedom and Constraint in Adjudication: a Critical Phenomenology' (1986) 36 *Journal of Legal Education* 547; J Finnis, 'Law and What I Truly Should Decide' (2003) 48 *American Journal of Jurisprudence* 111; and Posner, 'The Law and Economics Movement' (n 37 above) 5.

[41] See eg, RL Abel, 'Judges Write the Darndest Things: Judicial Mystification of Limitations on Tort Liability' (2002) 80 *Texas Law Review* 1554, 1572.

[42] See A Altman, *Critical Legal Studies: a Liberal Critique* (Princeton, Princeton University Press, 1990) 53–4; and Campbell, 'The Point of Legal Positivism' (n 9 above) 83–4. For similar examples on racial issues in US constitutional law, see RA Epstein, *Forbidden Grounds: the Case Against Employment Discrimination Laws* (Cambridge, Harvard University Press, 1992) 91–115; and M Klarman, *From Jim Crow to Civil Rights: the Supreme Court and the Struggle for Racial Equality* (Oxford, Oxford University Press, 2004) 294. This possibility is not ruled out by one of the very representatives of CLS, Horwitz, although he

Because the tendency to pursue different values is part of the very nature of law (due to its flexibility) and law-making (because of its open character), the theories representing the embedded model implicitly assume that the influence of politics (either as a value of efficiency, common good or dominance) is so diffused in every aspect of the law and in the working of the law-making, that it is pointless to limit the investigation only to the processes occurring in the moment of transformation.[43] As a result, the embedded model's legal theories tend to not pursue any specific investigations with respect to this transformational moment.

The legal theories within the embedded model naturally diverge when it comes to detecting the values to which the law tends more to adapt itself. The majority of natural law scholars have focused their attention on investigating the ultimate values that should be at the bottom of a legal order in order to legitimise it as such (eg ideas of justice, democracy, rights and the more procedural fidelity of Fuller). These values, despite the different appearances and momentary defeats, are always present in the consciousness of the majority of human beings, and therefore are reflected in the human construction known as legal phenomenon.[44]

For law and economics, the primary values to take into consideration are those functional to the improvement of the economic activities of a community; therefore they stress the idea of economic efficiency as the cornerstone on which the entire legal order is built. Therefore, law and economics scholars likewise have paid the largest part of their attention to trying to prove the existence of a derivative connection between judicial decisions and the value of economic efficiency (or, more recently, the value of wealth maximisation).[45]

Finally, for CLS scholars, the values realised by the legal machine are those of the political, economic and cultural elites; their task therefore is to expose such monopolies and to give a space in the legal arena to all the voices in a community. Despite their programmatic statement, CLS' primary focus in the end has also been on discovering which political values certain legal categories and concepts hide. The primary target,

discusses it as to another legal issue, namely the legal nature of corporation and the anti-corporate attitude of the conservative US Supreme Court at the end of the nineteenth century. See M Horwitz, *The Transformation of American Law 1870–1960: the Crisis of Legal Orthodoxy* (Oxford, Oxford University Press, 1990) 92–3.

[43] See G Peller, 'The Metaphysics of American Law' (1985) 73 *California Law Review* 1182. See also J Finnis, 'On Reason and Authority in Law's Empire' (1987) 6 *Law and Philosophy* 374; and G Calabresi and DA Melamed, 'Property Rules, Liability Rules, and Inalienability: One View of the Cathedral' (1972) 85 *Harvard Law Review* 1105.

[44] See J Boyle, 'Reasons for Action: Evaluative Cognitions that Underlie Motivations' (2001) 46 *American Journal of Jurisprudence* 197.

[45] See Posner, 'The Law and Economics Movement' (n 37 above) 3–5, about the law and economics' attempt at finding such derivative connection between economic values and areas of law not immediately of economic nature, eg family law.

similar to all the theories covered by the embedded model, is to reveal the 'hidden motives that the judge themselves would treat as illegitimate if forced to confront them'.[46]

The embedded model's legal theories then focus most of their efforts on determining which political, moral and economic instances correspond (or should correspond) to the existing legal categories and concepts. The problem of how and why legal concepts and categories are shaped and used by judges and legislators to implement into the community such values of efficiency, justice or simply the interests of the ruling class, these crucial questions tend to be left at the periphery of the analyses put forward by the embedded model's legal theories.

Similarly to the autonomous model, the embedded model's theories recognise the existence of such links between law and politics, in the sense that political messages are transformed into legal categories and concepts. However, these links are left theoretically explored in an inadequate manner: they remain grey boxes where some inputs come in (the value formed in the surrounding environment) and some outputs come out (the legal category or concept). What happens inside those boxes tends more or less to remain a mystery. The theories covered by the embedded model focus more on the premises (politics) and on the results (legal categories and concepts) of the transformational processes than on the processes themselves.

One article by Posner typifies the inclination, on one side, of recognising the importance of the transformational moment in the law-making and, on the other side, of leaving it mostly unexplored. In 'The Problematics of Moral and Legal Theory', Posner tries to prove how moral values do not work as moulding forces for important judicial decisions, that is for judicial decisions of a law-making nature such as the US Supreme Court's decision in *Roe v Wade*. On the other hand, since 'the standard sources of positive law in our system do not resolve most of the novel issues that judges must decide', judges build new legal categories and concepts, moulding them from other kind of values.[47] For Posner, the legality of abortion is not based on moral considerations, for example, but on the preservation of the professional autonomy of doctors.[48] Moreover, it is true that Posner initially states that his goal is to show that the legal categories of judicial formation are not the result of a transformation of moral values but of other kinds of values. In the end, however, he focuses

---

[46] D Kennedy, 'The Structure of Blackstone's Commentaries' (1979) 28 *Buffalo Law Review* 219. See also D Kennedy, 'Form and Substance in Private Law Adjudication' (1976) 89 *Harvard Law Review* 1732; and A Hutchinson, 'Introduction' in A Hutchinson (ed), *Critical Legal Studies* (Totowa, Rowman & Littlefield Publishers, 1989) 4–6.

[47] Posner, 'The Problematics of Moral and Legal Theory' (n 37 above) 1693.

[48] See *ibid* 1703. Compare J Noonan, 'Posner's Problematics' (1998) 111 *Harvard Law Review* 1768.

his attention only on the issue of what kind of values (freedom of choice vs autonomy of medical profession) corresponds to the legal category built by the courts (the legalisation of abortion).[49]

Posner does not develop any explanation for the two main events occurring in the transformational process from the values to law produced in *Roe v Wade*. Hypothetically, the justices can be viewed as being faced with two alternative and equally strong values, f (preserving the autonomy of the doctors) and e (preserving a human life with respect to the foetus). Why would a judge choose one instead of the other? Moreover, why would a judge consider a legal category, such as l (the decriminalisation of certain actions by doctors) as the category best reflecting in the legal world the value f (preserving the autonomy of the doctors)? Posner tends to focus more on the part values generally play in the administrative and adjudicative procedures of the law, leaving the questions concerning the very 'way' through which such moral values enter into the legal world inadequately investigated. Posner finds that the decision of the US Supreme Court built a bridge between a value (autonomy of professions) and a legal category (decriminalisation of abortion), but he does not explain why the bridge has been built there and how it has been built.

IV. THE TRANSFORMATIONAL MOMENT AND THE INTERSECTING MODEL

The centrality of the moment of the transformation of values into legal concepts and categories is also evident for the theories within the intersecting model. Like the previous models, the two major features attached by the intersecting model to the law and law-making in their relations with politics render the transformational moment a necessary and important stage of the processes through which the political phenomenon interacts with the legal world.

It is a necessary stage because of the idea of the legal realists of the law as having a partially rigid nature towards the political phenomenon. Because of the partial rigidity of the legal concepts and categories, the functioning of the law tends to obey, to a certain extent, its own rules and way of (legal) reasoning. This limited functional autonomy of the legal phenomenon then forces the political environment to take into consideration the specificity of the law and to adapt the values the political actors desire to be implemented into the community to it. This limited rigidity of

---

[49]　See Posner, 'The Problematics of Moral and Legal Theory' (n 37 above) 1638. See also R Dworkin, 'Why Efficiency? A Response to Professors Calabresi and Posner' (1980) 8 *Hofstra Law Review* 564; and R Dworkin, 'Is Wealth a Value?' (1980) 9 *Journal of Legal Studies* 200.

the law implies, similar to legal positivism for instance, that all the values expressed in the political world, in order to be introduced into the legal arena, have to take a new shape and nature, namely that of legal categories and concepts.[50]

For the legal realists, it is in this moment of transformation that the key figures, judges (for the American legal realists and Ross) and/or legislators (for the other Scandinavian realists) decide to give to the indeterminate political statement the nature of legally relevant statements.[51] It is the moment in which the values produced in the political world are allowed to enter into the legal world, taking the partially rigid form and nature of legal concepts and categories. Llewellyn's article regarding letters of credit is an example of the necessity of values being transformed into legal categories in order to become relevant for the legal order. He stresses the importance of the law-making processes as led by the common-law courts in constructing the legal category of letters of credit in order to satisfy the various needs coming from the economic world, such as the elimination of risk and dispute in economic transactions.[52]

Law is seen by legal realists as a tool to be used in order to implement certain values in a community. The transformational moment is the moment during which the primary legal actors decide which legal categories and concepts correspond to the values produced inside the political world. For example, Ross states that the goal of a legal realist is to show how:

> the juridical theory of guilt is really ... a more precise rendering of current moral ideas *adapted to the special needs of the institutions of law*.[53] (emphasis added)

In addition to being a necessary step, the transformational moment also acquires a key position in the legal realists' idea of the law-making process.

---

[50] See J Frank, *The Place of the Expert in a Democratic Society* (Philadelphia, Brandeis Lawyers' Society, 1945) 4–5, 38; K Llewellyn, 'The Normative, the Legal, and the Law-Jobs: the Problem of Juristic Method' (1940) 49 *Yale Law Journal* 1364; and K Olivecrona, *Law as Fact* (2nd edn, London, Stevens & Sons, 1971) 252–4. See also B Leiter, 'Rethinking Legal Realism: Toward a Naturalized Jurisprudence' (1997) 76 *Texas Law Review* 279; and J Bjarup, 'Scepticism and Scandinavian Legal Realists' in T Endicott *et al*, *Properties of Law: Essays in Honour of Jim Harris* (Oxford, Oxford University Press, 2006).60–4.

[51] 'Within the law ... rules *guide*, but they do not *control* decision. There is no precedent the judge may not at his need either file down to razor thinness or expand into a bludgeon.' K Llewellyn, *Bramble Bush: On Our Law and Its Study* (Dobbs Ferry, Oceana Publications, 1996) 180. See also K Llewellyn, *The Common Law Tradition: Deciding Appeals* (Boston, Little, Brown & Company, 1960) 179–80; and Olivecrona, *Law as Fact* (n 50 above) 186–93.

[52] See K Llewellyn, 'Some Advantages of Letters of Credit' (1929) II *Journal of Business* 1. See also V Lundstedt, *Legal Thinking Revised: My Views on Law* (Stockholm, Almqvist & Wiksell, 1956) 179.

[53] A Ross, 'Preface' in A Ross, *On Guilt, Responsibility and Punishment* (London, Stevens & Sons, 1975) v. See also JW Singer, 'Legal Realism Now' (1988) 76 *California Law Review* 483; and, for a concrete application to public law of such programmatic statement, A Ross, *Why Democracy?* (Cambridge, Harvard University Press, 1952) ch VIII.

This primary position is given to the transformational moment by an essential feature of the law-making: its openness towards the political order. Because of this openness of the law-making, the legal phenomenon becomes directly affected in its production of legal categories and concepts by the different choices and the dominant actors inside the political world. The legal actors involved in the transformational process (primarily judges and legislators), on one hand have at disposal their own arsenal of weapons (the partial rigidity of the law), while on the other hand they are under constant and strong pressure to participate on behalf of one side or the other in the battles taking place inside the political arena.

The struggles judges and legislators have among the different legal concepts and categories somehow tend to mirror not so much the struggles between what is the right and the wrong solution according to internal legal standards, such as those of coherence or consistency to the legal system as a whole. They tend instead to mirror more the struggles occurring inside the political world among the different actors, each political actor proposing different values. This idea of the legal conflicts as mirroring the political battles is also confirmed by the fact that the legal realists, both American and Scandinavian, heavily stressed the problem of the possible indeterminacy of the legal language, indeterminacy resulting by such language being the mirror of the often conflicting value-producing environment.[54]

This opening of the law-making, together with its rendering of the law as only a partially rigid structure towards political influences, makes the transformational moment central for the legal realist's entire idea of law and politics. During this moment, judges and legislators have to decide, under the influence of the political environment (through the openness of the law-making), the legal categories and concepts, either new or already existing, which better correspond to the values expressed by the political arena (partial rigidity of the law).

It is exactly in the transformational moment, more than elsewhere, that the final goal behind the adoption of an intersecting model of interpreting the relation between law and politics comes to the surface. The transformational moment is the point, in fact, where legal realists try to combine two apparently incompatible features of the relation between law and politics. On one hand, there is an opening of the law-making towards politics by the legal actors portrayed as open to the influences of the

---

[54] See W Cook, 'The Logical and Legal Basis of the Conflict of Laws' (1942) 33 *Yale Law Journal* 467; Olivecrona, *Law as Fact* (n 50 above) 252–67; J Frank, *Courts on Trial: Myth and Reality in American Justice* (Princeton, Princeton University Press, 1950) 384–8; and M Radin, 'My Philosophy of Law' in *My Philosophy of Law: Credos of Sixteen American Scholars* (Boston, Boston Law Book, 1941) 297–8. See also W Rumble, 'American Legal Realism and the Reduction of Uncertainty' (1964) 13 *Journal of Public Law* 45; and Cotterrell, *The Politics of Jurisprudence* (n 6 above) 198–9.

political environment in which they live and work. On the other hand, the legal realists present an idea of a partial rigidity of law towards politics by arguing the rigidity of the tools at the disposal of the legal actors, used to implement those values that the legal actors sponsor.

As a result of this combination, the legal realists reject the idea of this transformational moment as a unique bridge transferring values from the political world to the legal world (as in the theories covered by the autonomous model). They also discard the idea that these worlds actually are connected by an almost infinite series of highways where values travel more or less freely from politics to law (as in the embedded model). Legal realists try to arrive at some sort of intermediate solution, where the values are transferred into the legal arena from the political world through several paths (varying with the political or value positions of the legal actors). However, the paths are limited both in their extent and in their number.[55]

They are limited in their extent because of the limits of extending the significance of certain legal concepts and categories to encompass the different values expressed by the political arena (and expressed directly inside the legal world through the political positions of judges and legislators). Despite their position in favour of an indeterminacy of the legal concepts and categories, the legal realists never reach the radical conclusion, as did CLS, of a fundamental *global* vagueness of the legal language. Using Leiter's expression, for the legal realists it remains an indeterminacy *localised* to some circumscribed class of cases.[56]

The paths that the values have to follow in order to become law are also limited in their number. The legal phenomenon is a socio-psychological phenomenon and, therefore, it brings with it a need in the law-making to take into consideration the actual dimension of the legal phenomenon. In transforming values into law, the legal actors must avoid the risk of producing mere law-in-books (as for the American legal realists) or mere valid-law (as for the Scandinavian legal realists). They are therefore required to keep in the law-making process a certain adherence to the paths previously followed and considered as law by the addressee community or its judicial representatives. Only by observing the paths previously followed and considered as law, will the final result of the transformational moment have a chance to be real law, ie the law-in-action or the law-in-force.[57]

---

[55] For these series of limitations, see eg, Llewellyn's chapter 'Major Steadying Factors in Our Appellate Courts' in Llewellyn, *The Common Law Tradition* (n 51 above) 18–51.

[56] See B Leiter, 'Legal Realism' in D Patterson (ed), *A Companion to the Philosophy of Law and Legal Theory* (Oxford, Blackwell Press, 1996) 267.

[57] This limitation to the law-making and the transformational moment in particular is well described by Llewellyn's idea that a 'sound sociology of law is the precondition to sound legal technique'. K Llewellyn, 'My Philosophy of Law' in *My Philosophy of Law* (n 54 above) 197. See also Olivecrona, *Law as Fact* (n 50 above) 71.

A. The Transformational Moment in the Legal Realists' Analysis

Similar to other contemporary legal theories, the legal scholars adopting an intersecting model then put the transformational moment as the centre point of their ideas about how the law and law-making interact with the political world. However, in contrast to legal positivism or natural law theories, they also try to make the analysis of such moments as one of the central points of their legal investigations. The legal realists constantly stress the fact that judges and legislators and their actions (eg in the form of processes ending with judicial decisions or legislative acts) should be placed at the centre of any legal investigation concerning how law relates to politics. In the legal realist vision of law-making:

> it will often be he [the lawyer] who, after experts have had their say, will undertake the weighing and balancing of all considerations, and achieve the formulation that best integrates all the motivating components.[58]

The legal realists push their efforts so far in this direction that, as stated in chapter one, they end up considering the legal investigation simply as the study of the law-making processes of legal actors such as judges (American legal realists and Ross), and legislative bodies (Scandinavian legal realists). Not only do the theories covered by the intersecting model then recognise the centrality of the transformational moment, but they also focus their efforts on trying to disclose the processes occurring at that point. This is done by putting the issue of how juries (Frank) or appellate courts (Llewellyn) or legislators (Olivecrona) reason and behave at the centre of their legal analysis. In this way, legal realists can focus on the modalities through which the values coming from the political arena are legalised or, in other words, transformed into the specific discourse represented by the categories and concepts of the judicial and legislator's legal reasoning.[59] For example, according to Ross, a fundamental part of a legal investigation is the exploration of how and to what extent the values of judges have entered into their decisions under the guise of legal concepts and categories.[60]

Considering the centrality of such a transformational process in the legal realists' investigations, it is then not a coincidence that American and Scandinavian legal realists, although coming from different directions, have

---

[58] Ross, *On Law and Justice* (n 27 above) 330. See also Llewellyn, 'The Normative, the Legal, and the Law-Jobs' (n 50 above) 1392–5; and Olivecrona, *Law as Fact* (n 50 above) 212–16. Against *ibid* 4.

[59] See eg, K Llewellyn, 'On Reading and Using the Newer Jurisprudence' (1940) 40 *Columbia Law Review* 593; and Ross, 'Preface' (n 53 above) v.

[60] See Ross, *On Law and Justice* (n 27 above) 104. See also K Llewellyn, 'Some Realism about Realism' (1931) 44 *Harvard Law Review* 1240, in particular at point (a).

both arrived at the same conclusion. Either by elimination of the metaphysical elements in the legal language and thinking (as for the Scandinavians) or by exposing the law-makers' activities as influenced by and influencing the fluctuating socio-political reality (as for the Americans), the legal realists join as to stressing the importance for legal scholars to offer criteria for making such transformational moments more regular and predictable, both in their legislative and judicial dimension.[61]

In the end, judges and legislators live in and work with a law-making which is open towards politics (eg a judge shares a political conservative value-system). Consequently, legal realists converge their investigations towards the fact that the major function played by the legal actors is to sense the values created in the political arena and to transform them into legal categories and concepts. This central and active role that the legal actors have in sensing the values and transforming them into legal categories, is the precondition for the legal realists for their concept of legal activity as social engineering. The law is directed to *shape* certain values into a community more than simply to *transport* them from the political world into the legal one.

Another factor contributing to the central position of the transformational moment in the legal realists' investigation is their concern for the scientific character of their legal investigation. They desire to see how the process of transformation occurs in order to discover (or confirm their theories about) the true essence of the final product: the law as a carrier of political values but also as a shaper of its own tools (ie legal categories and concepts) for the legalisation of such values. This dual essence given to the law by the transformational moment, ie as *political*, for it is constructed in order to carry values into a community, and as *legal*, for the bridges used in such construction are legal categories and concepts, makes the apparently contradictory assertions by some scholars that legal realists are the legal philosophical root of movements such as CLS, and by others about legal realism, in its turn, leaning towards legal positivism, more comprehensible.[62]

---

[61] See N Duxbury, *Patterns of American Jurisprudence* (Oxford, Clarendon Press, 1995) 131. See also M Martin, *Legal Realism: American and Scandinavian* (Bern, Peter Lang, 1997) 109–13, 205; and B Anderson, '*Discovery' in Legal Decision-Making* (London, Kluwer Academic Publishers, 1996) 5–11. See eg, Llewellyn, *The Common Law Tradition* (n 51 above) 215–17; W Cook, 'My Philosophy of Law' in *My Philosophy of Law* (n 54 above) 59; Ross, *On Law and Justice* (n 27 above) 336–9; and Lundstedt, *Legal Thinking Revised* (n 52 above) 140–1. But see Olivecrona, *Law as Fact* (n 50 above) 110–13.

[62] For the traditional legal positivist aspects of legal realism, see eg, L Fuller, 'Reason and Fiat in Case Law' (1946) 59 *Harvard Law Review* 383; and Note, ''Round and Round the Bramble Bush: from Legal Realism to Critical Legal Scholarship' (1982) 95 *Harvard Law Review* 1676. For realism as the father of CLS, see eg, B Bix, *Jurisprudence: Theory and Context* (3rd edn, London, Sweet & Maxwell, 2003) 186; and Martin, *Legal Realism* (n 61 above) 209–15. Against Duxbury, *Patterns of American Jurisprudence* (n 61 above) 424–6;

This centrality of the investigation of the transformational moment in the scholarship of the legal realists is also confirmed by the fact that the very attention of legal realists on this moment, in its turn, has given birth to much criticism directed towards both the American and Scandinavian versions of this movement. As stressed by many critics, one of the weak points of the legal realisms is the fact that they tend to dismiss the true essence of the law, ie its normative nature, by their very focusing on mostly non-normative elements as decisive in determining the work of the legal actors and, consequently (at least according to a legal realist), the nature of the law.[63] The very focus of the realists on the empirical underpinnings of the transformational moment allows critics to point out how the normativity of the law disappears into all the realist socio-psychological explanations of how law-making interacts with the political order, transforming political ideologies into legal categories and concepts. This has, for example, led some of Frank's early critics to label his entire legal philosophy as 'breakfast jurisprudence'.[64]

This disappearance of the normativity of the law into all the realist socio-psychological explanations is even more difficult to justify if, as in this work, the normative nature of law is considered as originally accepted by the realists as qualifying their idea of a (partial) rigidity of the law towards political categories. The legal realists in the end are able to illuminate the box in which values become law only from the side abutting to the legal world and its discourse. They explore the socio-psychological constitutive and influencing factors in the work of the legal actors during the law-making processes, but they still leave unexplored what Hart would define as the internal perspective that the very legal actors have of what they are doing. What is still valid in those criticisms is the fact that the legal realists' attempts at enlightening the transformational moment, even if successful, leave a part of the box in the shadows, a very important part: the normative face of the box, ie the one facing the legal world into which the values enter.

Leiter, 'Rethinking Legal Realism' (n 50 above) 271–4; and EG White, 'From Realism to Critical Legal Studies: a Truncated Intellectual History' (1986) 40 *Southwestern Law Journal* 833.

[63] See HLA Hart, 'Scandinavian Realism' (1959) 1959 *CLJ* 238; Bix, 'Law as an Autonomous Discipline' (n 38 above) 979–80; and JW Harris, 'Olivecrona on Law and Legal Language:the Search for Legal Culture' (1981) 94 *Tidsskrift för Rettsvitenskap* 636. See also Martin, *Legal Realism* (n 61 above) 70–6.

[64] This negative idea of legal realism's explanations of the law-making and law-applying processes is still present, even if in a gentler way, in the works of many contemporary legal theoreticians and philosophers. See eg, J Murphy and J Coleman, *The Philosophy of Law: an Introduction to Jurisprudence* (Totowa, Rowman & Allanheld, 1984) 40–1; J Bjarup, 'Scandinavian Legal Realism' in CB Gray (ed), *The Philosophy of Law: an Encyclopedia* (New York, Garland Publishing, 1999) 773–7. But see Cotterrell, *The Politics of Jurisprudence* (n 6 above) 181–5; cf. B Leiter, 'Legal Realism, Hard Positivism, and the Limits of Conceptual Analysis' in Coleman (ed), *Hart's Postscript* (n 7 above) 369.

V. SOME FURTHER LIGHT ON THE GREY BOX

Beside the legal realists, other contemporary legal scholars and philosophers have attempted to systematically investigate the fundamental issues relating to the transformational moment. These are issues such as the modalities through which this central node of the law-making process works, the individuation of the main actors participating in it, and the magnitude of the influence of what happens in that moment in the law-making and in the law in general.

Among the works specifically directed at investigating the modalities and actors of the transformational moment of the law-making process, a large majority is represented by the theoretical literature focusing on public law.[65] A *raison d'être* of such interest in the transformational moment by the public, and in particular constitutional law scholars, is traceable to the very object of constitutional investigation. It is in the constitutional field where the frictions between the legal world and the political world are, if not more intense, certainly particularly evident. More often than in other parts of the legal system, it is in the very legal structuring and regulating of the relations among powers that the issue surfaces of whether the political goals are 'blunted both by the failure to translate political commitments into law, and the inability of participants to recognise the constraints of the governing legal frameworks'.[66] One example is the problem of translating, at the constitutional level, the support of the vast majority of the political world for the death penalty into legal categories, a measure very difficult to harmonise with a hypothetical constitutional prohibition as to cruel and unusual punishment.[67]

Jeremy Waldron and his traditional legal philosophical perspective is another relevant example of an investigation specifically devoted at enlightening the issue of the transformational moment. Starting from the legal philosophical contributions offered by Aristotle, Hobbes, Locke and

---

[65] Just to mention some examples, see JH Ely, *Democracy and Distrust: a Theory of Judicial Review* (Cambridge, Harvard University Press, 1980) ch 6; M Tushnet, 'Principles, Politics, and Constitutional Law' (1989) 88 *Michigan Law Review* 53, 68–74, 76–80; and B Ackerman, 'Constitutional Politics/Constitutional Law' (1989) 99 *Yale Law Journal* 526.

[66] C Harvey, 'On Law, Politics and Contemporary Constitutionalism' (2003) 26 *Fordham International Law Journal* 996. See also N Luhmann, *Law as a Social System* (Oxford, Oxford University Press, 2004) 403–10; B Cardozo, *The Nature of the Judicial Process* (New Haven, Yale University Press, 1945) 17; Habermas, *Between Facts and Norms* (n 4 above) 384; and F Frankfurter, 'Social Issues before the Supreme Court' in A MacLeish and E Prichard (eds), *Law and Politics: Occasional Papers of Felix Frankfurter 1913–1938* (Gloucester, Peter Smith, 1971) 48–9. See also the famous decision by the US Supreme Court in *Marbury v Madison*, 5 U.S. 164–67 (1803).

[67] See eg, R Bork, *The Tempting of America: the Political Seduction of the Law* (New York, Touchstone/Simon and Schuster, 1990) 213–14; and the criticism by R Dworkin, *Freedom's Law: the Moral Reading of the American Constitution* (Cambridge, Harvard University Press, 1996) 300–1.

Kant, Waldron focuses on one of the central regulatory mechanisms of the transformational process: the principle of majority decision. Waldron also scans the modalities through which such a principle operates in one of the central figures of the law-making process: the legislative body. This legal-philosophical investigation is done in order 'to recover and highlight ways of thinking about legislation that present it as a dignified mode of governance and a respectable source of law'.[68]

Looking more specifically at the representatives of the various models, one can notice how some of them actually do stress the necessity of investigating more and in a deeper way the transformational moment. For example, MacCormick has repeatedly emphasised, both in his articles and in his books, the idea that both the law-making and law-applying processes are 'central to legal activity, and that studying the rational structure of this process is central for explaining the character of legal reasoning as a branch of practical reasoning', ie a branch dealing with the criteria and the values the legal actors have to face in situations of choices of different legal solutions and categories.[69]

Luhmann also represents an example of attention to the transformational coming from the autonomous model. In particular, he points out the necessity of investigating as a central element for defining the law what he terms the 'structural couplings' between the legal phenomenon and the surrounding worlds, *in primis* politics and economics.[70] However, Luhmann's analysis suffers, at least from a legal theoretical perspective, from an original sin: it is not a normative perspective of the transformational moment. Luhmann explicitly and exclusively aims at investigating the legal system only as far and as long as it is considered as a mere subsystem functional of the general social system, as a system 'solely to bring about certainty of expectations'.[71] Neglecting the internal point of view of the law, Luhmann focuses then exclusively on the necessity of inserting the transformational moment into a more general external perspective, evaluating from the outside how law and the surrounding environments

---

[68] J Waldron, *The Dignity of Legislation* (Cambridge, Cambridge University Press, 1999) 2. See also J Waldron, 'Legislation, Authority, and Voting' (1996) 84 *Georgetown Law Journal* 2109; and J Waldron, 'Legislation and Moral Neutrality' in J Waldron, *Liberal Rights: Collected Papers 1981–1991* (Cambridge, Cambridge University Press, 1993) 153.

[69] N MacCormick, *Legal Reasoning and Legal Theory* (Oxford, Clarendon Press, 1997) ix. See also MacCormick, *H.L.A. Hart* (n 11 above) 110–15, 118–20; and N MacCormick, 'The Concept of Law and "The Concept of Law"' (1994) 14 *OJLS* 10. In a similar manner, stressing attention on the transformational moment in the judicial law-making, is J Gardner, 'Concerning Permissive Sources and Gaps' (1988) 8 *OJLS* 459; and Kramer, *Where Law and Morality Meet* (n 26 above) 60–1.

[70] See Luhmann, *Law as a Social System* (n 66 above) ch 10. As to Luhmann's idea of the transformational moment, *see ibid* 152 and ch 2.

[71] *Ibid* 164. See eg, Luhmann's analysis of legal argumentation from an external point of view in *ibid* ch 9.

interact.[72] In short, Luhmann attempts to describe how values are transformed into law and the role legal actors play in it without listening to what the legal actors say about it.

Among the scholars embracing the embedded model for explaining the relations between law and politics, Julius Stone has promoted a systematic investigation of the transformational moment. Stone stresses the social and economic dimensions of the law, that is the embedded position of the legal phenomenon into the surrounding environment of a political nature. As to this issue of the transformational moment, however, Stone seems to have a vision closer to that of the legal realists. In particular, he stresses the importance of studying the transformational moment, as it is one of the points where the *relative* character of the flexibility of the law towards the signals sent from the political world comes to the surface.[73]

A position similar to Stone's is that of the law and society movement. Despite embracing an idea of law embedded into politics, this movement adopts an attitude towards the transformational moment similar in some respects to the one expressed by the legal realists. Friedman openly recognises, for instance, the existence of the transformational moment, underlining the:

> process of transforming attitude—the legal culture—into structures of law ... the process of choosing which legal tools to use, or how those tools are shaped, and the institutional forms they take. The process is certainly not automatic.[74]

The law and society movement stresses the importance of investigating this stage in the law-making process, by using in particular conceptual tools and a perspective of a non-normative character, mainly sociological but also political, historical and economic.[75]

One final example of legal scholars attempting to investigate the moment of the transformation of values into legal concepts and categories can be found in the public choice theory approach to legal phenomenon. In particular, public choice scholars make use of the micro-economic analysis (eg transactions costs theory) in order to build up models of how such interests are transformed into legal categories and concepts. One of the

[72] See *ibid* 142.

[73] See eg, J Stone, *Social Dimensions of Law and Justice* (London, Stevens & Sons, 1966) 609–16; and J Stone, *Legal System and Lawyers' Reasoning* (n 27 above) 29. For a similar attempt to disclose the transformational moment, see M Kelman, 'Interpretative Construction in the Substantive Criminal Law' (1981) 33 *Stanford Law Review* 591.

[74] L Friedman, *Total Justice* (New York, Russell Sage Foundation, 1985) 148. See also B Tamanaha, *A General Jurisprudence of Law and Society* (Oxford, Oxford University Press, 2001) 131–2; and White, 'From Realism to Critical Legal Studies' (n 62 above) 825–30.

[75] See R Cotterrell, 'Introduction' in R Cotterrell (ed), *Law and Society* (New York, New York University Press, 1994) xii–xiii. See eg, Tamanaha, *A General Jurisprudence of Law and Society* (n 74 above) 154–5, 210–11; or L Friedman, *American Law in the 20th Century* (New Heaven, Yale University Press, 2002) 399–406.

basic functions of such models is to demonstrate the fundamental fallacy of the idea that the grey box of the transformational moment is dominated by randomness and anarchy.[76]

VI. CONCLUSION

This chapter has focused on one fundamental moment of the relations between law and politics: when values become legal categories and concepts (the transformational moment). In particular, how such a transformational moment, on one hand, occupies and plays a central position in the different portrayals that all three models (autonomous, embedded and intersecting) draw of the relations between law and politics, has been demonstrated. On the other hand, this moment, for different reasons, has somehow been left by most contemporary legal theories at the margins of their investigations. For the theories covered by the autonomous model, the moment where values become law is important because it clearly marks where politics ends and law begins. However, it is not considered as belonging to the proper domain of legal inquiries. Just the opposite, for scholars embracing the embedded model, law per se is so permeated by political concepts and categories that it is almost futile to tackle the issue of where and how in the law-making process the value-world becomes the world of legal concepts.

Among the contemporary legal theories, legal realism has probably paid the most attention to the transformational moment, making its investigation one of the cornerstones of the legal realist inquiries. However, the illumination of the grey box by legal realists has been done mainly from sociological and psycho-linguistic perspectives, therefore leaving one fundamental face of the box unexplored, namely the normative one. Finally, this chapter has briefly discussed, both within and outside the main legal theories investigated up to now, those legal scholars who, from different angles (philosophical, quasi-sociological or normative) have directed their efforts at systematically penetrating the transformational box.

One final step is now necessary before commencing the voyage that will lead to redressing this problem and to framing a field of systematic studies of such a crucial transformational moment in the law-making processes. In chapter three, the analysis is directed at investigating the transformational moment as seen from another point of observation, a perspective naturally involved in the debate about the relations between the legal and the political phenomena: the perspective of political science.

---

[76] See D Farber and P Frickey, 'The Jurisprudence of Public Choice' (1987) 65 *Texas Law Review* 901. See also D Farber and P Frickey, *Law and Public Choice: a Critical Introduction* (Chicago, University of Chicago Press, 1999) 1; and Bix, *Jurisprudence* (n 62 above) 208.

3

Law and Policy

C HAPTER TWO SHOWED how the transformational moment plays a crucial role in the images of the relations between law and politics as portrayed by contemporary legal theories. Moreover, most legal theoretical movements, for different reasons, have left such a moment at the borders of their legal inquiries. The first part of this chapter is devoted to the exploration of the empirical conditions in which such ambivalent attitudes by most contemporary legal theory originate. In particular, the investigation is directed at the system of opposing forces acting on the law in the world today, simultaneously pushing the legal phenomenon away and toward the political world.

The second part of this chapter is devoted to the first step as to a possible solution to such ambivalence in contemporary legal theory. In particular, the middle-range enterprise of framing a field of investigation dealing specifically with the transformational moment will be commenced. As a preliminary step, the possibility of borrowing some of the concepts employed in one of the sciences that have investigated the relations between law and politics, political science, will be explored. In particular, the focus will be on the distinction made by political scientists between the *politics* and *policy* dimensions of the processes of forming and implementing political decisions.

I. THE TRANSFORMATIONAL MOMENT IN THE DIFFERENT MODELS: AT THE CENTRE OF THEIR LAW-MAKING

Though in different ways, all the models relating law and politics recognise the centrality of the transformational moment in the law-making process. They see the transformation of values into legal categories and concepts as one of the cornerstones of the working of law-making. The extent and intensity of the conversion of values into legal categories and concepts vary considerably according to the kind of model the legal theories have embraced.

As seen in chapter two, the positions of legal scholars range from a design of the transformational moment as occupying a narrow and restricted space between the legal and political fields (autonomous model), to a moment as a large and always open gate granting politics an almost free entrance into law (embedded model).[1] Nevertheless, the transformational moment, across the vast majority of contemporary legal literature, still maintains its function as one of the central crossroads where the legal and political paths meet. This central position, and the transformational nature of the points of contact between law and politics, can be explained mainly by two concurring and equally strong forces operating on contemporary law: its *politicisation* and its *specialisation*.

A. The Politicisation of Contemporary Law

The politicisation of the law is the phenomenon by which political and legal actors make increasing use of the law, having as a primary (and often exclusive) criterion the implementation of their own values, of their own politics. In other words, the politicisation of the law here means the phenomenon through which, by using law, the actors belonging both to the political and the legal arenas tend to submerge the traditional internal rules superseding the working of the law-making (*eg* the formal consistency of the legal order) in favour of a more pragmatic approach, a getting-things-done approach (*eg* introducing a certain model of behaviour into a community).

Using the Weberian ideal-types, one can speak of a politicisation of the law when the actors involved in the law-making process (both in its legislative and judicial forms) tend to reason in terms more of substantive rationality than of formal rationality. This happens when the legal production is attained and justified looking primarily to the observation of criteria and the fulfilment of needs positioned outside the system of law and traditional legal reasoning (*eg* reaching a political goal at the expense of the logic of the legal order).[2]

The phenomenon of the politicisation of the law certainly did not originate in the twentieth century. Historically, political powers (here comprehending also powers of a moral, religious, social, cultural and economic nature) have made a quantitatively extensive use of the law in

---

[1] See eg, H Kelsen, *The Pure Theory of Law* (Berkeley, University of California Press, 1970) 245–9; and D Kennedy, 'Freedom and Constraint in Adjudication: a Critical Phenomenology' (1986) 36 *Journal of Legal Education* 562.

[2] See M Weber, *Economy and Society* (G Roth and C Wittich (eds), Berkeley, University of California Press, 1978) 654–8. See also N Luhmann, *A Sociological Theory of Law* (London, Routledge & Kegan Paul, 1985) 224.

order to get their values implemented into a community.[3] That which is typical of modern times, at least in the Western legal order, is the fact that the politicisation of the law has reached a different qualitative level. The law, previously, was considered one among other tools at the disposal of the political powers. Nowadays, it is considered the instrument of choice for enforcing values into a community, because:

> [t]oday the most common form of legitimacy is the belief in legality, the compliance with enactments which are *formally* correct and which have been made in the accustomed manner.[4] (emphasis original)

One effect of this new qualitative level reached by the politicisation of the law is traceable in a contemporary phenomenon affecting almost every legal order around the world on both a practical and theoretical level: the intensification of the debate concerning judicial activism. Judicial activism is when 'the courts impose a judicial solution over an issue erstwhile subject to political resolution' by intervening and, for example, striking down properly enacted legislation.[5] Judicial activism is a sign of the politicisation of the law since it identifies a judicial activity directed at stretching the formal structures and letter of the law (in particular at the constitutional level) in order to fill the gaps left by politicians. Judges do this in order to implement those values the political actors are unable to sense in the community or are unable to transform into legislative measures or which are simply part of the political baggage of the judges.[6]

The legal phenomenon is then conceived, both in the political and in the legal worlds, as one of the privileged tools in the hands of political actors in order to reach their goals, to realise their ideologies. In particular, Carl Schmitt has stressed this feature of the modern relations between law and

---

[3] One example is the use of Roman law in the thirteenth to fourteenth centuries by jurists loyal to the emperor as against the legal foundation of the pope's authority. See G Sabine, *A History of Political Theory* (3rd edn, New York, Holt Rinehart & Winston, 1964) 277–80.

[4] Weber, *Economy and Society* (n 2) 37. See also R Cotterrell, *Law's Community: Legal Theory in Sociological Perspective* (Oxford, Clarendon Press, 1995) 319; and J Habermas, *Between Facts and Norms: Contributions to a Discourse Theory of Law and Democracy* (Cambridge, The MIT Press, 1998) 171.

[5] DL Anderson, 'When Restraint Requires Activism: Partisan Gerrymandering and the Status Quo Ante' (1990) 42 *Stanford Law Review* 1570. See also R Bork, *The Tempting of America: the Political Seduction of the Law* (New York, Touchtone/Simon and Schuster, 1990) 3; M Tushnet, 'Comment on Cox' (1987) 47 *Maryland Law Review* 147; and G Jones, 'Proper Judicial Activism' (2002) 14 *Regent University Law Review* 142.

[6] In this way, judicial activism tends to be value-free or, as strikingly expressed by Duxbury, implies that 'for every *Brown* there is likely to be a *Lochner*'. N Duxbury, 'The Theory and History of American Law and Politics' (1993) 13 *OJLS* 252. See also FH Easterbrook, 'Do Liberals and Conservatives Differ in Judicial Activism?' (2002) 73 *University of Colorado Law Review* 1405. But see J Ferejohn, 'Judicializing Politics, Politicizing Law' (2002) 65 *Law and Contemporary Problems* 49, 55–7.

politics. His position goes to the extreme of rendering the legal phenomenon not only as instrumentally but also ontologically fully dependent on
the political one. According to Schmitt, law is not only used by politics but
also 'is' because of politics.[7]

As a result of the politicisation of the law, contemporary legal theories
are all forced to recognise in their ideas of law and law-making the
centrality of the transformational moment, ie of the moment in which
political actors get in touch, more or less intensely, with the legal tools. As
seen, though to a very different extent, all legal theories hold a partition of
the legal phenomenon from the political one. If there is a contemporary
tendency towards law becoming a privileged instrument to do politics, it
then becomes of primary importance for legal theories not only to put into
their portrayals of the relations between law and politics a (thin or thick)
wall still delimiting their area of investigation; it also becomes structurally
important to project in the centre of such theoretical portrayals the door(s)
through which the increasing and manifest political instances enter into the
legal field.[8]

B. The Specialisation of Contemporary Law

There is also the 'other' feature of the modern relations between law and
politics: the specialisation of the law. Political actors increasingly use the
law as an instrument to influence society, becoming more and more
complex, more specialised and therefore requiring a specific and unique
core of knowledge for production and functioning. The specialisation of
law, due to the increasingly detailed 'marking out of what counts as legal
knowledge, legal reasoning and legal issues', leads to the progressive
marginalisation of the political discourse from the mechanisms (though not
the content) of law-making, as well as their substitution by the specific
knowledge and discourse provided by specific actors, the lawyers.[9]

As with politicisation, the specialisation of the legal phenomenon is not
a product of the twentieth century. From antique Roman times through the
Middle Ages, a branch of human knowledge and a group of actors dealing

---

[7] See C Schmitt, *Verfassungslehre* (Berlin, Duncker & Humblot, 1928) 22.

[8] See eg, R Summers, 'My Philosophy of Law' in R Summers, *Essays in Legal Theory*
(Dordrecht, Kluwer Academic Publishers, 2000) 99–108.

[9] Cotterrell, *Law's Community* (n 4 above) 12. See also R Summers, 'Law as a Type of
"Machine" Technology' in Summers, *Essays in Legal Theory* (n 8) 49; J Raz, 'The Inner Logic
of the Law' in J Raz, *Ethics in the Public Domain: Essays in the Morality of Law and Politics*
(Oxford, Clarendon Press, 1994) 236–7; Luhmann, *A Sociological Theory of Law* (n 2 above)
159–60; and B Tamanaha, *A General Jurisprudence of Law and Society* (Oxford, Oxford
University Press, 2001) 71–6.

specifically with the law and its making have existed.[10] What characterises the contemporary legal phenomenon is the high degree of its specialisation, leading to and paralleling (somehow connected) an equally strong politicisation of the law:

> As legal thought is invaded by the challenges of social complexity and its autonomy and identity are questioned and threatened it spins increasingly intricate networks of doctrine ... Thus, ironically, as legal doctrine's relations with the contexts of its social existence become more important topics for lawyers and legal scholars, this doctrine seems to retreat further into moral and social obscurity. It is as though, while society presses in on law, dissolving it into a diversity of regulatory practices, law hides from society's gaze behind dense webs of proliferating technical detail.[11]

This growing specialisation is echoed in the degree of penetration of the law in different areas of human activity, *eg* with the phenomenon of over-regulation both in the United States and in the European Union. This also increases the specificity of the area of expertise required of lawyers; for example, a main distinction historically was between civil and criminal lawyers. Today, one can find lawyers dealing exclusively with the legal aspects of corporate take-overs. This growing specialisation is also visible in the training required for future lawyers, *eg* in the increasing number of specialised courses and curricula given by law faculties. Last but not least, this tendency towards a lawyers' law can also be traced in the contemporary evolution of legal philosophy 'from the philosopher's or politician's to the lawyer's legal philosophy'.[12]

This high level of specialisation has then made contemporary legal theorists well aware of the fact that law, because of its larger use by the political arena, has become a very complex phenomenon, with its own rules, its own actors, and its own very detailed conceptual apparatus. As a consequence, the (increasing number of) contacts between law and politics

---

[10] See eg, A Watson, *Roman Law and Comparative Law* (London, University of Georgia Press, 1991) 104.

[11] Cotterrell, *Law's Community* (n 4) 299. See also Weber, *Economy and Society* (n 2 above) 895; Summers, 'Law as a Type of "Machine" Technology' (n 9 above) 52; P Bourdieu, 'The Force of Law: toward a Sociology of the Juridical Field' (1987) 38 *Hastings Law Journal* 835; and A Hunt, 'The Politics of Law and the Law of Politics' in K Tuori *et al* (eds), *Law and Power: Critical and Socio-Legal Essays* (Liverpool, Deborah Charles Publications, 1997) 82–3.

[12] W Friedmann, *Legal Theory* (5th edn, New York, Columbia University Press, 1967) 4. See also R Ellickson, 'Taming Leviathan: Will the Centralizing Tide of the Twentieth Century Carry into the Twenty-first?' (2000) 74 *Southern California Law Review* 101; A Abbot, *The System of Professions: an Essay on the Division of Expert Labor* (Chicago, University of Chicago Press, 1988) 248–54; and E Vink and E Veitch, 'Curricular Reform in Canada' (1977) 28 *Journal of Legal Education* 438. But see MDA Freeman, *Lloyd's Introduction to Jurisprudence* (7th edn, London, Sweet & Maxwell, 2001) 15–19.

are not perceived by contemporary legal theoreticians as simple transfer-points where the value-instances produced inside the political arena are poured into the law-making and become law. Rather, these moments of contact between law and politics are characterised in all three models as having a transformational nature, ie as implying an (onto)logical alteration of the political values (*eg* protection of life) into a specific code (*eg* the legal category of criminalisation of abortion).[13]

Only a few contemporary legal scholars claim an independence of legal concepts from values and interests or, in the opposite, the absolute interchangeability of legal and political categories. The vast majority of contemporary legal theories provide for moments where the values, in order to make an entrance into the legal world, have to change their structure, as in the autonomous model, or at least have to put on some additional legal vestiges, as in the embedded model.

In the end, in their portrayals of the relations between law and politics, contemporary legal theories are affected by what Bourdieu has defined as:

> [t]he constant tension between the available juridical norms, which appear universal, at least in their form, and the necessarily diverse, even conflicting and contradictory, social demand.[14]

In particular, the increasingly specialised character of the law and the growing use of the law by the political actors forces legal scholars to require both a (more or less extensive) transformation of values into something recognisable as belonging to the legal world and to place such a transformational process as a central moment of the more general law-making process.[15]

II. ... BUT SOME QUESTIONS ARE STILL OPEN

With the exceptions presented in the previous chapter, the attitude of contemporary legal theories towards the transformational moment can be generally defined as tending towards ambivalence. Despite the recognition of the crucial position occupied by such transformational moments in the relations between law and politics, contemporary legal theories tend to

---

[13]   See Bourdieu, 'The Force of Law' (n 11 above) 828.

[14]   *Ibid* 841. Bourdieu more generally recognises the simultaneous operation of these two factors as constitutive of the juridical field. See *ibid* 816.

[15]   See G Teubner, 'How the Law Thinks: toward a Constructivist Epistemology of Law' (1989) 23 *Law and Society Review* 745.

leave the investigation of such moments at the periphery of their theoretical analysis.[16] This marginalisation of any systematic study of the transformational process is rooted in different reasons. They range from grounds of an ontological nature (eg Kelsen's restrictive idea of what belongs to the law and to its study, or CLS' view of the law as per se deeply mixed with politics), to considerations of a more epistemological character (eg Hart stressing the clarification of legal concepts as the privileged task of legal scholars).

Regardless of the reasons, contemporary legal scholars tend to leave aside the full and systematic investigation of the questions concerning what is happening inside this moment of conversion of values into legal categories and concepts. They leave unexplored the possibility of framing and building inside a more general vision of how law and politics relate, the possibility of having a more specific subtheory expressly directed to answer some of the most fundamental questions of the law-making process: what happens inside the moment of the transformation of values into legal categories and concepts? Why and how do legal actors transform a certain value into a certain legal category? Which actors play a role in these transformational processes?

These questions demonstrate that there is an opportunity of opening and theoretically framing a field for a middle-range legal theory of the transformational moment, ie the opportunity of establishing a type of _legal investigation_ with the task of exploring what happens and how the processes operate in this crucial transformational moment. Legal investigation here means the complex of intellectual operations directed at explaining that segment of the law-making process from a Hartian internal perspective, ie 'that of a participant in such practice who accepts the rules as guides to conduct and as standards of criticism'.[17]

It is true that many legal realists have aimed at systematically answering the questions relating to transformational processes. However, as seen previously, they tend to focus on the non-normative elements of such moments, eg the psychology of judges and juries (Frank) or the social behaviours activated by the use of legal language (Olivecrona). Legal realists aim at pointing out the factual dimension and the factual position of the transformational process: to locate the transformational moment within an empirical reality (law-as-fact) and to frame it with components directly observable in the same reality (law-in-action). For example, Frank

---

[16] Another similar ambivalent position is eg the one taken by contemporary legal theory on the notion of 'functions of law', as pointed out by J Raz, 'On the Functions of Law' in AWB Simpson (ed), _Oxford Essays in Jurisprudence (Second Series)_ (Oxford, Clarendon Press, 1973) 278.

[17] HLA Hart, 'Postscript' in HLA Hart, _The Concept of Law_ (PA Bulloch and J Raz (eds), 2nd edn, Oxford, Clarendon Press, 1994) 255.

and Lundstedt lean towards placing the transformational moment in the social context represented by the ideas shared by a community or part of it, and framing it with the complex of concrete behaviours taken by the population or by part of it.[18]

In this way, the legal realists somehow overlook the investigation of the normative internal dimension of why and how, during such moments, legal actors reason and operate in a certain way. Because of the very external perspective adopted, the legal realists end up using explanatory concepts of a non-normative nature. 'Social welfare' or 'actual or potential social consequences' are some of the criteria that, according to the legal realists, are (or should be) directly embraced by the legislator or judge in choosing among the different legal categories and concepts.[19] Using Hart's criticism, the legal realists can then be considered as unable to give birth to a systematic *legal* investigation of the transformational moment because they place themselves in an external perspective, different from the one taken by the legal actors.[20]

For example, a legal realist tends to focus the investigation on proving that strict liability is a legal construction directed at implementing a certain economic value expressed by the community (the protection against certain dangerous but necessary activities). In this way, he or she tends to dismiss as formalistic the question of why legal actors prefer to transform this value into a tort legal concept of strict liability instead of into a legal category of a fiscal nature (such as increasing the taxation on cigarettes according to the dangerousness of the activity exercised in order to cover the possible future expenses suffered by the community).

The problem is not that legal realists give an account of the empirical framework of the field within which the transformational work of judges and law-makers takes place. The problem is that they move no further, failing to enter into this field:

> There is ... nothing in that behaviour [investigated by the legal realists] which manifests the internal point of view characteristic of the acceptance of rules.[21]

The legal realists do not consider some basic questions of the transformation from the lawyers' perspective: How do the legal actors reason when

---

[18] See J Frank, *Courts on Trial: Myth and Reality in American Justice* (Princeton, Princeton University Press, 1950) 271–4; and V Lundstedt, *Legal Thinking Revised. My Views on Law* (Stockholm, Almqvist & Wiksell, 1956) 150–72. See also A Ross, *On Law and Justice* (London, Stevens & Sons, 1958) 354–7; and K Llewellyn, *The Common Law Tradition: Deciding Appeals* (Boston, Little, Brown & Company, 1960) 121–32.

[19] As examples of the excessiveness reached by the 'external' perspective by some of the legal realists, see Lundstedt, *Legal Thinking Revised* (n 18 above) 171–89; Frank, *Courts on Trial* (n 18 above) 342–3; and J Frank and B Frank, *Not Guilty* (Garden City, Doubleday, 1957) 199–209.

[20] See HLA Hart, *The Concept of Law* (Oxford, Clarendon Press, 1961) 134.

[21] *Ibid* 135. See also Ross, *On Law and Justice* (n 18 above) 11–18.

they transform values into law? How and why do they build or choose a certain legal category in order to implement a value into the community?[22] To fulfil their goal of being scientific, legal realists not only pretend to look to the law as external spectators; in order to be as objective as possible, they fail to take a step into the field they are investigating. In other words, they miss considering in general the normative aspect of the law, the internal perspective of the players. In the specifics of the law-making process, the legal realists thus miss a central element in the investigation of the transformational moment: the way the legal actors perceive (and act according to) the relations between law and politics.[23] In the end, both legal realisms and the other contemporary legal theories, although for different reasons, leave from a lawyers' perspective untouched, taken for granted or inadequately answered, the fundamental questions of whether, why and how a certain value is transformed into a certain legal category.

One should consider, for example, the question of why the value of equality for human beings regardless of sex finds its way into the legal system as a statutory quota-system for the working place. Most legal scholars would answer such a question by either stating that this is an issue of a political nature and therefore, although it is relevant for the content of the law, lies outside the reach of the legal discipline (autonomous model). Alternatively, they would say that it is only a matter of words and the real aim of a legal investigation is directed at critically unveiling the real values (produced by the dominant political, economic or moral forces) behind the legal jargon (embedded model). Or, finally, they would say that because the law is a phenomenon taking place in the space-time dimension, the legal investigation has to be directed towards exposing the actual patterns of behaviours adopted by the legal actors in the transformation of the equality-value into a statutory quota-system (intersecting model).

All these answers still leave some fundamental questions open: How and why do the legal actors operating in the law-making process consider the value of gender equality represented in a statutory quota-system for the working place? Which legal reasoning is applied to the transformation of equality into a quota-system? Why has the latter legal category been preferred over the other legal categories, eg tax law measures directed at aiding equality-oriented employers?

---

[22] For example, the American realist Underhill Moore considers the transformational moment as having mainly a psychological nature, a position also shared by some of the Scandinavians (eg Olivecrona). See U Moore and C Callahan, 'Law and Learning Theory: a Study in Legal Control' (1943) 53 *Yale Law Journal* 1.

[23] See L Fuller, 'American Legal Realism' (1934) 82 *University of Pennsylvania Law Review* 461. See also M Moore, 'The Need for a Theory of Legal Theories: Assessing Pragmatic Instrumentalism. A Review Essay of 'Instrumentalism and American Legal Theory' by Robert S. Summers (Book Review)' (1984) 69 *Cornell Law Review* 1009.

Even if the transformational moment is depicted as a central point of law-making by almost all the legal theories considered, there is still the need and the space to develop a middle-range legal theory of the transformational moment. This is a theory that momentarily leaves aside the general issue of how law and politics relate and builds around the task of specifically and systematically dealing with, and answering from, a lawyers' perspective the questions of why, how and to what extent values are transformed into certain legal categories or concepts.

The first step in developing and framing this middle-range theory of the transformational moment is to conceptually mark the theory's field, ie to find a concept that clearly identifies its object of investigation.[24] Since an answer has to be found (centrality of the transformational moment) and since contemporary legal theory does not provide an adequate and specific conceptual apparatus on the issue (periphery of their investigation), the search for such a concept of marking has to begin by borrowing it from somewhere else, namely political science.

This choice is not only dictated by the fact that political scientists are those who, besides legal scholars, have developed a strong analytical interest in the relations between the legal and the political phenomenon.[25] Political science is also one of the areas noted by the legal realists as helpful in understanding the complex world of the relations between law and politics, ie the movement that as a whole has tried more than the others to develop a systematic investigation of the transformational moment.

III. THE CONCEPT OF POLICY IN POLITICAL SCIENCE

The previous chapter revealed how little attention most legal theories have given the intermediary moment that allows politics to enter into the law. It seems then natural to search for possible theoretical tools for exploring such moments in a field of knowledge that, outside the legal discipline, can further help investigate the relationship between law and politics: political science.

The concept of *politics* embraced by political scientists differs considerably from the one presented up to now, ie politics as seen from a legal perspective. Usually, although not exclusively, most political science definitions start with Weber's characterisation of politics as 'a striving for a share of power or for influence on the distribution of power, whether it is between states or between the groups of people contained within a single

---

[24] See HLA Hart, 'Definition and Theory in Jurisprudence' in HLA Hart, *Essays in Jurisprudence and Philosophy* (Oxford, Clarendon Press, 1983) 21–2. See also B Bix, *Jurisprudence: Theory and Context* (3rd edn, London, Sweet & Maxwell, 2003) 14.

[25] See eg, M Shapiro, 'Political Jurisprudence' (1964) 52 *Kentucky Law Journal* 294.

state'.[26] Starting from this general definition, the leading political scientists of the twentieth century have then further described politics as dealing with 'power, rule and authority' (Dahl), as the 'shaping and sharing of power' (Lasswell) or as the 'authoritative allocation of values' (Easton).[27]

During the second half of the twentieth century, political science scholars in particular have produced a series of works and debates about a fundamental moment of the study of politics: *policy*. Similar to the idea of law in the legal discipline, the positions of the concept of policy in political science are stretched on a very broad and articulated spectrum of definitions.

The term 'policy' exists in so many places in the general political phenomenon that sometimes it is even questioned whether policy is really so different from politics.[28] Moreover, in political science and more generally in the political discourse, the term policy usually stands for the more specific one of 'public policy,' ie 'whatever the controllers of the state institutions decide to do', in other words, policy as a 'state action using bureaucratic organisational forms' such as agencies or departments.[29] However, in reality the public dimension of policy (ie its dealing with bureaucracy's actions) often interacts and is mixed with its private dimension, that is the policies expressed by the markets and the community, such as private organisations.[30]

There is also a more tangible sign of the complexity of the problems and of the intense debate associated with the use of term 'policy'. Many political national arenas, such as those in France, Germany or Spain, do not possess in their linguistic kits a specific term indicating policy as

[26] M Weber, 'The Profession and Vocation of Politics' in P Lassman and R Speirs (eds), *Weber: Political Writings* (Cambridge, Cambridge University Press, 1994) 311.

[27] R Dahl, *Modern Political Analysis* (5th edn, Englewood Cliffs, Prentice Hall International, 1984) 8; D Easton, *A Systems Analysis of Political Life* (Chicago, University of Chicago Press, 1979) 21–33; HD Lasswell and A Kaplan, *Power and Society: Framework for Political Inquiry* (New Haven, New Haven Press, 1950) xiv. See also generally, HD Lasswell, *Politics: Who Gets What, When, How* (New York, Meridian Books, 1958). For a mixed definition, see A Heywood, *Political Theory: An Introduction* (2nd edn, London, Macmillan Press, 1999) 52–63. Compare C Hay, *Political Analysis: a Critical Introduction* (New York, Palgrave, 2002) 69–71.

[28] See eg, J Plano *et al*, 'Politics' in J Plano (ed), *The Dictionary of Political Analysis* (2nd edn, Santa Barbara, ABC-Clio, 1982) 94–5; or L Allison, 'Policy' in I McLean and A McMillan (eds), *The Oxford Concise Dictionary of Politics* (2nd edn, Oxford, Oxford University Press, 2003) 412.

[29] MJ Hill, *The Policy Process in the Modern State* (3rd edn, Englewood Cliffs, Prentice Hall, 1997) 16–17.

[30] See H Colebatch and P Larmour, *Market, Bureaucracy and Community: A Students' Guide to Organisation* (London, Pluto Press, 1993) 17. As the focus in this work is on the concept of policy and the law, and since the latter necessarily has a public nature (as in the definition presented in the Introduction), the terms policy and public policy will be here used synonymously.

different from politics; they are both encompassed by one single word: *politique*, *Politik* or *politica* respectively.[31]

However, three main features frequently are present when looking at the evolution of the idea of policy in the modern political science debate. The first is a general desire by scholars to point out that policy is not only the result of the work of the political order. Efforts are generally made in developing an idea of policy, which breaks, or at least modifies, the identification of policy with the decisions, of an authoritative nature, coming from the political order. This development is directed at illustrating that under the labelling of policy, there are more than the resolutions taken by the political order, resolutions directed at creating certain outputs in the surrounding environment. When speaking of policy, one also has to take into consideration the processes through which such decisions were taken or created, policy processes defined as 'the given set of methods, strategies and techniques by which a policy[-decision] is made'.[32] As stated by Easton, a policy 'consists of a web of *decisions and actions* that allocate values'[33] (emphasis added).

The second feature generally characterising the concept contemporary political scientists have of policy concerns its range, which tends to reject the identification of policy as one single process leading to one single decision coming out of the political order. Instead, political scholars tend to stretch the surface covered by the concept of policy. This stretching goes in another, although parallel, direction than the one including in policy both processes and decisions. The stretching now goes into a more chronological direction of including in one policy several processes leading to several resolutions. The idea of policy requires both the process leading to the decisions and a chronological contextualisation of both processes and decisions along a certain period of time. Dealing with policy not only

---

[31]   For a detailed political-historical investigation of the reasons behind such an absence in the continental European languages, see A Heidenheimer, 'Politics, Policy and Policey as Concepts in English and Continental Languages: an Attempt to Explain Divergences' (1986) 48 *Review of Politics* 3.

[32]   W Jenkins, *Policy Analysis: a Political and Organizational Perspective* (London, Martin Robertson, 1978) 16. See also R Ripley, *Policy Analysis in Political Science* (Chicago, Nelson-Hall Publishers, 1985) 49. The idea of matching the policy moment with its products (authoritative outputs) is still present in S Nagel, 'Trends in Policy Analysis' in SA Theodoulou and MA Cahn (eds), *Public Policy: the Essential Readings* (Englewood Cliffs, Prentice Hall, 1995) 181–5.

[33]   D Easton, *The Political System: An Inquiry into the State of Political Science* (2nd edn, Chicago, University of Chicago Press, 1981) 130. See also H Heclo, 'Policy Analysis' (1972) 2 *British Journal of Political Science* 85. But see R Dahl, 'Decision-Making in a Democracy: the Supreme Court as a National Policy-Maker' (2001) 50 *Emory Law Journal* 564 (reprint 1957); and H Jenkins-Smith and P Sabatier, 'The Study of the Public Policy Process' in P Sabatier and H Jenkins-Smith (eds), *Policy Change and Learning: an Advocacy Coalition Approach* (Oxford, Westview Press, 1993) 3–4.

means dealing with one process that leads to one decision; it means dealing with '*a course* of action *or a web* of decisions rather than one decision'[34] (emphasis added).

The third and final feature of the contemporary idea of policy developed inside political science has to do with the function played by policy inside a political order. The web of actions and decisions defined as policy is characterised as being a moment of conversion in the life of a political order. Most political scientists tend to see policy as the moment when certain actions or processes are taken in order to transform certain inputs (or demands) coming from the environment, into outputs (or decisions), those also directed at the surrounding environment. The transformation actually is the very core of the policy process:

> policy making is the pivotal stage of the political process, the point at which effective political demands are converted into authoritative decisions.[35]

It is in the policy process that the political system decides to transform certain demands into outputs of different natures, with the goal that the impact of the outputs on the environment will fulfil the original demands. This can, for example, be the transformation of the ideological demand of full employment in a certain community into the economic outputs of reduced taxation of employers' re-invested profits; this in order to have a further impact on the environment by encouraging employers to expand their activities.

It is worth mentioning that the transformation analysed here is a procedural transformation. It is not a random transformation process but conducted according to certain rules and mechanisms. For example, the transformation has to proceed from the ideology of full employment to tax reduction because it follows the economic mechanism that decreasing taxation will give birth to higher investments through freed financial resources. Moreover, the transformation has to respect the legal borders

---

[34] Hill, *The Policy Process in the Modern State* (n 29 above) 7. See also J Anderson, *Public Policy-Making* (3rd edn, New York, Holt, Rinehart and Winston, 1984) 8; HD Lasswell, 'The Emerging Conception of the Policy Sciences' (1970) 1 *Policy Sciences* 6; R Hofferbert, *The Study of Public Policy* (New York, Bobbs Merrill, 1974) 23; and R Heineman *et al*, *The World of the Policy Analyst: Rationality, Values, and Politics* (3rd edn, Chatham, Chatham House Publishers 2002) 49.

[35] GA Almond and G Bingham Powell, *Comparative Politics: System, Process, and Policy* (2nd edn, Boston, Little Brown, 1978) 232. This model of policy is actually a simplification of the more sophisticated and articulated policy models produced within political science in the last 50 years. See *ibid* 9–10; Jenkins, *Policy Analysis* (n 32 above) 17–18, 22; and G Smith and D May, 'The Artificial Debate between Rationalist and Incrementalist Models of Decision-making' in M Hill (ed), *The Policy Process: A Reader* (2nd edn, London, Prentice Hall, 1997) 164–7.

present along this economic path. Such legal borders, for example, can be the legal rules superseding the enactment by the legislature of a budget for the financial year.[36]

The policy seen by political scientists can then be defined as that network of processes and decisions where inputs into the political order coming from the surrounding environment are converted into outputs of an authoritative nature designed to have an impact on the environment. For example, because of inflation, a reduction of real income occurs among certain groups in a population. The groups then address (usually mediate through other actors, eg trade unions) demands (inputs) to the political order of preserving their income. As a result, the political order converts (policy process) such demands by choosing a group of authoritative measures (policy decision A), eg repressive measures directed at price control, instead of another group (policy decision B), eg financial measures directed at increasing welfare payments. These measures are taken in order to provoke an effect of 'more value for money' on the market (outputs).[37]

These three major features of policy as generally designated by political scientists (being a *network* of both *processes and decisions* with a *conversional function* of inputs into outputs) can then be extremely helpful in order to better define, from a legal perspective, that which up to now has been called the 'transformational moment' of the relationships between law and politics. Chapter four investigates the possibility of whether such transformational moments in the life of a legal order can be defined as the policy of law. Before that, however, a preliminary step has to be taken looking into the meanings and significance the legal world has now to ascribe to the concept of policy.

IV. THE CONCEPT OF POLICY IN THE MINDS OF LAWYERS

The concept of policy as developed by political science focuses on its being a complex of processes and authoritative decisions by which a conversion of certain inputs into certain outputs occurs. This almost naturally leads to an investigation of the possibility of redefining as the policy moment of the law that which has been previously defined as the transformational moment of the legal phenomenon, ie the moment where values-inputs are transformed into legal categories-outputs.

---

[36] See Almond and Powell, *Comparative Politics* (n 35 above) 14–15, chs VIII–X. See also Raz, 'On the Functions of Law' (n 16 above) 301–2.

[37] The example described here is an adaptation of a similar case presented in Almond and Powell, *Comparative Politics* (n 35 above) 10. Another helpful example is in CJ Fredrich, *Constitutional Government and Democracy: Theory and Practice in Europe and America* (4th edn, Waltham, Blaisdell Publishing Company, 1968) 379.

In order to proceed with this evaluation, however, it is first necessary to see whether, and if so how, contemporary legal actors have been using the idea of policy in their investigations of the normative phenomenon. This investigation of the policy moment is directed at scrutinising the entire spectrum of legal actors, from the most theoretical approaches to the law (eg legal scholars) to the more practical ones (eg traceable in a judicial decision or legislative act). This work has explicitly adopted a legal theoretical orientation, and therefore the focus will primarily be on the attention paid by contemporary legal theory to the policy phase. This perspective obviously does not exclude the parallel treatment of several judicial and statutory acts, used in particular to point out the strong similarity the idea of policy has among theorists and practitioners of the law. This analytical interaction between legal theory and legal practice is particularly necessary when one considers that the concept of policy has been developed or used mainly in the Anglo-American legal environment. This is an environment that has often intensely felt the necessity of crossing the barrier between the law-in-books and the law-in-action.[38]

A. Policy at the Border of the Lawyer's Attention

Political scientists have made many efforts to investigate and penetrate the law and its world with categories and concepts constructed around the concept of policy. In particular, the law and its system has often been considered by political scientists as central tools in the hands of the political order in order to convert certain demands, produced by the surrounding environment, into certain outputs. In the political science context, the definition of outputs characterising policy as 'authoritative decisions' refers to the fact that the expected attitude among the addressees is obedience.[39] This mind-set is required regardless of whether the addressees share the needs or values giving rise to the inputs activating the political order. The basic source of this authoritative nature, however, is the fact that the addressees recognise in general the legitimacy of the actors creating the policy's outputs, a legitimacy which is often given to the policy outputs by their being endorsed in legal forms.[40]

---

[38] See eg, OW Holmes, *The Common Law* (New York, Dover Publications, 1991) 48 and his contribution to *Gompers v United States*, 233 U.S. 612 (1914). See also M Tushnet, 'The Logic of Experience: Oliver Wendell Holmes on the Supreme Judicial Court' (1977) 63 *Virginia Law Review* 1010, 1023–5.

[39] D Easton, 'An Approach to the Analysis of the Political System' (1957) 9 *World Politics* 384.

[40] See Anderson, *Public Policy-Making* (n 34 above) 5. See also Weber, *Economy and Society* (n 2 above) 212–16.

Lasswell and McDougal, for example, have examined legal phenomenon from a policy perspective. They try to answer, from a non-normative perspective, the questions of the roles the law and legal order play in a more general (political) process, ie how the law relates to the political questions 'of "[w]ho" says "what" in which "channel" to "whom" with what "effect"'.[41] Nagel has also produced similar works, investigating the relations between law and policy from a political science perspective, using in particular mathematical models to explain the legal process. He offers a depiction of the position and nature of law in policy studies that can be considered as generally representing the idea political scientists have of the normative phenomena as a step in a broader inputs-outputs process:

> The basic conceptual scheme … involves thinking of law and the legal process *not* as something to be studied in itself, the way a lawyer would … Instead, law and the legal process are viewed as phenomena which produce various kinds of effects.[42]

In contrast, legal scholars have not made so many attempts to systematically penetrate the policy momentum of a law-making process by exploiting normative analytical tools and categories. In particular, few studies have attempted to build a legal-theoretical structure from which to analyse from a legal perspective the role the law plays in the processes of conversion constituting the essence of the policy moment. The legal process approach has to be counted among the few legal schools that have attempted the construction of a systematic investigation of the law-policy relations.

This stream was already present in American legal thinking in the 1950s, focusing on identifying the best among both legal institutions (who) and legal procedures (how) for resolving the practical problems raised before a court or a legislative assembly. In this way, law is perceived as a policy science, ie an institutional process that mediates law and the world of values.[43] In contrast to political scientists, however, followers of the legal process approach base their investigation on two traditional legal dogmas.

First, they assume that both the judicial and legislative law-making institutions function within established and firm limits of power and

---

[41] HD Lasswell, 'Lasswell on Collaboration with McDougal' in HD Lasswell and M McDougal, *Jurisprudence for a Free Society: Studies in Law, Science and Policy* (New Haven, New Haven Press, 1992) xxxvi. See also HD Lasswell and M McDougal, *Jurisprudence for a Free Society: Studies in Law, Science and Policy* (New Haven, CT, New Haven Press, 1992) vol 1, pt 2.

[42] S Nagel, *Improving the Legal Process: Effects of Alternatives* (Lexington, Lexington Books, 1975) 1. See also S Nagel and L Bienvenue, *Social Science, Law, and Public Policy* (London, University Press of America, 1992) 6–12, 265–89.

[43] See W Eskridge and P Frickey, 'The Making of the Legal Process' (1994) 107 *Harvard Law Review* 2031, 2040. See also N Duxbury, *Patterns of American Jurisprudence* (Oxford, Clarendon Press, 1995) 242–51.

propriety. These boundaries reduce in particular the law-making function of judges.[44] Secondly, legal process scholars take for granted that the best procedure the judge or legislator should be encouraged to adopt is the one which is most 'reasoned'. A reasoned procedure is the procedure that, regardless of the rightness or wrongness of the particular result, is most faithful to the inner-criterion of the Weberian formal rationality of a legal order.[45] These two main features of the legal process approach to the law-policy relations, have led to a position quite distant from the one reached by political science studies of the law. In particular, this approach ends up in 'repress[ing] politics by devoting its energies to form instead of substance and to technical accomplishment at the expense of social and political insight'.[46]

If policy can be defined as the moment of conversion of something (inputs) into something different (outputs), this general inadequacy by contemporary legal theory of systematically framing a field of legal analysis around the policy moment, can then be explained as a part of a broader phenomenon by contemporary legal theories of pushing the transformational moment of a legal system to the periphery of their interests. In other words, legal scholars are not very interested in policy because it is somehow identified with the transformational moment, ie the complex of processes and decisions where something (values) is transformed or converted into something else (legal categories and concepts).[47]

B. Policy at the Centre of the Lawyer's Work

As with the transformational moment, this lack of interest in any systematic scrutiny of the concept of policy has not impeded its use in the legal discourse. Lawyers, both in their theoretical (scholars) and practical roles (lawyers, judges and collaborators in the legislative process) have always used the concept of policy, both in their reasoning and in their analysis of legal phenomena. The expression 'policy of law' appears already in both

---

[44] See Eskridge and Frickey, 'The Making of the Legal Process' (n 43 above) 2035.

[45] See H Hart and A Sacks, *The Legal Process: Basic Problems in the Making and Application of Law* (Cambridge, Tentative edition-mimeographed copy, 1958) 3, 165–7. See also H Hart, 'The Power of Congress to Limit the Jurisdiction of Federal Courts: an Exercise in Dialectic' (1953) 66 *Harvard Law Review* 1366.

[46] M Horwitz, *The Transformation of American Law 1870–1960: the Crisis of Legal Orthodoxy* (Oxford, Oxford University Press, 1990) 253. See also Bix, *Jurisprudence* (n 24 above) 85; and Duxbury, *Patterns of American Jurisprudence* (n 43 above) 232–41, 251–6.

[47] See J Bell, *Policy Arguments in Judicial Decisions* (Oxford, Clarendon Press, 1983) 5–6, extending this refusal of discussing about policy (while using it) to the English judiciary.

Blackstone's Commentaries and early American legal literature.[48] The concept of policy has always also been present in the language of American judicial decisions. For example, the term policy is widely used by the US Supreme Court, from the beginning of the nineteenth century up to the twenty-first century; from the (in)famous *Dredd Scott v Sanford* (1856) to the recent *Eldred v Ashcroft* (2003).[49]

The use made by legal actors of the concept of policy somehow resembles the one produced by political science. Contemporary legal theory uses policy as recalling a moment of the life of a (legal) system where a conversion occurs. It is a conversion of values produced in the outside world (ie the political world in the lawyer's case) into guidelines or standards at the disposal of the legal world. Policies are often defined as standards that can be, and often are, used by courts or legislative bodies in the same way as moral standards: to insert into the legal order non-legal values (such as 'good' or 'bad') either through the creation of new legal categories or through the modification of the old ones.[50] There are, however, two main features that distinguish policy as generally intended by the legal scholars, and in some way restrict it, in comparison to the one developed by political scientists.

C. Policy as a Political Phenomenon

First, contemporary legal theory tends to give to the idea of policy a different collocation. For the political scientist, the moment of conversion (policy) is a central part of the (political) system that they have as a main object of their investigation. This centrality is so pervasive that a specific field of studies inside political science has been opened in order to investigate this moment: policy studies.[51]

In contrast, the position of policy is detected by contemporary legal theory outside or (for the most benevolent of scholars) at the periphery of the legal system under scrutiny. Policy is placed in the political arena, that

[48] See W Blackstone, *Commentaries on the Laws of England*, vol. II, *Of the Rights of Things* (Chicago, University of Chicago Press, 1979) 191; and A Blanding and DJ McCord, 'The Effect of Foreign Divorces on South Carolina Marriages' (1831) 1 *Carolina Law Journal* 379.

[49] See *Dredd Scott v Sanford*, 60 U.S. 414 (1856); and *Eldred v Ashcroft*, 123 S.Ct. 780, 783–85, 814 (2003).

[50] An example of such idea of policy can be traced in MA Eisenberg, *The Nature of the Common Law* (Cambridge, Harvard University Press, 1991) 26–37. See also Bell, *Policy Arguments in Judicial Decisions* (n 47 above) 35–6; and G Hughes, 'Rules, Policy and Decision-Making' in G Hughes (ed), *Law, Reason, and Justice: Essays in Legal Philosophy* (New York, New York University Press, 1969) 111.

[51] See Jenkins, *Policy Analysis* (n 32 above) 18 (figure 2), 50 (figure 4). For a brief history of the birth of policy studies, see Heineman *et al*, *The World of the Policy Analyst* (n 34 above) 9–29.

is in the arena where the values and goals, which are to be pursued and introduced into a community by the legal order, are selected. Policy is not only produced by the political system *stricto sensu*, but also by other value systems such as the economic system (eg industrial policy and business law) or the cultural system (eg cultural policy and welfare-related statutes).[52]

This tendency of considering policy as something not belonging to the legal world can already be traced in the early history of legal thinking and production. One example is in the issues of the short-lived *Carolina Law Journal*, published between 1830 and 1831. Here the different usages of the idea of policy point towards a common denotation of policy as the evaluations by the courts and lawyers of the 'general interests of the community'.[53] More recently, Dworkin stated: '[I]t is uncontroversial (I suppose) that the decision whether to build a highway in a particular direction is, absent of special circumstances [eg threat tof life or health] ... a matter of policy.' As a consequence, continues Dworkin, this brings the position of such decisions outside the legal world or, in other words, the fact that '[n]o individual or group has a right in the strong sense against that decision'.[54] Policy is so integral a part of the political moment of the law-making process for legal scholars such as Kelsen and Raz, that they use politics and policy synonymously.[55]

Moving to the practical dimension of law, the term policy is also there used to identify something that does not completely fit into the legal world. Already in the nineteenth century, the US Supreme Court stated: 'It is not the province of the court to decide upon the justice or injustice, the policy or impolicy, of these laws.'[56]

The judges then consider policy as an external element of the legal system, an element that locates itself in the same position occupied by that which previously has been defined as the world of politics (in the language of the US Supreme Court, the justice-injustice value dilemma). The US Supreme Court throughout the twentieth century has upheld this political position of policy, its belonging entirely to the environment surrounding that which traditionally is defined as the legal world. In *Chevron v Natural Resources Defense Council* (1984), the US Supreme Court held the policy choices of an administrative agency to be outside the jurisdictional review

---

[52] See Bell, *Policy Arguments in Judicial Decisions* (n 47 above) 68–77.

[53] TC, 'Coloured Marriages' (1830) 1 *Carolina Law Journal* 95.

[54] R Dworkin, *A Matter of Principle* (Cambridge, Harvard University Press, 1985) 78. See also R Dworkin, *Taking Rights Seriously* (Cambridge, Harvard University Press, 1978) 226. For this interpretation of the concept of policy in Dworkin, see Habermas, *Between Facts and Norms* (n 4 above) 207–8.

[55] See eg, Kelsen, *The Pure Theory of Law* (n 1 above) 259; or J Raz, 'Legal Principles and the Limits of Law' (1972) 81 *Yale Law Journal* 841.

[56] *Dredd Scott v Sanford* (n 49 above) 406.

of a judge. Otherwise, the result would be an invasion by the judiciary into an area of the Constitution left to the exclusive domain of the political branch. Policy is excluded from judicial jurisdiction because it does not deal with the law but with political decisions.[57]

Legal actors, by stressing this feature of policy as an entirely political phenomenon, tend to then focus almost exclusively on the issue as to which relationships occur between *law and policy*, the latter perceived as a subproduct of the political system. They concentrate on the relationships between the two as different systems interacting with each other. This consideration of law and policy as belonging to two different worlds is also a general approach among the vast majority of legal scholars. It is diffuse even among those scholars, such as Dworkin or Kennedy, that more than others stress the tight and frequent interactions between law and policy. The emphasis on the idea of a 'tight and frequent interaction' necessarily presupposes the designation of law and policy as belonging to two different (although intermingling) systems and discourses.[58] Likewise, the majority of the criticisms directed at Dworkin's concept of policy take the different natures of policy and law for granted. Such criticisms articulate a discussion not of whether law and policy are two different systems, but whether or not these two systems (should) interact.[59]

In contrast to the general consensus of political actors around the existence of a *policy* (phase) *of politics*, legal actors in general do not recognise a possibility of having a distinct *policy* (phase) *of law*, ie a moment signalling the point of transformation of inputs coming from the surrounding environment (politics, in the case of lawyers) into outputs of the system in focus (legal categories and concepts). Even in the few cases in which a legal actor inside a legal context has brought up the expression 'policy of law', it has been used in order to indicate the general principles, of political origin, by which the public authorities are guided in using the law for reaching their goals.[60]

Legal scholars also use the policy moment as a transformational moment, but just as for the US Supreme Court, it remains a conversion that, from a legal perspective, appears to be from the political to the

---

[57] See *Chevron v Natural Resources Defense Council*, 467 U.S. 865–66 (1984). See also the dissenting opinion by Judge William Andrews in the famous *Palsgraf v Long Island Railroad*, 248 N.Y. 352 (1928).

[58] See eg, D Kennedy, *A Critique of Adjudication (fin de siècle)* (Cambridge, Harvard University Press, 1998) 101. But see *ibid* 135–6.

[59] See eg, K Greenawalt, 'Policy, Rights and Judicial Decision' (1977) 11 *Georgia Law Review* 1033. See also N MacCormick, *Legal Reasoning and Legal Theory* (Oxford, Clarendon Press, 1997) 262.

[60] See eg, *Hoffman Plastic Compounds, Inc v National Labor Relations Board*, 122 S.Ct. 1275 (2002).

political. The transformation takes place from non-legal values to standards not directly relevant in the legal arena or, in other words, non-legal concepts and categories.[61] This idea of policy as entirely political by nature can be found in the majority of the legal scholars using such a concept, from at least the late 1800s up to today.

Holmes, for example, distinguishes between two levels of legal phenomenon: the logical surface of the statutes (or judicial decisions) and the deeper 'competing legislative grounds' (or 'question of legislative policy'). Such grounds or policies are the ideological underpinnings of the law. They are purely political decisions or value-choices upon which the logical surface of the legal rules and categories are built. For example, a policy is the limitation of liability 'to cases where a prudent man might have foreseen the injury'.[62] This functions as a ground for the legally relevant instruction of a judge to a jury 'that an employer is not liable to an employee for an injury received in the course of his employment unless he is negligent'.[63]

Many contemporary legal scholars, even those who usually are more open to a law and policy discussion, tend to follow the Holmes' path of externalising, although from different approaches, and making the nature of policy in general political as towards the legal material and the legal phenomenon. The consideration of policy as a foreign/political element in the legal world is evident even in the legal theories embracing the idea of law as embedded into politics. For example, the legal process movement can be considered as belonging to the embedded model in conceiving the relations between law and politics. Despite considering law as embedded into politics, the legal process school draws a clear-cut line between legal rules and standards on one side, and policies and principles on the other side. Although the latter influence and intervene in the work of legislators and judges, principles and policies are still formed and shaped outside the legal arena. In particular, policy is defined as:

> a statement of objective ... eg full employment, the promotion of the practice or procedure of collective bargaining, national security, conservation of natural resources, etc., etc., etc.[64]

The legal process school then considers policy as a statement of values that needs to be transformed into legal categories before their implementation by means of law into the community.

---

[61] See eg, Kennedy, *A Critique of Adjudication (fin de siècle)* (n 58 above) 83.
[62] OW Holmes, 'The Path of the Law' (1897) 10 *Harvard Law Review* 465.
[63] *Ibid* 467. See also Holmes, *The Common Law* (n 38 above) 35.
[64] Hart and Sacks, *Legal Process* (n 45 above) 159. See also Eskridge and Frickey, 'The Making of the Legal Process' (n 43 above) 2044.

Even if following a different theoretical path, Dworkin arrives in the end at the same idea of the political nature of the policy moment. According to him, policies are among those kinds of criteria that are used, in particular in the presence of hard cases, by the judiciary as alternative means to the traditional legal categories and concepts:

> when lawyers reason or dispute about legal rights and obligations, particularly in those hard cases when our problems with these concepts seem most acute, they make use of standards that do function as rules, but operate differently as principles, policies, and other sorts of standards ... *these standards are not rules.*[65] (emphasis added)

As for other legal actors, policy still maintains its non-legal nature for Dworkin, although entering and, to some extent, being a constitutive part of the legal phenomenon. In particular, Dworkin defines the policy of a statute as its ultimate goals, that is the goals lying outside the legal world, the world in which the statute has an impact. For example, the policy of a statute that awards damages for business practices reducing market competition (impact on the legal world), is to 'encourage investment, create jobs, reduce inflation, and otherwise contribute to the general good', ie political goals external to the legal system.[66]

This basic common position of considering the policy moment as political by nature, however, does not prevent contemporary legal theories from differing as to the issue of the weight such non-legal standards known as policies should have in judicial and legislative law-making activities. The answers range from encouraging a further opening of the legal arena to the entrance of policy, such as with the American legal realists or CLS, to an attitude of closing the legal order towards foreign political entities as represented by policies, as with Dworkin and Scalia.

According to the legal realists, the legal arena should be open to the political elements as represented by policy at several and different levels: at the legislative level, at the judicial level and the legal-educational level.[67] CLS carries to the extreme the legal realist proposition of opening the law to the political world. CLS promotes the complete assimilation of the legal arena and all its actors (eg scholars, judges and politicians) into the political environment as represented by policy evaluations. Many CLS scholars so extensively absorb the law into policy that it gives rise to a

---

[65] Dworkin, *Taking Rights Seriously* (n 54 above) 22.

[66] Dworkin, *A Matter of Principle* (n 54 above) 73–4. See also R Dworkin, *Law's Empire* (Cambridge, Harvard University Press, 1997) 390.

[67] See eg, F Cohen, 'Field Theory and Judicial Logic' (1950) LIX *Yale Law Journal* 260; J Landis, *The Administrative Process* (New Haven, Yale University Press, 1938) 111–17; K Llewellyn, 'Remarks on the Theory of Appellate Decisions and the Rules or Canons about how Statutes are to be Construed' (1950) 3 *Vanderbilt Law Review* 400; and R Pound, 'A Survey of Social Interests' (1943) 57 *Harvard Law Review* 4, 4–6, 30–1.

certain confusion. CLS scholars in the legal phenomenon often freely interchange political evaluations with policy evaluations. In other words, CLS does not distinguish, as do political scientists, between the ultimate values that the surrounding environment asks to be implemented (politics) and the outputs in which those values have been transformed (policy).[68]

In contrast to CLS, both Dworkin and Scalia openly recognise but do not approve of the fact that judges make use of this political or foreign element called policy. According to Dworkin, policy is a compromise between different collective demands or values. Therefore, in order to respect the idea of democracy, it would be better if policy arguments would be limited as deciding criteria to the law-making process occurring in the legislative arena and not be allowed inside the judicial arena. The legislative authorities are specifically 'designed to produce an accurate expression of the different interests that should be taken into account' in the policy process.[69]

Scalia's ideas as to the position of policy in the law-making process are clearly stated in his comments to *Chevron v Natural Resources Defense Council*. First, the consideration of policy consequences is included in that which Scalia defines as the 'traditional tools of statutory construction' at the disposal of the courts.[70] Secondly, from a constitutional perspective, Scalia does not see any impediment to the policy-making role of the judiciary. Finally, allowing the courts to take into account policy consequences gives the entire system (both in its judicial, political and legislative aspects) more flexibility. However, Scalia continues, the judicial ideology is first of all so imbued with traditional legal categories of interpretations that policy evaluations by lower judges are probably destined to be rejected by higher courts. Moreover, the *Chevron* decision recognises the agency's law-making discretion in the form of policy or, in other words, the US Supreme Court's interpretation gives to governmental agencies (ie political actors) and not to the courts (ie legal actors) the legal power of deciding as to the implementation of value f instead of value e.[71]

D. Policy as Standards

From this collocation by legal actors of the policy moment inside the political world, that is policy as mainly constituted by values and value-choices, the second feature of the policy moment according to the lawyers

---

[68] See eg, K Klare, 'Judicial Deradicalization of the Wagner Act and the Origins of Modern Legal Consciousness, 1937–1941' (1978) 62 *Minnesota Law Review* 301, 301–2, 338–9.

[69] R Dworkin, 'Hard Cases' (1975) 88 *Harvard Law Review* 1061. See also Dworkin, *Law's Empire* (n 66 above) 241–3; Dworkin, *Taking Rights Seriously* (n 54 above) 85; and B Leiter, 'Positivism, Formalism, Realism: Legal Positivism in American Jurisprudence by Anthony Sebok (Book Review)' (1999) 99 *Columbia Law Review* 1146.

[70] A Scalia, 'Judicial Deference to Administrative Interpretations of Law' (1989) *Duke Law Journal* 515.

[71] See *ibid* 516–21.

is also derived: its being constituted only of standards. This second feature of the concept of policy as understood by the legal actors (policy as standards) cannot be easily separated from the first (policy as political phenomenon). The difficulty of dividing the political nature of policy from its being shaped in the form of standards is primarily caused by the perception legal actors have of the policy moment. Many legal actors tend to characterise policy standards as separate from other types of standards, which can become relevant in the law-making and law-applying processes (eg moral standards), by the very fact that policy standards have their origin mainly in the political world.[72]

The connection of 'policy as standards' to their political nature (ie their being created in the environment surrounding the legal world) is evident in Dworkin and his controversial distinction between policies and principles. As pointed out by Bell, Dworkin characterises policy as the category of non-ethical standards. Dworkin's non-ethical standards are those that are designated by that which here has been defined as the political arena. They are set out in order to justify a decision by showing that it fulfils certain goals of a political, economic or social nature. These goals, for example, are greater wealth for the community or a better environment. In contrast, Dworkin's principles are ethical standards. They have the moral nature of being used in order to justify a result by making reference to a certain 'valuable in itself' value, for example fairness.[73]

It should be noted that this 'de-moralisation' and politicisation of the idea of policy is further stressed in Dworkin's legal theory by one other element. Dworkin adopts the presence of goals as a qualifying element in order to speak of policy. This allows him to distinguish policy from morals and incorporate it into a *stricto sensu* politics, as for Dworkin the goal is 'a nonindividuated political aim, that is, state of affairs whose specification does not ... call for any particular opportunity or resource or liberty for particular individuals'.[74]

Most contemporary legal theories seem to have also embraced such an idea of policy as standards. Similarly to Dworkin, American legal realists tend to limit their idea of policy to the area of (political) standards as opposed to the traditional formal-legal rules. For example, Llewellyn characterises the Grand Style of the common law tradition in terms of a

---

[72] See eg, the distinction between moral principles and policy as sketched by Eisenberg, *The Nature of the Common Law* (n 50 above) 14–37.

[73] See Bell, *Policy Arguments in Judicial Decisions* (n 47 above) 23. See also Dworkin, *Taking Rights Seriously* (n 54 above) 90–1; S Guest, *Ronald Dworkin* (Edinburgh, Edinburgh University Press, 1992) 61–4; and for a similar distinction Hart and Sacks, *Legal Process* (n 45 above) 159.

[74] Dworkin, 'Hard Cases' (n 69 above) 1068. But see MacCormick, *Legal Reasoning and Legal Theory* (n 59 above) 263–4; and Greenawalt, 'Policy, Rights, and Judicial Decision' (n 59 above) 996–1003, 1035–42.

legal thinking focused on the use, both in law-making and in law-interpretation, of policy standards. It is this very use that distinguishes this Grand Style from the Formal Style, in which a dominant role is played instead by the legal rules and the traditional legal logical principles. Moreover, Llewellyn continues, the modalities through which such political standards have been reached (policy as process) belong to neither the law nor to its investigation.[75]

Even Posner, who is extremely sceptical as to the distinction between policies and principles as drawn by Dworkin, does not question the identification of the term policies with the (limited) meaning of standards constructed for the purpose of gaining certain collective goals. For him, the processes directed at producing such standards also remain in a field outside the law, a field to be investigated either by policy or ethical analyses.[76]

Another typical example of identifying policy with standards produced inside the political environment as surrounding the legal arena, can be found in the *Chevron* judgment. The main message of the Court appears to be to exclude policies from judicial review, that is those standards produced by the interpretative activity of a public administration agency in the case of vague or incomplete statutory regulation as enacted by Congress.[77] The identification of policy with standards for behaviour for public authorities is also present in more recent decisions, such as *Miller-El v Cockrell* (2003) (policy by a County District Attorney's Office excluding minorities from jury service) and *Eldred v Ashcroft* (policy followed by Congress treating existing and future copyrights in parity).[78]

V. THE LAWYER'S POLICY AS POLITICAL STANDARDS

The perception of policy among legal actors, and in particular among legal scholars, is similar in one respect to the one shared by a large segment of political scientists. In both cases, policy indicates a spectrum of standards expressing the result of a process through which the political system

---

[75] See Llewellyn, *The Common Law Tradition* (n 18 above) 59–60. See also F Cohen, 'Transcendental Nonsense and the Functional Approach' (1935) 35 *Columbia Law Review* 833; and W Twining, *Karl Llewellyn and the Realist Movement* (London, Weidenfeld & Nicolson, 1973) 212 Table 1.

[76] See R Posner, *The Problems of Jurisprudence* (Cambridge, Harvard University Press, 1990) 105, 238–9.

[77] See *Chevron v Natural Resources Defense Council* (n 57 above) 2792–3. See also L Silberman, 'Chevron: the Intersection of Law and Policy' (1990) 58 *George Washington Law Review* 823.

[78] See *Miller-El v Cockrell*, 537 U.S. 334 (2003); and *Eldred v Ashcroft* (n 49 above) 780. Legislative bodies also take a similar position. See eg, USCA Const. Art I § 9, Cl 8, or National Agricultural Research, Extension, and Teaching Policy Act ss 1409(A), 1411, 1421 (1977).

converts certain demands coming from the surrounding environment into inputs relevant for the system in question, whether legal or political. When it comes to the nature of the relevancy of policy as to the law, the positions of legal scholars can vary considerably, according to whether they consider the law as inside, outside or intersecting politics.

For example, for the theories within the autonomous model, policy tends to have an indirect effect on the legal phenomenon. The standards of policy affect the legal arena through a narrow and single channel represented by the Basic Norm or Rule of Recognition as in the legal world. Political standards, such as equality between men and women, have to be either constitutionalised in a first Constitution or somehow recognised by the legal community in order to then affect the legal decisions of judges.[79] For the embedded model, in contrast, the nature of the effect of policy is of a more direct character, since policy, once formed in the political surroundings, then moves directly into the legal phenomenon. In such a case, the judge directly takes into consideration the equality standard in the decision's reasoning, picking it directly from the political surrounding.[80]

Despite these divergences, and in contrast with political science, the large majority of legal actors, and in particular most legal scholars, lean towards a common idea of policy: policy is constituted entirely by exogenous (*political*) standards, that is they originate and are formed in the environment surrounding the one in which the legal actors work (ie the legal world). Moreover, for political scientists, as seen above, policy identifies both the processes and the results that transform certain inputs into certain political outputs. In contrast, for legal actors, policy becomes relevant for their work only when it arrives inside the legal world, only in terms of results of a certain process occurring in the political surrounding environment, results that can influence the legal working. Lawyers and legal scholars therefore identify policy with the standards chosen by the environment surrounding the legal world (*policy as standards*). That part of policy dealing with the mechanisms behind the production of such results, the idea of policy as the processes of evaluation and selection of the goals to be pursued through the legal order, remains outside the horizon of legal actors, belonging to another landscape (the political one).[81]

---

[79] See eg, HLA Hart, 'Positivism and the Separation of Law and Morals' (1958) 71 *Harvard Law Review* 614. Cf Hughes, 'Rules, Policy and Decision-Making' (n 50 above) 113–19, 127–31.

[80] See Kennedy, *A Critique of Adjudication (fin de siècle)* (n 58 above) 108–11. According to Kennedy, policy arguments have a legal character in the sense that a legal actor uses them. When it comes to the nature of policy, Kennedy admits the different nature of policy by defining it as a Trojan horse within the legal world, see *ibid* 109.

[81] For Kennedy, 'policy argument *presupposes* a "force field" model of the decision process'. Kennedy, *A Critique of Adjudication (fin de siècle)* (n 58 above) 99 (emphasis added).

In summary, both contemporary legal scholars and, in general, legal actors by and large, tend to perceive policy as a spectrum of *standards* (policy as results) whose production and nature is *political* in relation to the legal order (externality of the policy process). Policies are generally perceived as paths with a political nature because they are produced outside the legal world, and through which, political evaluations and decisions are inserted (to a greater or lesser extent) into the legal system.[82]

VI. MODELS OUTLINING POLICY ACCORDING TO CONTEMPORARY LEGAL THEORY

How the vast majority of contemporary legal scholars and practitioners tend to conceive of policies in a similar way has been seen above: political standards that can penetrate and have a (direct or indirect) relevancy for the making and applying of legal categories and concepts. In other words:

> the term 'policy' is used to refer to a community's values, culture or expectations, whether they be social, political, or economic (Dworkin's 'policies') or ethical or moral (Dworkin's 'principles') ... a policy is the stuff of which a rule (a standard of behavior) is made ... A policy, in short, is a community norm.[83]

It is now possible to place such common concepts of policy as espoused by legal scholars into the more general and diversified panorama of how the relations between law and politics have been portrayed by contemporary legal theory. The following explanatory models (Figures 3.1, 3.2 and 3.3) roughly illustrate the positions and roles of policy in the relationships between law and politics, according to the different models outlined in chapter one. This is a conceptualisation of policy similar to the one developed by political science, as in the legal world policy also tends to indicate something occurring in the political world and affecting the world of regulations (ie the legal world), that is something happening between the transmission of some inputs (f) and the production of different outputs (f[1]).[84] The perception of policy phenomenon by legal actors, however, presents considerable differences from the perception held by contemporary political scientists.

First, for legal actors in general and legal scholars in particular, the goal of using policy is to introduce into the legal world value(s) produced in the

---

[82] Exemplary in this sense are Podgórecki's ideas of policy in the legal phenomenon. See A Podgórecki, *Law and Society* (London, Routledge & Kegan Paul, 1974) 242. See also A Podgórecki, *A Sociological Theory of Law* (Milan, Dott A Giuffrè Editore, 1991) 195–232.

[83] RL Brooks, 'The Use of Policy in Judicial Reasoning: a Reconceptualization before and after *Bush v. Gore*' (2002) 13 *Stanford Law and Policy Review* 36.

[84] Policy 'is understood as situated between the paradigmatically legal appeal to authority and the paradigmatically extra- or nonlegal appeal to "politics" or ideology'. Kennedy, *A Critique of Adjudication (fin de siècle)* (n 58 above) 109.

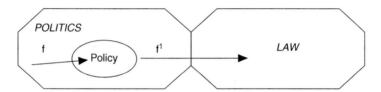

Figure 3.1: Policy as viewed by the autonomous model

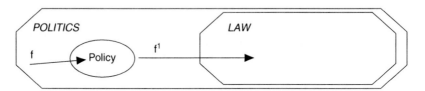

Figure 3.2: Policy as viewed by the embedded model

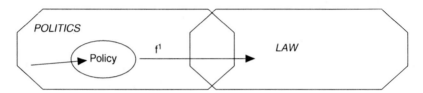

Figure 3.3: Policy as viewed by the intersecting model

political world (*policy as standard*). Policies are simply standards that (to a greater or lesser extent) are used by judicial and legislative powers in their law-making and law-applying activities. Policies are generally perceived by legal scholars and practitioners as relevant for the legal world only as results (f^1 in Figures 3.1, 3.2 and 3.3) of external processes occurring in the political world.[85]

As a consequence, and this is the second major difference between lawyers and political scientists, the processes through which such standards/policies have been formed and/or selected (ie how f became f^1), do not belong to the concept of policy as embraced by the legal world. Policies are considered as originating and developing entirely inside the political world (in Figures 3.1, 3.2 and 3.3, f is fully positioned inside the politics area). In other words, the formation of such political standards occurs externally to the legal system, and this affects the very nature of the

---

[85] See eg, Bell, *Policy Arguments in Judicial Decisions* (n 47 above) 22–3; or T Grey, 'Judicial Review and Legal Pragmatism' (2003) 38 *Wake Forest Law Review* 479. Compare S Nagel and M Neef, 'Legal Policy Optimizing Models' (1977) 29 *Journal of Legal Education* 32.

policy, depriving it of its more legal aspects (*policy as a political phenomenon*).[86] Even if the idea of the relations between law and politics (and consequently the figure) changes according to the legal theory under scrutiny, the idea of policy still keeps the same position across the vast majority of contemporary legal thought: inside the political arena and outside the legal one, in which it, however, becomes directly or indirectly relevant in terms of results or standards (f^1).[87]

The positions of law and politics can vary considerably according to the different legal theories: law can either be autonomous from, embedded in, or intersecting with the area of politics. Nevertheless, when it comes to policy, legal actors in general and legal scholars in particular tend to arrive at the same idea of policies as those standards produced inside the political world, affecting legal actors in their law-making and in their law-applying moments. In summary, it is then possible to consider how policy for lawyers is limited to the meaning of standard(s) introducing political problems and solutions into the legal world, ie problems originating in the world of non-legal values and the solutions reached following patterns of reasoning and argumentation of a non-legal nature.[88]

This attitude seems even more peculiar when confronted by the highly articulated and sophisticated production on the same issue by political scientists. There is a possible explanation for such a self-limiting attitude carried on by the legal world in general as to a systematic investigation about and around policy issues, an underlying feature shared by the vast majority of different legal ideologies, cultures and theories produced and embraced in the twentieth century. As pointed out by de Sousa Santos:

[i]n the twentieth century, and particularly after the Second World War, the law underwent a ... metamorphosis. It gave up resistance in docile submission to the whole range of values and beliefs—sometimes complementary, sometimes contradictory—that the different social and political forces imposed upon it. In sum, law became a camel, and the welfare state is the most salient feature of this process of 'camelisation' of the law.[89]

---

[86] See eg, Hart and Sacks, *Legal Process* (n 45 above) 1179.

[87] See eg, MacCormick, *Legal Reasoning and Legal Theory* (n 59 above) 149; or the features of policy according to W Clune, 'Law and Public Policy: Map of an Area' (1993) 2 *Southern California Interdisciplinary Law Journal* 3.

[88] See R Pound, *The Ideal Element in Law* (Calcutta, Calcutta University Press, 1958) 88–90. See eg, PS Atiyah and R Summers, *Form and Substance in Anglo-American Law: a Comparative Study of Legal Reasoning, Legal Theory, and Legal Institutions* (Oxford, Oxford University Press, 1987) 389; and Bell, *Policy Arguments in Judicial Decisions* (n 47 above) 1–7.

[89] B Sousa Santos (de), 'Law: a Map of Misreading. Toward a Postmodern Conception of Law' (1987) 14 *Journal of Law and Society* 279.

As a result, as for the autonomous model, or as a reaction, as for the embedded model, to such a phenomenon, contemporary legal scholars and practitioners have always been so much concerned with the question of whether and where to draw a line between law and politics and their respective investigations that, in the end, they tend not to pay enough attention to how the disciplines inside the political world have evolved spectacularly in the last century.[90] It is then not a coincidence that this purposive lack of systematic attention has been underlined by legal realism, ie the theory embracing that which has been previously defined here as probably the most modern among the models relating politics and law (the intersecting model).

VII. CONCLUSION

The approach the majority of contemporary legal theories have to the transformational moment mirrors the general dilemma law now faces. Because of the high degree of politicisation of the legal phenomenon, legal scholars tend to place the transformational moment (although attaching to it different natures and functions) in a central position in their models of the law and of the working legal order.

In order to commence framing this moment in the life of a legal order, and in particular in the law-making, the debate developed inside political science has been investigated. Residing specifically within the concept of policy is the most suitable analytical tool to help legal theories penetrate the transformational moment. This is true if one accepts the political scientist's definition of policy as a *network* of both *processes and decisions* with a *conversional function* of inputs into outputs. This definition, as developed inside political science, moreover brings to the surface the deficiencies of the idea of policy as used by lawyers today; a legal perspective that limits the meaning of policy to only one part of the phenomenon as identified by political scientists, ie to only the final result (standards) in the form of political evaluations and decisions affecting the legal world.

This investigation will now proceed in chapters four and five to transfer the idea of policy as developed inside political science (as conversional processes and results) into the legal world and legal disciplines, a two-step path. The first, starting from the conceptual findings reached by political scientists, will target the opening of a field of investigation for legal

---

[90] See F Ross, 'Political Science and the New Legal Realism: a Case of Unfortunate Interdisciplinary Ignorance' (1997) 92 *Northwestern University Law Review* 314; Kennedy, *A Critique of Adjudication (fin de siècle)* (n 58 above) 112; and Cotterrell, *Law's Community* (n 4 above) 54–5.

scholars: the policy of law (or the transformational moment). The second will endeavour to identify and sketch the foundational constitution of a branch of legal studies dealing specifically with the processes and results of the transformation of values into law: the policy of law analysis.

4

The Policy of Law: Opening and Framing the Field

THE PREVIOUS CHAPTERS revealed the central role the processes of transformation play in law-making as portrayed by most contemporary legal theories, as well as the necessity for a systematic investigation, from a legal-theoretical perspective, regarding such processes. This chapter proceeds in the effort to satisfy this need, starting with the results reached by contemporary political science and its concept of policy.

This analysis is structured in the direction of developing a model to explain the position and function of the transformational moment in the law-making process. In particular, through progressively refined models of the process, a space can be opened in the law-making activity between the formation of values in the political world (politics of law) and the impact of the newly-made law on the community (policy of law outcomes). This space is defined as the 'policy of law', a space in which values entrenched in political decisions are transformed into law, having an effect on the existing legal system. These changes in the legal system, in their turn, affect the behaviours of the persons within the community at large. It will also be demonstrated how, in contemporary Western legal orders, this space of policy of law is mainly (but not exclusively) the domain of the work and reasoning of the actors belonging to the legal world.

I. OPENING THE FIELD OF THE 'POLICY OF LAW'

To introduce policy as a field relevant for the legal actor and, at the same time, a field in which legal investigations are possible, it is necessary to preliminarily open the meaning of policy as traditionally seen by lawyers and legal scholars. This opening can lead to the possibility of using this renewed concept of the policy of law as a central point for explaining that which has been shown here to be one of the least systematically investigated moments of the law-making process: the transformational moment. The effort here is to try to use the idea of policy of law as an analytical tool in order to better illuminate the grey box in which politics becomes law; this can be done in particular by defining the transformational moment as the moment where the policy of law processes (and results) take place.

A preliminary and necessary step in order to absorb the transformational moment into a legal idea of policy is a realignment of the somehow abbreviated policy as invoked by legal actors with the more developed and articulated concept of policy built inside political science. This can be done through the introduction into the legal concept of policy some new constitutive components working in the direction of transforming the traditional dualism of 'policy and law' into a unified concept of the 'policy of law'. In other words, new ingredients can assist in separating the policy moment from its purely political nature and becoming more normative, ie directly relevant both for and because of the existence of a normative system known as law.[1]

A. The Policy of Law as Rational Processes Leading to Legal Categories

The first action to be taken in the realignment is to modernise the legal concept of policy with respect to the procedural aspects of the policy moment. As pointed out in chapter three, policy for political scientists is more than authoritative outputs, policy is *a web of both decisions and processes* through which such decisions are taken.

Taking such a definition as the basis, one can see how the concept of policy employed by legal actors already comprehends the component of decisions as a constitutive element of policy. In particular, as seen in the previous chapter, legal actors view policy in terms of *decisions* or standards of certain (political) processes which are introduced, under the mantle of legal categories or legal concepts, inside an already existing general system of legal norms. This is done to achieve certain results in the community, mostly in terms of behaviours by the members of the community.

The first consequence of inserting into the legal discourse the political scientist's definition of policy as a web of decisions and processes, is that the final results of the policy process can be defined in terms of *legal categories* (or *concepts*) and not of a single statute, judicial decision or, more generally, a single legal rule.[2] The policy of law cannot be identified by one single political process leading to one single legal decision. It is

---

[1] See G Hughes, 'Rules, Policy and Decision-Making' in G Hughes (ed), *Law, Reason, and Justice: Essays in Legal Philosophy* (New York, New York University Press, 1969) 111–15. Compare D Kennedy, *A Critique of Adjudication (fin de siècle)* (Cambridge, Harvard University Press, 1998) 97–101; and S Coval and JC Smith, 'The Causal Theory of Rules' in DN Weisstub (ed), *Law and Policy* (Downsview, Osgoode Hall Law School, 1976) 126–7.
[2] See eg, J Bell, *Policy Arguments in Judicial Decisions* (Oxford, Clarendon Press, 1983) 40–3; N MacCormick, *Legal Reasoning and Legal Theory* (Oxford, Clarendon Press, 1997)

more a question of several processes leading to the production, often through several statutes and/or judicial law-making decisions, to a legal category or legal concept. The latter can be defined as a group (often scattered) of rules and normative regulations that aim, through their co-ordination and combination, at building an interaction responding to the criteria required by the formal rationality of the law (eg consistency or coherence).[3]

This rationalised interaction of rules, in its turn, forms a theoretical matrix with the primary classificatory and normative functions of diagnosing and systematising legal problems occurring both in the creation and interpretation of the law. Legal concepts and categories play both a classificatory and a normative function because, as pointed out by Tuori:

> [l]egal concepts included in the general doctrines play an important role in systematising surface-level legal material. New statutes issued by the legislator do not function in isolation but are inserted into the legal order's totality. Their location in this totality is determined by legal concepts, which indicate to the newcomers their domicile in the systematics of the legal order.[4]

The legal category or concept then becomes the primary tool through which the complexity of political values can find their place and/or be 'discovered' by the legal actors inside the legal system. For example, the value of considering that which is 'best for the child' in family law issues can be transformed into the legal category known as joint custody. This is not composed of one single rule but is more a question of a co-ordinated (either by the same law-making authority or by doctrine) complex of rules imposing several duties and rights on the parents, child and supervising public authority.[5]

The second innovative element of transferring the idea of policy as developed by political sciences into the legal discourse, consists of taking into account in the legal concept of policy the *processes* through which such policy-decisions or standards are reached. In law-making, the policy

---

259. But see RL Brooks, 'The Use of Policy in Judicial Reasoning: q Reconceptualization Before and After Bush v. Gore' (2002) 13 *Stanford Law and Policy Review* 36 n 20.

[3] See HLA Hart, 'Problems of the Philosophy of Law' in HLA Hart, *Essays in Jurisprudence and Philosophy* (Oxford, Clarendon Press, 1983) 93; and M Weber, *Economy and Society* (G Roth and C Wittich (eds), Berkeley, University of California Press, 1978) 656–7.

[4] K Tuori, *Critical Legal Positivism* (Aldershot, Ashgate Publishing, 2002) 218. Compare R Pound, *The Ideal Element in Law* (Calcutta, Calcutta University Press, 1958) 84 (in particular the dividing line between normative 'legal concepts' and mere classificatory 'juristic concepts').

[5] See eg, K Kurki-Suonio, 'Joint Custody as an Interpretation of the Best Interests of the Child in Critical and Comparative Perspective' (2000) 14 *International Journal of Law, Policy and the Family* 187–99. See also W Hohfeld, 'Fundamental Legal Conceptions as Applied in Juridical Reasoning' (1916–17) 26 *Yale Law Journal* 712; and Å Frändberg, 'An Essay on the Systematics of Legal Concepts: A Study of Legal Concept Formation' (1987) 31 *Scandinavian Studies in Law* 81.

of law processes are the complexity of actions taken by a single actor (eg a judge) or by groups of actors (eg the legislature) in order to produce a decision (legal category or concept). These actions are characterised by two elements.

First, the actor(s) attach to their actions a *common subjective meaning*: the intention of transforming a value into a legal category. Subjective meaning of an action, according to Weber, can be defined as 'the theoretically conceived pure type of subjective meaning attributed to the hypothetical actor or actors in a given type of action'.[6] The expression *common subjective meaning* is used here then in order to denote the fact that the actions constitutive of the policy of law process are considered by most of the actors (both legal and political) as having the same ideal-typical purpose: the transformation of values into law.

The ideas of the actors, of course, can, and usually do, fluctuate very much as to which values are to be or not be implemented. These can differ so much that they also include the values of those actors for whom the actual legal system has to be preserved, that is of those against the very transformation of any new value and for the maintenance of the status quo of the existing legal system. The conservative actors implicitly recognise the transformational function played by the policy process when considering the entrance of new values as risky and, therefore, try to 'sabotage' the policy process. This can be done, for example, by lowering the degree of comprehensibility of the language used in a new statute.[7] Nevertheless, while the specific end of the policy process can vary considerably, eg realising value f instead of value e, the common subjective meaning of the process tends to be the same: transforming values into law.

The second element characterising the process of policy of law is that the complex of actions becomes a process because they present a *rational* character. The actors or groups of actors operating inside the moments of the policy of the law organise their actions, that is they choose the appropriate means on the basis of the actual situation, in such a way as to achieve certain ends.[8] In particular, the actors act according to the common

---

[6] Weber, *Economy and Society* (n 3 above) 4. See also Talcott Parsons' n 3 in *ibid* 57; and SP Turner and RA Factor, *Max Weber: the Lawyer as Social Thinker* (London, Routledge, 1994) 30–2. For a separation of the policy and purpose of a statute, see M Radin, 'Statutory Interpretation' (1930) 43 *Harvard Law Review* 875.

[7] See eg, AE McCormick, 'Dominant Class Interests and the Emergence of Anti-Trust Legislation' (1979) 3 *Contemporary Crises* 399; and M Horwitz, *The Transformation of American Law 1870–1960: the Crisis of Legal Orthodoxy* (Oxford, Oxford University Press, 1990) 79–85. See also V Aubert, 'Some Social Functions of Legislation' (1966) 10 *Acta Sociologica* 105; and L Sossin, 'The Sounds of Silence: Law Clerks, Policy Making and the Supreme Court of Canada' (1996) 30 *University of British Columbia Law Review* 280 n 5.

[8] See Weber, *Economy and Society* (n 3 above) 5. See also the criticisms by J Habermas, *Between Facts and Norms: Contributions to a Discourse Theory of Law and Democracy* (Cambridge, The MIT Press, 1998) 71–3.

subjective meaning in the policy of law process of transforming a certain value into law either by choosing among the existing legal categories or by inventing new legal concepts. This choice or invention is done primarily taking into consideration the globality of the legal system and/or of the socio-political environment in which the chosen or new legal concepts are to operate.[9]

In the policy of law process, political actors can (and usually do) have a primary goal of a non-legal (eg economic) nature and therefore, they mainly take into consideration the surrounding political environment (substantive rationality). In contrast, particularly in Western legal systems, the legal actors primarily aim at affecting the legal system and therefore, mainly take into consideration the latter's logical structure (formal rationality).[10]

The policy of law, then, is more than simple *decisions* or standards. It also includes the complex of actions, or *process*, through which certain actors take certain decisions with the aim of transforming values into legal categories and concepts to be inserted in the existing legal system. Consideration of the procedural aspects of the policy of law is particularly present in the works produced by some of the legal scholars adopting an idea of the legal phenomenon as embedded in the political world. For example, the process can take the shape of a logical *determinatio* from general moral values into a more legally relevant category (Finnis) or of a judicial reasoning leading to the insertion into the legal forms of the economic value of efficiency (law and economics).[11]

B. The Policy of Law as More than a Political Phenomenon

A second action must be taken in the realignment in order to arrive at a definition of policy directly relevant for the legal order (policy of law): the cleansing of certain segments of the political nature within the concept of policy. This feature absolutely does not mean that policy processes and decisions are independent of the political arena. Just the opposite, policy seen from a legal perspective maintains and strengthens its function as a bridge between the political and the legal arenas.

[9] See A Ross, *On Law and Justice* (London, Stevens & Sons, 1958) 335. See also O Weinberger, *Law, Institution and Legal Politics: Fundamental Problems of Legal Theory and Social Philosophy* (Dordrecht, Kluwer Academic Publishers, 1991) 222.

[10] See Weber, *Economy and Society* (n 3 above) 657. See also Tuori, *Critical Legal Positivism* (n 4 above) 36–9.

[11] See eg, R Posner, 'A Theory of Negligence' (1972) 1 *Journal of Legal Studies* 32. See also N Duxbury, *Patterns of American Jurisprudence* (Oxford, Clarendon Press, 1995) 409–14.

Policy is those processes and decisions directed at transforming certain political inputs into legal categories and concepts. The cleansing of certain segments of the political nature within the concept of policy then simply identifies the operation directed at distinguishing, from a legal point of view, the political dimension of the law from its policy dimension. It entails, in other words, a demarcation often overlooked by the few works specifically devoted to the concept of policy of law, denoting as two different phenomena the selection and the emission of values (politics) and their transformation into legal categories and concepts (policy).[12]

As already discussed, politics usually identifies the complex of values that are to be implemented into a community by means of the law. Politics designates the complex of ideas or values embraced by the legal system in general, either by a series of laws or a single statute. Such ideas or values are to be realised through the promulgation (or not) of specific legal norms or, more generally speaking, through the adoption of a certain concerted course of legal measures, ie a policy of law.

Policy, on the other end, should not be directly identified with ideas and values. Policy deals with the processes and results of the transformation of such ideas and values into legal categories and concepts. Policy does not directly concern the process of choosing the values aimed at penetrating into a community by passing through the legal order. When discussing policy, one should actually refer more to the process of choosing the legal paths to follow in order to implement the values previously identified by the political process.[13]

Politics from a legal perspective, for example, deals with choosing the value of an absolute protection of human life as a principle inspiring the actions of a repressive (penal) apparatus of the state. Policy focuses, instead, on the choice that a conservative legal arena has by defining the expression 'human life' as having a legally binding status (in the sense that it legally binds the public authorities as to intervening and defending it) already when an egg has become fertilised by a sperm (in this way criminalising abortion). Moreover, the conservative legislator or law-making judge can decide that the best way to legally protect this value (or, in other words, to transform it into a legally relevant category) is to ensure

---

[12] See eg, M Samu, 'Legal Policy' in CB Gray (ed), *The Philosophy of Law: an Encyclopedia* (New York, Garland Publishing, 1999) 653; and A Podgórecki, *A Sociological Theory of Law* (Milan, Dott A Giuffrè Editore, 1991) 209. This confusion of policy of law and legal politics in the law-making process is also quite common among non-English speaking legal scholars. See eg, M Rehbinder, *Rechtssoziologie* (3rd edn, Berlin, Walter de Gruyter, 1993) 32; or Weinberger, *Law, Institution and Legal Politics* (n 9 above) ch XI.

[13] See G Teubner, 'How the Law Thinks: toward a Constructivist Epistemology of Law' (1989) 23 *Law and Society Review* 748; and Kennedy, *A Critique of Adjudication (fin de siècle)* (n 1 above) 165–6.

as a compulsory legal consequence the death penalty in cases of the violation of the prohibition against abortion.

This category creates a series of legal obligations for the public authorities to intervene and stop abortion even if, paradoxically, the certain practical outcome of the authorities' intervention can be the defiance of the value chosen by the political arena. This is a hypothetical example not far from the reality of certain legal systems where, in order to implement the value of the protection of life, the legislature and/or judges introduce into the legal system the legal category of an unconditional criminalisation of abortive practices, ie regardless of the physical or psychological conditions of the mother (eg the mental or physical risks to her life in carrying a child).[14]

II. AN UPDATED CONCEPT OF POLICY OF LAW

It is now possible to insert this separation of the policy moment in law-making from its political origins, into the re-elaborated traditional legal concept of policy, ie the one obtained by adding two further constitutive elements (*legal categories* and *processes*). The models described in chapter three (Figures 3.1, 3.2 and 3.3) as a result can be further developed into Figure 4.1, defining the actual position and role of policy of law arising from transferring into the legal discourse the conceptual results reached by political science. Policy of law is a kind of consequential moment of conversion, constituted by actions and standards, fitting in between the values to be implemented (politics) and the tools to be used for this purpose (law).

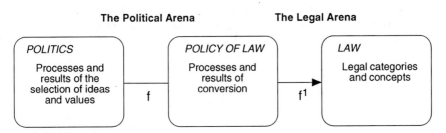

Figure 4.1: Position of the policy of law between politics and law

---

[14] See eg, the position of the Irish Government in the renowned decision by the Supreme Court of Ireland *Attorney General v X and others*, [1992] 1 IR 11. See also R O'Connell, *Legal Theory in the Crucible of Constitutional Justice: a Study of Judges and Political Morality in Canada, Ireland and Italy* (Aldershot, Dartmouth Publishing Company, 2000) 176–80.

The political value f (protection of life) presents a different nature and shape from the legal categories and concepts that are the legal version of the values inside the legal arena (legal category f^1 or compulsory death penalty in case of abortion). As Habermas points out:

> Legal statutes certainly contain teleological elements [typical of the political discourse], but these involve more than just the hermeneutic explication of shared value orientations.[15]

This actually is one of the major contributions of the autonomous model's theories to the debate on the relations between law and politics: underlining the different natures (some would even say ontologies) of the values and legal categories standing for those values in the legal world.[16]

III. LEGALISATION OF THE POLICY OF LAW

This manoeuvre of detaching the policy moment from the political arena can actually be brought even further. A fourth feature can be introduced into the concept of policy from a legal point of observation: the increasing *legalisation* of the policy of law processes transforming values into law. The phenomenon of the legalisation of policy is actually only a part of a more general tendency of the legal world to occupy the surrounding spaces (eg politics, economy, society), a tendency typical for contemporary Western legal cultures. As already pointed out by Weber:

> [t]o an outstanding degree, politics today is in fact conducted in public by means of the spoken or written word. To weigh the effect of the word properly falls within the range of the lawyer's tasks.[17]

More recently, Dworkin began his critical enterprise against legal positivism with the same premises, considering it an established truth that '[w]e live in and by the law. It makes us what we are: citizens and employees and doctors and spouses and people who own things.'[18]

---

[15] Habermas, *Between Facts and Norms* (n 8 above) 282. See also J Simmons, *Moral Principles and Political Obligations* (Princeton, Princeton University Press, 1979) 16–23.

[16] See eg, HLA Hart, *The Concept of Law* (Oxford, Clarendon Press, 1961) 86–8, 181–2; H Kelsen, *Introduction to the Problems of Legal Theory* (Oxford, Clarendon Press, 1996) 15–16; J Austin, *The Province of Jurisprudence Determined and the Uses of the Study of Jurisprudence* (London, Weidenfeld and Nicolson, 1954) 184; and N Luhmann, *Law as a Social System* (Oxford, Oxford University Press, 2004) 187.

[17] M Weber, 'Politics as a Vocation' in HH Gert and C Wright Mills (eds), *From Max Weber: Essays in Sociology* (Oxford, Oxford University Press, 1991) 95. See also J Habermas, 'Law as Medium and Law as Institution' in G Teubner (ed), *Dilemmas of Law in the Welfare State* (Berlin, Walter de Gruyter, 1986) 213–17; and P Bourdieu, 'The Force of Law: toward a Sociology of the Juridical Field' (1987) 38 *Hastings Law Journal* 830.

[18] R Dworkin, *Law's Empire* (Cambridge, Harvard University Press, 1997) vii. See also L Friedman, *Total Justice* (New York, Russell Sage Foundation, 1985) 42; M Loughlin, *Sword*

The legalisation of policy denotes, in particular, the phenomenon by which the policy processes and the policy results become increasingly normative in nature. The process of the transformation of values into law, and their results, can be better understood by using mainly a Hartian internal perspective, that is by taking into account as crucial the perspective lawyers have as to the issue of transforming value (f) into a category or concept which is directly relevant for the legal order (f^1).[19] For example, in order to understand the criminalisation of abortion, the legal concept of 'human life' that judges sitting in a supreme court or legal advisors of a government have becomes fundamental, regardless of the general sentiments in the community, the religious authorities or the medical experts' opinions on the issue.

The recognition of the centrality of legal actors in law-making in general and in the policy moment in particular is actually one of the major accomplishments of the analysis performed by the legal realists. They point out not only the complexity of the relationships between law and politics, but also stress the determinant role legal actors can play in such relationships, either in their theoretical functions as legal scholars advising law-making authorities (as in Scandinavian legal realism) or in their more direct and practical role of judges, legislators and law professors (as with most American legal realists).[20]

The reasons for such a transference of the policy moment inside the legal arena or, in other words, for the growing importance of the views of lawyers as to issues of how and why politics is transformed into law, are mainly two. The first is that practically all Western legal and political orders have adopted the rule of law (or in Europe *Rechtsstaat*) as one of the models according to which the regulations of the relations between the public authorities and the private individual are sculpted.

The rule of law and the *Rechtsstaat* provide a model focusing attention on the respect public authorities have to accord the law (and, in the case of

---

and Scales: an Examination of the Relationship between Law and Politics (Oxford, Hart Publishing, 2000) 229–35; and P Steiner, 'The Legalization of American Society: Economic Regulation' (1983) 81 *Michigan Law Review* 1289.

[19] See eg, L Friedman, *The Limits of Law: a Critique and a Proposal* (Siegen, Center for Studies on Changing Norms and Mobility, 1986) 27–8. See also MacCormick, *Legal Reasoning and Legal Theory* (n 2 above) 235–7; and R Cotterrell, *Law's Community: Legal Theory in Sociological Perspective* (Oxford, Clarendon Press, 1995) 240–8.

[20] See eg, Ross, *On Law and Justice* (n 9 above) 330–1; K Olivecrona, *Law as Fact* (2nd edn, London, Stevens & Sons, 1971) 86–9, 92–3; K Llewellyn, 'The Normative, the Legal, and the Law-Jobs: the Problem of Juristic Method' (1940) 49 *Yale Law Journal* 1395; and J Frank, *Courts on Trial: Myth and Reality in American Justice* (Princeton, Princeton University Press, 1950) 239–42. Cf J Sundberg, 'Scandinavian Unrealism: Co-report on Scandinavian Legal Philosophy' (1986) 9 *Rechtstheorie* 312; and Duxbury, *Patterns of American Jurisprudence* (n 11 above) 149–55.

the rule of law, also certain basic rights), and therefore shift the transformational moment of the law-making process towards the law and the legal system. The values espoused by the public authorities have to fit into the latter and, therefore, both the legal vestiges (legal categories and concepts) taken by the values and, more in general, the views of the same transformation the legal actors have (in particular the judges and the legal scholars) become of primary importance.[21] Despite their very different ideas as to the meaning of the expression 'the respect public authorities have to pay to the law', the vast majority of contemporary legal theories recognise one of the functions that the rule of law plays in the Western legal systems: it allows law to occupy some spaces which previously were the monopoly of politics.[22]

The other reason that encourages the shifting of the policy moment into the legal arena is connected to the specific features the legal phenomenon has acquired in contemporary legal history. One of the constitutive elements of the law-making process is the fact that, in the end, such a process must externalise itself in the form of specific linguistic utterances, with an authoritative nature and a performative function, expressed in an oral or written form by specific actors or groups of actors (eg judge or legislature).

In recent centuries, it is possible to see an increasing *professionalisation* of both such externalising actors and their linguistic utterances. Professionalisation means that a specific training (eg a law degree) and a specific legitimation (usually of a legal nature itself, eg a selection according to specific legal procedures) is usually required of individuals or groups of individuals in order to give a binding character to their linguistic utterances, ie in order to become institutional actors in the law-making process. Moreover, such linguistic utterances are (or should be) translations done by

---

[21] See R Summers, 'A Formal Theory of the Rule of Law' in R Summers, *Essays in Legal Theory* (Dordrecht, Kluwer Academic Publishers, 2000) 167–8; Habermas, *Between Facts and Norms* (n 8 above) 134–5; Luhmann, *Law as a Social System* (n 16 above) 362–3; and Kennedy, *A Critique of Adjudication (fin de siècle)* (n 1 above) 13–14. See also J Raz, 'The Politics of the Rule of Law' in J Raz, *Ethics in the Public Domain: Essays in the Morality of Law and Politics* (Oxford, Clarendon Press, 1994) 359–61; J Waldron, 'Lex Satis Iusta' (2000) 75 *Notre Dame Law Review* 1845; and O Kirchheimer, 'The Rechtsstaat as Magic Wall' in F Burin and K Shell (eds), *Politics, Law and Social Change: Selected Essays of Otto Kirchheimer* (New York, Columbia University Press, 1969) 433.

[22] See H Kelsen, 'Foundations of Democracy' (1955) LXVI *Ethics* 77; R Dworkin, *A Matter of Principle* (Cambridge, Harvard University Press, 1985) 11–13; and K Llewellyn, *Jurisprudence: Realism in Theory and Practice* (Chicago, University of Chicago Press, 1971) 130–5. But see D Kairys, 'Introduction' in D Kairys (ed), *The Politics of Law: a Progressive Critique* (3rd edn, New York, Basic Books, 1998) 6.

qualified translators from the political will into a particular kind of language, the legal language, which differs from other languages (eg political *stricto sensu* or moral).[23]

The political will can be expressed in forms that are relevant for the legal order either directly (eg with the delegation of the legislative power as to a particular issue from the legislature to a legislative drafting committee) or simply indirectly (eg through a mass-media campaign while awaiting a decision from a supreme court as to a hard case). Usually, the direct or indirect relevance of the political will for the legal order tends to be connected respectively to a normal mode (ie through the established legal apparatus) or to an extraordinary mode (ie with the participation of public opinion) of posing and settling problems in a community:[24]

> [Legal actors] are of vital importance in producing in contemporary Western societies the ideological effects of law ... They carry before state agencies (for example through litigation, demands for legal reform, and technical and consultancy work for public administrative agencies of all kinds) contradictions thrown up by confrontations between legal doctrine and particular social circumstances ... Hence they tend to promote through highly developed techniques of legal argument and doctrinal reasoning the idea of law as a rational integrated system of knowledge.[25]

Therefore, the function played by the 'interpreters of the political will' or, in other words, by the actors having the job of transforming the values expressed in the political arena into a specific language, becomes crucial for the entire law-making process. Even in conflicts with the values expressed by the political arena, it is usually the final product of the work of such interpreters (statute or judicial decisions) that, in the end, becomes the law in force that actually binds and shapes the behaviour of the members of the community. An example of the increasing legalisation of the policy process and results, is the fact that in most contemporary legal orders, politicians sitting in the legislature have staff or experts specifically educated in law. The main function of these persons is to draft in legal language (ie making use of legal categories and concepts) the ideas and proposals (ie the values) promoted by the political actors.[26]

---

[23] See Bourdieu, 'The Force of Law' (n 17 above) 834–9. See also R Summers, 'How Law is Formal and Why it Matters' (1997) 82 *Cornell Law Review* 1204.

[24] See Habermas, *Between Facts and Norms* (n 8 above) 352–9. As an example of the indirect relevance for the law of the political will, see A Addis, 'Hell Man, They Did Invent Us: the Mass Media, Law, and African Americans' (1993) 41 *Buffalo Law Review* 629.

[25] R Cotterrell, *The Sociology of Law: an Introduction* (2nd edn, London, Butterworths, 1992) 203–4. See also Luhmann *Law as a Social System* (n 16 above) 79–88. See eg, RP Malloy, 'Framing the Market: Representations of Meaning and Value in Law, Markets, and Culture' (2003) 51 *Buffalo Law Review* 83.

[26] See eg, N Lund, 'Rational Choice at the Office of Legal Counsel' (1993) 15 *Cardozo Law Review* 452. See also J Stone, *Social Dimensions of Law and Justice* (London, Stevens &

To counter-balance the shifting of the policy moment towards the legal arena, direct legal relevance has been given to legislative preparatory work in certain Western legal systems, making them one of the sources for the interpretation of law.[27] If legislative preparatory works are a source for the interpretation of law (and therefore for its law-making version), then the legal arena is forced to take into consideration that which the political actors 'actually meant', acting as political subjects (eg representing certain values inside the legislative committee), while adopting a certain legal concept.

However, one should not over-estimate this attempt to prevent the shifting of the policy process towards the legal arena. First, legal actors usually rank legislative preparatory works as a secondary source, mostly for their very nebulous and conflicting form typical of the political discourse (or at least perceived as such by the formal legal perspective embraced by the participants to the legal discourse). For example, in the famous decision *Pepper v Hart* (allowing the use of preparatory work in the English legal system), the Law Lords made it perfectly clear that the legal language of the statute under consideration is the primary source for tracing back the actual meaning of the political actors.[28]

Secondly, the decisive power, in the end, tends always to remain in the hands of the legal actors. Other legal actors (eg justices in the national highest court) are those who usually have the jurisdiction to evaluate whether a certain implementation by regulation or judicial decision actually pursues, or is in conflict with, the political meaning of the law. Left to the legal actors is the legal, and therefore binding, power to ascertain the legislative intent and whether the regulation or the decision reflects the original value fixed by the political actors in the preliminary works.[29]

To sum up, two major factors contribute to the legalisation of policy. First, the diffusion of the rule of law (or *Rechtsstaat*) obliges the political arena to transform its values into, and according to, the categories and

---

Sons, 1966) 56–62; Ross, *On Law and Justice* (n 9 above) 35; Kennedy, *A Critique of Adjudication (fin de siècle)* (n 1 above) 219; and M Van Hoecke, *Law as Communication* (Oxford, Hart Publishing, 2002) 133.

[27] See eg, for England, the decision by the House of Lord in *Pepper v Hart* [1993] 1 All ER 64. As for the United States, the situation is less clear. See R Summers, 'Interpreting Statutes:Should Courts Consider Materials of Legislative History?' in Summers, *Essays in Legal Theory* (n 21 above) 252–3, 263–4. See also MDA Freeman, *Lloyd's Introduction to Jurisprudence* (7th edn, London, Sweet & Maxwell, 2001) 1411–19.

[28] See *Pepper v Hart* (n 27 above) 50. See also M Healy, 'Legislative Intent and Statutory Interpretation in England and the United States: an Assessment of the Impact of "Pepper v. Hart"' (1999) 35 *Stanford Journal of International Law* 247; and Summers, 'Interpreting Statutes' (n 27 above) 256–62.

[29] See D Jabbari, 'Critical Theory in Administrative Law' (1994) 14 *Oxford Journal of Legal Studies* 201. For a diametric view of the effect of *Pepper v Hart*, see S Styles, 'The Rule of Parliament: Statutory Interpretation after Pepper v. Hart' (1994) 14 *Oxford Journal of Legal Studies* 153.

concepts provided by the legal order. Secondly, this transformation, which requires professional skills and language, usually occurs 'under the guardianship' of the legal actors.[30] For the working of such concurring (and often interrelated) factors, the processes and the results constituting the policy of law have not only to be removed from the monopoly of the political arena, but they also have to be at least partially incorporated into the activities occurring inside the legal arena.

IV. A TRADITIONAL LAW-MAKING MODEL

The model relating politics and law as represented in Figure 4.1 can now be further developed. The process of the creation and implementation of values into legal norms can be placed in a model in which the 'legalised' policy process plays a central role, appearing as in Figure 4.2. This figure is a preliminary and rudimentary model of law-making as occurring in Western-based legal systems and cultures. According to this view, the law-making process starts in the political arena, that is in the arena where the representatives of the community crystallise the people's will in a series of values to be implemented though legislative and judicial measures.[31]

A. Formation of the Legal Political Inputs and Policy of Law Process

In imaging a very basic process of implementation of certain values inside a community by using the law, one should begin at square one, ie the political arena. From a normative perspective, or from the Hartian internal aspects of a legal system, the political arena can be defined as the *ideal* place where certain actors or groups of actors decide that value f has to be implemented into a community by law (in Figure 4.2, legal political inputs). An example of a very basic process of implementation of values inside a community as described by Figure 4.2 is then the case in which value f represents equality between men and women in employment hiring procedures, a value that certain political parties and non-governmental organisations (NGOs) have decided to strengthen through the legal system in the national community.

---

[30] This expression is borrowed from Cotterrell, *The Sociology of Law* (n 25 above) 179.
[31] See eg, FC von Savigny, *Vom Beruf unserer Zeit für Gesetzgebung und Rechtswissenschaft* (Heidelberg, Mohr und Zimmer, 1814) 16–26; or R Bork, *The Tempting of America: the Political Seduction of the Law* (New York, Touchtone/Simon and Schuster, 1990) 4–5. The model represented in Figure 4.2 is an adaptation in this work of the classical model designed originally by D Easton, 'An Approach to the Analysis of the Political System' (1957) 9 *World Politics* 384 and developed by R Dahl, *Modern Political Analysis* (5th edn, Englewood Cliffs, Prentice Hall International, 1984) 23. But see R Summers, 'Law as a Type of "Machine" Technology' in Summers, *Essays in Legal Theory* (n 21 above) 46–7.

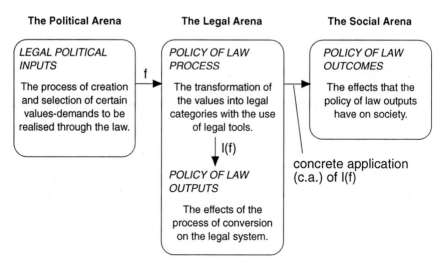

Figure 4.2: Position of the policy of law

The political arena is defined as an 'ideal' place in order to stress the fact that in reality, the political moments, from which the transformational process of values into law begins, actually tend to be both subjectively and chronologically fragmented. It is often very difficult to individuate the subjects which have decided whether and which values have to be implemented into a national community through the law. For example, members of a legislature proposing a certain draft in reality tend usually to act as a mere driving belt for decisions actually taken inside their political parties.[32]

Similarly, and partially as a consequence of the subjective fragmentation, it is sometimes also difficult to focalise a political decision, which gives birth to a policy of law process, at one or several distinct chronological points. Working against this chronological focalisation of legal political decisions, for example, can be the political interactions between local and federal powers. A decision taken by a federal government in favour of the implementation of a certain value can be considerably delayed in its

---

[32] See Habermas, *Between Facts and Norms* (n 8 above) 455; A Marmor, *Interpretation and Legal Theory* (Oxford, Clarendon Press, 1992) 159–65; L Fuller, *The Anatomy of Law* (New York, Praeger, 1968) 89–93; Olivecrona, *Law as Fact* (n 20 above) 73–7; and J Waldron, *The Dignity of Legislation* (Cambridge, Cambridge University Press, 1999) 25–8. See also F Easterbrook, 'Statute's Domain' (1983) 50 *University of Chicago Law Review* 547.

transmission to the community' by the local authorities. The latter can purposefully delay the nomination of their representatives in the lower implementing organs as prescribed by the federal decision. It is then difficult to establish when a certain decision of legal politics has been made, it being fragmented into several moments on a time-line, eg when the federal government decides or when the local government (at the end) accepts such a decision in favour of certain values.[33]

A depiction reproducing the reality of the political arena should then show several (almost infinite) series of political arenas distributed along a tortuous chronological line.[34] Despite this actual fragmentation of the political arena, this work focuses on the policy process and the law and therefore, for the sake of space and clarity, it presupposes that such different political moments happen inside one single ideal arena, the political arena.

In order to be carried via the law into a community, the values expressed by the political arena need to go through a more or less radical process of transformation into legal categories and concepts. 'Radicalism' is the degree of change into the legal language the value expressed inside the political arena, ie in a political language, has to go through in order to be accepted into the legal order. Such a degree depends, among other things, on the national legal order under consideration, on the branch of law and also on the dominant legal culture among the different legal actors.[35] In any case, as pointed out by Teubner:

> [j]ust as a domestic court does not apply foreign law authentically in the international law of conflicts, legal discourse does not all of a sudden act in an authentic manner morally, ethically, scientifically, economically or politically when it uses non-legal arguments. In both situations, foreign concepts are radically reconstructed.[36]

---

[33] See eg, W Jenkins, *Policy Analysis: a Political and Organizational Perspective* (London, Martin Robertson, 1978) 87–8. See also S Vago, *Law and Society* (6th edn, Upper Saddle River, Prentice Hall, 2000) 178–9.

[34] See eg, Jenkins, *Policy Analysis* (n 33 above) 22, figure 3; or J Anderson, *Public Policy-Making* (3rd edn, New York, Holt, Rinehart and Winston, 1984) 38–42. On the legal theoretical front, one of the most vital contributions coming from the CLS movement is pointing out this very complexity of the legal political moments. See J Standen, 'Critical Legal Studies as an Anti-positivist Phenomenon' (1986) 72 *Virginia Law Review* 996.

[35] See Summers, 'Law as a Type of "Machine" Technology' (n 31 above) 50. See also Pound, *The Ideal Element in Law* (n 4 above) 69; and Luhmann, *Law as a Social System* (n 16 above) 366–7. See eg, the idea of an (almost) almighty legislative power in Tuori, *Critical Legal Positivism* (n 4 above) 162. Compare to the restriction to state legislative power in *Griswold v Connecticut*, 381 U.S. 484–86 (1965).

[36] G Teubner, 'Altera Pars Audiatur: Law in the Collision of Discourses' in R Rawlings (ed), *Law, Society and Economy: Centenary Essays for the London School of Economics and Political Science 1895–1995* (Oxford, Clarendon Press, 1996) 165. See also, more in general as to the diffidence of legal actors towards the political discourse, J Waldron, 'Legislation, Authority, and Voting' (1996) 84 *Georgetown Law Journal* 2185

The necessity of this step of reconstruction is particularly evident in contemporary general Western culture, in which the ideology of legality dominates and heavily affects the law-making process: '[T]he modern state's specific form of legitimacy is its appeal [to the value] that its commands be recognized as binding because *legal,* that is because issued in conformity with properly enacted, general rules.'[37] In legal theory, for example, legality as a constitutive element for the law-making process is shared by both natural law scholars and legal positivists.[38]

The process of transformation is usually carried through by specific actors devoted to such transformations (eg the legal staff of the members of a committee of a legislature). These actors in general consist of persons formally educated as to legal matters, an education that is based on the same way of thinking (legal rationality) and which (to a greater or lesser extent) gives birth to a specific legal arena. This can be defined as the ideal place in which the political goal of having values implemented into the community (with value-based reasoning) is taken over by the goal of transforming (with a legal rationality-based reasoning) the values into legal categories and concepts, inserting them into the existing legal order (policy of law process).[39]

Hypothetically, if the political actors (eg the director of an NGO or member of a legislature) would themselves do the work of transforming their values into a draft for a Bill, they still would be forced to make use of the legal language and, moreover, to take into consideration the structure of the legal system (at least at a constitutional level) in which their proposal for a statute is going to be inserted. For example, in South Africa during the apartheid regime, the white ruling minority was forced to adapt their arsenal of racist values to legal forms.[40]

---

[37] G Poggi, *The Development of Modern State: a Sociological Introduction* (Stanford, Stanford University Press, 1989) 132. See also P Nonet and P Selznick, *Law and Society in Transition: toward Responsive Law* (New York, Harper and Row, 1978) 51–2; JH Skolnick, *Justice Without Trial: Law Enforcement in Democratic Society* (3rd edn, New York, Macmillan College Publishing Company, 1994) 5–9, 16–21; Luhmann, *Law as a Social System* (n 16 above) 368–71; and Hart, *The Concept of Law* (n 16 above) 97–100.

[38] See eg, L Fuller, *The Morality of Law. Revised Edition* (London, Yale University Press, 1969) 96–7; and J Gardner, 'Legal Positivism: 5 ½ Myths' (2001) 46 *American Journal of Jurisprudence* 225. But see generally C Schmitt, *Legalität und Legitimität* (Berlin, Duncker & Humblot, 1932). Cf D Dyzenhaus, 'Introduction: Why Carl Schmitt?' in D Dyzenhaus (ed), *Law as Politics: Carl Schmitt's Critique of Liberalism* (Durham, Duke University Press, 1998) 11–12.

[39] See Tuori, *Critical Legal Positivism* (n 4 above) 161. See also A Abbot, *The System of Professions: an Essay on the Division of Expert Labor* (Chicago, University of Chicago Press, 1988) 52–7; and Cotterrell, *Law's Community* (n 19 above) 108–10.

[40] See eg, O Kirchheimer, *Political Justice: the Use of Legal Procedure for Political Ends* (Princeton, Princeton University Press, 1961) 124. See also Habermas, *Between Facts and Norms* (n 8 above) 241, 385–6.

Following the traditional (and probably never fully applied) idea of separation of powers, the actors operating inside the legal arena work as mere transformational belts of values sent into them by distinct political actors. The legal actors then normally succeed in locating (or inventing) such a legal category or concept, l, they assume to be the best translation into law (l(f) in Figure 4.2) of the original value f expressed by the political arena. In the previous example, political parties or NGOs give the mandate of transforming their equality value into legal proposals to other individuals, groups of individuals or institutions (eg their legal staff or an external legal think-tank). The latter, after searching among the available legal tools (ie legal categories and concepts), drafts a new statute realising in legal language the value/ideal of equality between men and women. The legal tool used by the legal actors for realising equality between the sexes in the job market can be a legally compulsory system of quotas (l), already pre-existing for implementing the value of helping physically challenged people in getting jobs (e) with the statute l(e).[41]

B. Policy of Law Outputs and Outcomes

The second step of the process occurring inside the legal arena consists of the legally relevant acceptance (usually) by other legal actors (eg by a vote of the legislature or by a decree of the competent Ministry) of the proposed legal category. As a consequence, the new legal category l(f) is enacted in the form of making it legally binding for the other legal actors and for the community, usually by incorporating l(f) in one unique or several different legally relevant documents (eg one or more statutes or several administrative regulations). L(f) means that the value f has been transformed (and somehow incorporated) into the legal category l. The latter represents the necessary legal corridor through which the value f has to pass in order to be implanted into the legal system or, in other words, to become relevant to the community as a legally binding statement.

This implanting of f into the legal system will normally have a (more or less extensive and deep) impact on this system, ie l(f) will to a various degree change the existing legal system (policy of law outputs), for example, the draft written by the lawyers of the political parties and NGOs goes unchanged through the entire parliamentary procedures and becomes a statute modifying both the legal duties of the employers and the legal rights to which women applying for jobs are entitled.

---

[41] As to the possible recycling of one legal category in order to implement a value different from the original one, *see* eg, US Supreme Court's decision, *Griswold v Connecticut* (n 35 above) 482–4, which transfers the legal concept of 'inviolable right' from the value of allowing political assemblies to the one of allowing birth control.

As the last stage of this extremely simplified law-making process, the binding legal category l(f) is then concretely applied (in Figure 4.2 c.a.[l(f)]) into the social arena of the national community.[42] This means, using an idea particularly developed by the legal realist movement, that the valid law becomes law in force (or in action) and actually implements into the social arena the original values (policy of law outcomes).[43] This concrete application of the legal category l(f) into the community can occur either with the direct participation of the legal actors or through a more indirect role. For example, the concrete application of a compulsory quota system in hiring women can happen through binding judicial decisions as by Dworkin's Judge, Hercules. It can also be that citizens voluntarily adhere to the behaviours prescribed in category l(f) in order to avoid possible sanctions from administrative or judicial bodies, as with Holmes' bad man.[44] In the previous example, employers are then forced to respect male-female quotas in their recruiting procedures and therefore actually employ more women than they otherwise would.

Two further specifications of the model of a simple law-making as presented in Figure 4.2 are required. First, it is important to note the distinction between *outputs* and *outcomes* made in the model presented here concerning the results coming out of the processes taking place in the policy of law moment. This separation of outputs from outcomes is actually an adaptation in the law-making process of the results reached by a long series of studies developed in political science.[45]

Relocated into the context of the process of policy of law, outputs are the impacts of the policy processes inside the legal arena in which the process itself has taken place (eg changes of the legal system concerning hiring procedures). The outcomes of the policy process, in contrast, mark the effects (intended or unintended) such impacts have on the surrounding

---

[42] See Cotterrell, *The Sociology of Law* (n 25 above) 56–8. The social arena in this work has a very broad and residual meaning, encompassing all those communities of actors, rationalities and processes, which somehow participate in the law-making and can be defined neither as political nor as legal (eg economic actors, religious organisations or ethnic communities). See also B Tamanaha, *A General Jurisprudence of Law and Society* (Oxford, Oxford University Press, 2001) 206–8; and Cotterrell, *Law's Community* (n 19 above) 325–32.

[43] See eg, Olivecrona, *Law as Fact* (n 20 above) 222–3. Compare Kennedy, *A Critique of Adjudication (fin de siècle)* (n 1 above) 63–4. Some contemporary legal theories (eg legal realists) consider this phase of social or economic effects of the law as *conditio sine qua non* for having a transformational moment. See eg, J Frank, *Law and the Modern Mind* (London, Stevens & Sons, 1949) 46–7; and Ross, *On Law and Justice* (n 9 above) 81. But see HLA Hart, 'Self-referring Laws' in HLA Hart, *Essays in Jurisprudence and Philosophy* (Oxford, Clarendon Press, 1983) 175–8

[44] See OW Holmes, 'The Path of the Law' (1897) 10 *Harvard Law Review* 459; and R Dworkin, *Taking Rights Seriously* (Cambridge, Harvard University Press, 1978) 105–10.

[45] See eg, J Thompson, 'Outputs and Outcomes of State Workmen's Compensation Laws' (1981) 43 *Journal of Politics* 1132. See also F Castles, *Comparative Public Policy: Patterns of Post-war Transformation* (Northampton, Edward Elgar, 1998) 248–92.

environment (eg changes in the concrete behaviours of the employers). For example, the distinction between policy of law outputs and policy of law outcomes is important in order to understand the fact that sometimes new legislation (different policy of law outputs) can have more or less the same practical effects on a community (same policy of law outcome) as those of the previous legislation.[46]

In legal theoretical terms, the distinction between policy of law outputs and policy of law outcomes can be important in order to point out the difference between a *valid* new law and an *in-force* new law. For example, a legislature promulgates a statutory provision of penal law criminalising abortion practices, proactively and retroactively. Before the decision is applied by any court or enforcement agency to a concrete case, the legislature then decides to change its construction because of strong criticism from the legal community. During this short period, the legal category of criminalising abortion has been valid, ie it has produced certain legal outputs. The criminalisation has provisionally changed the structure of criminal law (eg disregarding the legal principle of *nullum crimen sine lege*). On the other hand, the new legal category of punishing abortions retroactively has never been in force since it has not and never will produce any concrete results (outcomes) as to the behaviours of the members of the national community.[47]

The second specification deals with the fact that in the model represented in Figure 4.2, an additional arrow should be drawn showing how the policy of law outcomes of a law-making process influence the formation of legal political inputs.[48] It is a line representing, for example, the pressure employers put on political parties in order to change a newly enacted statute imposing a compulsory quota system.

The relationships between the policy of law outcomes and the political inputs naturally can have some effects on the legal arena since they deal with 'the central question of who can place issues on the [political] agenda'.[49] For example, the spreading among a population of a high

[46] See eg, Luhmann, *Law as a Social System* (n 16 above) 166. Though confined to the decision-making process, see the distinction between 'consequences' and 'juridical consequences' as developed by N MacCormick, 'On Legal Decisions and their Consequences: from Dewey to Dworkin' (1983) 58 *New York University Law Review* 247. This different kind of effects can be considered a consequence of the more general distinction between the normative and social functions of the law. See J Raz, 'On the Functions of Law' in AWB Simpson (ed), *Oxford Essays in Jurisprudence (Second Series)* (Oxford, Clarendon Press, 1973) 280. But see P Gabel, 'Reification in Legal Reasoning' (1980) 3 *Research in Law and Sociology* 25.

[47] See MacCormick, *Legal Reasoning and Legal Theory* (n 2 above) 54–5. See also N MacCormick, 'Institutional Normative Order: a Conception of Law' (1997) 82 *Cornell Law Review* 1063.

[48] See Habermas, *Between Facts and Norms* (n 8 above) 373–4; and M Perry, *Morality, Politics, and Law* (Oxford, Oxford University Press, 1988) 87.

[49] Habermas, *Between Facts and Norms* (n 8 above) 379.

degree of legitimacy (policy of law outcomes) of a supreme court newly established by constitutional law could increase that which Lundstedt would call 'the obedience to the law' among the political actors, ie their consideration for the legal actors' perspective on certain legal political issues.[50]

This connection between policy of law outcomes and legal political inputs, however, is not directly relevant for the model presented here. The latter has a normative perspective, and the line from the social to the political arenas belongs more to the area of the formation of the political and social ideas about the law, not of the formation of the lawyers' internal perspective on the legal phenomenon. In other words, these effects, although sometimes decisive for one or the other direction of the law-making, are only indirectly relevant from a legal perspective in order to explain the law-making process, ie the construction of legal categories by the legal actors.[51]

To conclude, the model represented in Figure 4.2 is a very simple illustration of a general law-making process in a national legal order of a Western country. In particular, it aims at evidencing, inside that process, a preliminary basic distinction between the political and the policy aspects of the law-making process. From a legal perspective, the politics of law designates both the processes of creation and the selection of certain values-demands (ie the processes occurring inside the political arena producing f) and the values themselves (f) that have to be introduced into a community by means of the law (*legal political inputs*). On the other side, the policy of law identifies the processes of transforming those values into legal categories, that is the processes occurring inside the legal arena and ending in the formation of l(f) (*policy of law process*). Moreover, the policy of law covers the effects of such processes on the legal system or, in other words, the insertion of l(f) into the existing legal system in terms of legal categories or concepts (*policy of law outputs*).

V. FRAMEWORKS AND ADJUSTMENTS OF THE POLICY OF LAW

In past decades, a trend has arisen in political science that refuses the explanatory linear model of policy as presented by Easton and Dahl and

---

[50] See V Lundstedt, *Legal Thinking Revised: My Views on Law* (Stockholm, Almqvist & Wiksell, 1956) 175. See also Waldron, 'Legislation, Authority, and Voting' (n 36 above) 2196–7, discussing 'the sense of respect for law.' See eg, the social role played, after the fall of the Communist regime, by the new Hungarian Constitutional Court in E Klingsberg, 'Judicial Review and Hungary's Transition from Communism to Democracy: the Constitutional Court, the Continuity of Law, and the Redefinition of Property Rights' (1992) 1992 *Brigham Young University Law Review* 64, 133–6.

[51] See Hart, *The Concept of Law* (n 16 above) 114–20.

here represented (with due modification) in Figure 4.2. This trend proposes instead a more articulated model for explaining the role and the position policy actually occupies inside the political process.[52] In a similar way, several adjustments of the model sketched in Figure 4.2 are required in order to more accurately depict the role and position of the policy of law procedures and results with that happening in reality. In the end, a model more faithful to the actual reality of the policy of law appears as Figure 4.3.

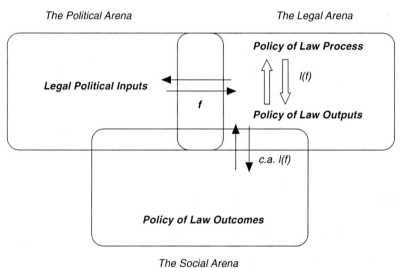

Figure 4.3: Intersections of the policy of law

A. Mutual Character of the Relations between the Arenas

The first fine-tuning of the model represented in Figure 4.2 deals with the nature of the relations between the three arenas, ie the ideal places where the value formation (the political arena), their transformation into law (the legal arena), and law implementation in society (the social arena) occur. In reality, the law-making process only rarely proceeds quietly from the proposal of a political party, for example, to the legislative works within the legislature and from that to the concrete application into a certain community of the value incorporated in the statute. As stressed by Raz:

---

[52] See Jenkins, *Policy Analysis* (n 33 above) 18 figure 2, 22 figure 3.

[a]rguably not all the intentions of legal institutions are transformed into law, and not all those which do affect the law have exactly their intended effects. Arguably the law is not exhausted by the scope of the intentions of law-making and law-applying institutions.[53]

It can actually happen that the legal political inputs do not find their way into the legal system in the form of legal outputs. This can happen because the legal actors, despite the pressures coming both from the political and social actors, do not succeed in finding or inventing a legal category or concept transforming the value into law. These hindrances to the law-making process have been particularly pointed out by the 'outsider jurisprudence' theories: feminist legal theory and critical race theory. For example, the legal actors can claim the impossibility of transforming the value of allowing abortion into a legal category; this because all the legal spaces are closed by a constitutional norm acknowledging 'the right to life of the unborn' and the duty of the state apparatus 'to defend and vindicate that right' (as in Article 40 of the Constitution of Ireland).[54]

Another possibility is that the legal category l actually transforms so much of the value f to make l(f) as having an effect on the legal system opposite to that originally intended when the political arena produced value f. Using a previous example, this 'distortion' can happen when the value of equality between men and women in employment is transformed, *per absurdum*, into a legal category that confers upon employers the legal right to hire more women. In this manner, the impact on the legal system would be to expand, instead of to limit, the legal tools in the hands of the employers during hiring procedures.

The relations among the three arenas are then not of a linear or one-way character (the one-way directional arrows in Figure 4.2). They are more complex and tend to have a reciprocal nature (the two-way arrows f and c.a. l(f) in Figure 4.3). The insertion of the two-way arrows in the model represented in Figure 4.3 aims at representing the factual phenomenon of that which happens inside each arena tending to influence the work of the other two; that which was the effect of a certain cause according to the previous model (Figure 4.2), in reality can be reversed.

The choice of legal category l(f) has been shown as the effect in the legal arena of the choice of value f made in the political arena. However, the choice of implementing value f by means of the law can have resulted as a

---

[53] J Raz, 'On the Autonomy of Legal Reasoning' in Raz, *Ethics in the Public Domain* (n 21 above) 314. See also A Thurman, *The Symbols of Government* (New Haven, Yale University Press, 1935) 34.

[54] See eg, M McBrien, 'Ireland: Balancing Traditional Domestic Abortion Law with Modern Reality and International Influence' (2002) 26 *Suffolk Transnational Law Review* 211; and O'Connell, *Legal Theory in the Crucible of Constitutional Justice* (n 14 above) 154–61. See also B Bix, *Jurisprudence: Theory and Context* (3rd edn, London, Sweet & Maxwell, 2003) 222; and Tuori, *Critical Legal Positivism* (n 4 above) 136–8.

consequence of the presence in the legal arena of legal category l. In the law-making process, the processes of creation or selection of certain value-inputs f to be sent to the legal world (politics of law) do not then take place in a *vacuum*, but are influenced by the existence and/or availability (or not) of certain legal categories l to be used during the policy moments (two-way arrows f in Figure 4.3). Sometimes, as pointed out by one legal scholar, legal 'rules sharply discipline the territory over which [political] argument can occur'.[55]

In addition to that stated by Waldron, one can affirm then that not only the *circumstances of politics* 'are indispensable for our understanding of procedural decision-making rules', but also that the *circumstances of law* are often vital for grasping certain processes taking place in the political arena.[56] As pointed out by Ramsay, for example, '[a]ny attempt to understand the politics of commercial law should capture issues of conflict, power ... as well as exploring *the interplay of structure and agency in the construction and reproduction of the "rules of the game"*', ie the policy of commercial law.[57] (emphasis added)

A more historical example can be taken from Weber's analysis of the birth and growth in Western nations of the capitalistic economic system and the role played in it by the corporation. It was the presence in the Western legal systems of the legal concept of a corporation that created in the political arena (or facilitated the consolidation of) the economic value of encouraging financial investment in economic activities, a basic value for contemporary capitalist economic systems. In its turn, this economic value activated (as legal political inputs) a series of law-making processes leading to the formation of the contemporary, extremely articulated legal conceptual apparatus surrounding the legal concept of a corporation (eg the legal figure of corporate limited liability).[58]

In short, the legal world can somehow create or facilitate the creation of values that, successively, this very world has the duty to translate into legal categories and concepts:

---

[55] C Sunstein, *Legal Reasoning and Political Conflict* (Oxford, Oxford University Press, 1996) 191. See also Luhmann, *Law as a Social System* (n 16 above) 140; J Raz, 'The Inner Logic of the Law' in Raz, *Ethics in the Public Domain* (n 21 above) 225–8; and Bell, *Policy Arguments in Judicial Decisions* (n 2 above) 60–7.

[56] Waldron, 'Legislation, Authority, and Voting' (n 36 above) 2198. See also J Waldron, 'Legal and Political Philosophy' in J Coleman and S Shapiro (eds), *The Oxford Handbook of Jurisprudence and Philosophy of Law* (Oxford, Oxford University Press, 2002) 352–3; and K Tuori, 'Law, Power and Critique' in K Tuori *et al* (eds), *Law and Power: Critical and Socio-Legal Essays* (Liverpool, Deborah Charles Publications, 1997) 16.

[57] I Ramsay, 'The Politics of Commercial Law' (2001) 2001 *Wisconsin Law Review* 573.

[58] See Weber, *Economy and Society* (n 3 above) 655, 687. See also Luhmann, *Law as a Social System* (n 16 above) 172; and A Harding, *Medieval Law and the Foundations of the State* (Oxford, Oxford University Press, 2001) ch 9.

Thus although legal discourse is in one sense driven by the underlying opposition of ideologized interests, it may also react back on the ideologies and the interest and transform them. The modern legal discourse of civil rights is as much a cause as an effect of civil rights thinking within liberal ideology at large.[59]

For example, actors operating inside the politics of law moment know that the legal order has already successfully (at least from a legal perspective) solved certain problems relating to the issue of 'equality in access to employment' in favour of physically challenged persons. The existence and availability of a well-established legal concept such as a compulsory quota-system can certainly create (or at least facilitate the expression of) the political actors' demands (inputs) of an implementation by law of the value of equality between men and women in employment.

A similar process of mutual influence can take place in the relationship between the policy of law outcomes and the policy of law process as well as the policy of law outputs (two-way arrows c.a. l(f) in Figure 4.3). While converting values (policy of law process), the actors operating inside the legal world can, and usually do, take into consideration the possible consequences on the community (policy of law outcomes) of their choice of a certain legal category instead of another (policy of law outputs).[60] Furthermore, certain policy of law outcomes of previous policies of law can encourage the creation or the change of legal categories available for the policy of law process among the legal actors.

For example, in the policy process, law-makers can prefer to incorporate a legal category of a compulsory quota system in a statute, instead of employing a taxation legal tool in the form of tax deductions available to employers hiring women. This choice can be made because the legal actors have witnessed a success with a previous similar compulsory quota system in fighting discrimination against physically challenged persons. In other words, the actors in the legal arena, looking at the effects on the community of a certain legal category (c.a. l(e)) previously chosen by them

---

[59]   Kennedy, *A Critique of Adjudication (fin de siècle)* (n 1 above) 152. See also Cotterrell, *Law's Community* (n 19 above) 250–2. But see M Klarman, *From Jim Crow to Civil Rights: the Supreme Court and the Struggle for Racial Equality* (Oxford, Oxford University Press, 2004) 448–50.

[60]   See Ross, *On Law and Justice* (n 9 above) 372–3; and C Varga, 'On the Socially Determined Nature of Legal Reasoning' in C Varga, *Law and Philosophy: Selected Papers in Legal Theory* (Budapest, Faculty of Law of Lórand Eötvös University, 1994) 326–7. In socio-legal terminology, the legal actors not only consider the *purpose* of the law (to change the legal system) but also its possible *function* (its impact on society). See Cotterrell, *The Sociology of Law* (n 25 above) 72.

(in the policy process leading to l(e)), can decide to modify the existing legal system by introducing a similar new legal category (l(f)) through a policy of law process.[61]

To sum up, the phenomenon of mutual influences among the different arenas is intended to point out how the policy of law outputs can be heavily influenced by their social impact and can themselves heavily influence the policy of law processes. In their turn, the existence of certain legal concepts can give birth to new values inside the political arena. This is represented in Figure 4.3 by the counter-clockwise direction of the process from the policy of law outputs via l(f) and f to the legal political inputs.

A final clarification of the model presented in Figure 4.3 has to be made. As already stated for Figure 4.2, in order to be more close to reality, two-way arrows should also be used even with Figure 4.3 between the politics of law and the policy of law outcomes, representing their mutual influences in the law-making process. They shows how the political actors are not only a representation of certain social demands but also how the presence of a certain political actor with a strong ideology (eg moral danger of using any kind of drugs) stimulates a social activism with respect to certain legal issues (eg in favour of categorising as a criminal felony the use of marijuana).[62]

This mutual relationship between the political and the social arenas can in policy of law sometimes be a decisive factor in determining the final legal outputs. On one side, the possible or actual effects on the community by the policy of law (policy of law outcomes) can create, eliminate or modify the demand, inside the political arena, of implementing certain values by law.[63] For example, it can be the case that a previous policy of implementing by law the hiring of physically challenged persons did not have any effects on the community. It is then possible that the political arena decides to implement the value of equal opportunity between men and women with tools other than legal ones, eg economic measures. On the other hand, the political arena can, in various non-legal ways, increase or decrease the effects of a certain policy of law into society; the political

---

[61] See eg, L Friedman and J Ladinsky, 'Social Change and the Law of Industrial Accidents' (1967) 67 *Columbia Law Review* 55. Even if focused mostly on the judicial law-making, see also EH Levi, 'An Introduction to Legal Reasoning' (1948) 15 *University of Chicago Law Review* 501.

[62] See eg, H Becker, *Outsiders: Studies in the Sociology of Deviance* (New York, Free Press, 1963) 121–46. See also I Jenkins, *Social Order and the Limits of Law: a Theoretical Essay* (Princeton, Princeton University Press, 1980) 341; and Vago, *Law and Society* (n 33 above) 199 (as to the political target of the influence of interest groups in the law-making processes).

[63] See, as a concrete example, D Dixon, *From Prohibition to Regulation: Bookmaking, Anti-Gambling, and the Law* (Oxford, Oxford University Press, 1991) 202–3, 215–18.

actors can affect legal outputs becoming legal outcomes.[64] For example, political actors can improve the possibility of a successful application of a quota-system by making significant use of political propaganda, the mass media and advertising. Such influences and in general all the intersections and influences within and between the political and social arenas can be important for explaining the policy of law process. However, these are considered outside the normative perspective of this work, belonging more to legal-political or legal-sociological investigations, as pointed out in chapter five.

B. Mutual Influences Internal to the Legal Arena

Moving to the second adjustment to the model presented in Figure 4.3, it is based on the consideration that the reciprocal influences described above occur not only among the arenas, but are also a feature of the relationships among the internal components of each arena. The main purpose of this chapter is to open and frame an explanatory field equipped with a normative nature: the policy of law. Therefore, attention is focused here on the internal mutual influences occurring in the legal arena.

One can notice in the latest model that a mutual process of influence and determination exists inside the legal arena between the conversion process and the legal outputs (l(f) in Figure 4.3). This means not only, as already described in Figure 4.2, that the policy of law process produces, with its results in the form of legal categories and concepts, certain changes in the legal system. It can also be the reverse; the legal system is not simply a passive target of the policy process but also heavily influences the very policy of law process. Legal actors can be stimulated by the very structure of the legal system (in particular in its constitutional forms) into transforming a certain political value into one legal category instead of another.[65] It is part of that which Dworkin defines as 'the chain of law', where:

> a group of novelists writes a novel *seriatim*: each novelist in the chain interprets the chapters he has been given in order to write a new chapter, which is then added to what the next novelist receives, and so on.[66]

An ideal-typical legal arena with a dominant legal positivistic culture, in particular, is more open to the likelihood that the considerations of the

---

[64] See W Evan, *Social Structure and Law: Theoretical and Empirical Perspectives* (London, Sage Publications, 1990) 109–20.

[65] See eg, Fuller, *The Morality of Law* (n 38 above) 105; and Pound, *The Ideal Element in Law* (n 4 above) 194–5. See also Summers, 'Law as a Type of "Machine" Technology' (n 31 above) 48–9 and B Auerbach, 'The Politics of Due Process: Incorporation and the Bill of Rights' in D Schultz (ed), *Law and Politics: Unanswered Questions* (Vienna, Peter Lang , 1994) 59–68.

[66] Dworkin, *Law's Empire* (n 18 above) 229.

possible outputs into the legal system deeply influence the policy process. This is mainly due to the fact that most of the legal actors are educated in the idea that their main task is to maintain the internal (logical) coherence and consistency of the legal system. In practice, they start looking at the possible impacts of their law-making decisions on the legal system. From that, the legal positivistic actors go back and choose in the policy of law process the solutions (policy of law outputs) that least jeopardise such ideals of internal coherence and consistency of the legal system.[67]

For example, a law-making authority can deny recognition of a claim as to a deceased's estate in the case of a same sex couple. It can base this refusal on the fact that recognition can jeopardise the coherence of the legal system, on one side, with respect to family legislation that denies marriage to persons of the same sex and, on the other side, the inheritance law that statutorily allocates a portion of an estate to a surviving spouse. Instead, the law-making authority preserves the coherence of the legal system by giving recognition to the interests of the living partner under the (hypothetical) business law category of 'de facto economic partnership'. The internal mutual influences between the policy of law process and the policy of law outputs is then about the influences the actual legal system can operate on the choice of legal category the value already chosen by the political arena has to assume in order to enter into the law.[68]

VI. LEGAL WITHINPUTS

The mutual nature of the relations between and inside the three arenas (political, legal and social) is not the only element needed in order to make the model of transformation of values into law more similar to that which happens in reality. A second phenomenon contributes to the formation of the more articulated model represented in Figure 4.3, that which in political science has been generally defined as 'withinputs'. This term is generally used to characterise the fact that the inputs to the political system can sometimes come from other actors within the system itself. A typical example of a withinput in political science is symbolic politics. This is a political decision created ad hoc by the political actors, ie without any initiative or pressure coming from the surrounding environment. This

---

[67] See Habermas, *Between Facts and Norms* (n 8 above) 202. See also J Raz, 'Legal Rights' in Raz, *Ethics in the Public Domain* (n 21 above) 249. But see G Radbruch, 'Anglo-American Jurisprudence through Continental Eyes' (1936) 52 *LQR* 530.

[68] See F Schauer, 'Rules and the Rule of Law' (1991) 14 *Harvard Journal of Law and Public Policy* 686, who grounds this feature of the law-making process on the principle of separation of powers. See also Cotterrell, *The Sociology of Law* (n 25 above) 132.

political decision is adopted, for example, in order to increase the general political support among the population.[69]

Transferring this concept to the model of the law-making process, one can easily notice that the withinputs can take place at every stage of the process of transformation described by the model depicted in Figure 4.3. The social and political arenas do not necessarily have to wait for stimuli coming from the other arenas to activate their own processes of influencing politics and initiating the law-making process respectively.[70] Based on its normative point of view, this work however takes into consideration only the withinputs of the law-making process occurring inside the legal world or, in other words, the withinputs taking place in the space occupied by the processes and results of policy of law (*legal withinputs*).

The withinputs in the legal arena can be described as the phenomenon of when the legal actors themselves activate the policy process of conversion, generating their own demands-inputs.[71] The process of the transformation of values into law represented in Figure 4.3 does not necessarily have to start in the political arena (with f), but can originate directly inside the legal arena, where the policy of law is (with l(f)).

In their *strong form*, legal withinputs mean that legal actors do not always take for granted the values indicated by the political actors and formally transmitted to the legal world for transformation. In many cases, the legal actors operate as autonomous actors, in the sense that they themselves extrapolate from the political arena the values that they assume are best. This choice of values made directly by the legal actors is done because such values are considered as being already admitted in the existing legal system, either under an explicit legal form (eg as constitutional norms) or somehow underlying the national legal order (eg as legal principles or as part of the legal culture).[72]

---

[69] See eg, M Edelman, *Politics as Symbolic Action: Mass Arousal and Quiescence* (New York, Academic Press, 1971) 2. See also Easton, 'An Approach to the Analysis of the Political System' (n 31 above) 388–9; D Easton, *A Framework for Political Analysis* (Englewood Cliffs, Prentice Hall, 1965) 114; and D Easton, *A Systems Analysis of Political Life* (Chicago, University of Chicago Press, 1979) 389.

[70] Law-making in the USSR during the Stalinist regime is an extreme example of a process where the legal political decisions were activated by evaluations of a purely political nature, ie without any influence from the social or legal arenas. See C Varga, *Transition to Rule of Law: On the Democratic Transformation in Hungary* (Budapest, Faculty of Law of Lórand Eötvös University and Institute for Legal Studies of the Hungarian Academy of Sciences, 1995) 21–2.

[71] See Raz, 'The Inner Logic of the Law' (n 55 above) 228–34. See also Raz, 'On the Functions of Law' (n 46 above) 297–9.

[72] See Dworkin, *Taking Rights Seriously* (n 44 above) 32; N MacCormick, 'A Moralistic Case for A-Moralistic Law?' (1985) 20 *Valparaiso University Law Review* 31; and H Bredemeier, 'Law as an Integrative Mechanism' in W Evan (ed), *Law and Sociology* (New York, Free Press of Glencoe, 1962) 79–80. See also K Tuori, 'Legislation Between Politics and Law' in LJ Wintgens (ed), *Legisprudence: a New Theoretical Approach to Legislation*

For example, the recognition of a strong form of legal withinputs allows the identification of a contemporary phenomenon of Western legal orders: the judicialisation of politics. By this is meant the role the judiciary and ideology plays in doing politics, in building and/or choosing themselves the values to implement through the law: 'Policy processes can be described as judicialised to the extent that constitutional jurisprudence, the threat of future constitutional censure, and the pedagogical authority of past jurisprudence' decisively determine the political arena's work.[73]

In their *weak form*, legal withinputs originate in the fact that in many parts of contemporary Western legal orders, a considerable portion of legal production is depoliticised and, to some extent, desocialised. The innovation and use of legal categories and concepts are not in response to actual or potential political requests or to values expressed by the social arena (cultural, economic, etc). The law-making process sometimes is begun in order to respond to requests and criticisms of a formal character, coming from the very legal actors, eg the courts or scholars.[74]

The very structure of the legal system or the very composition of the legal arena can be such that the legal actors can proceed in shaping new legal categories and concepts in order to solve purely doctrinal problems; in this way, such categories and concepts initially are neither the legal version of political values (f) nor the effects of the pressure by the social arena on the legal actors (c.a. l(f)). A concrete historical example can be found in the already mentioned Weberian investigation of the origins of the legal concept of corporation. The latter started as a withinput of the legal arena, ie as a doctrinal evolution mainly directed not at fulfilling some economic or *stricto sensu* political value, but at maintaining coherence in the legal system. According to Weber, the very origin of the legal concept of the modern corporation has to be traced back to the specific liturgical character the Norman administration had in England and its conceptual development in English legal history.[75]

(Oxford, Hart Publishing, 2002) 102–3; and Habermas, 'Law as Medium and Law as Institution' (n 17 above) 215. But see J Raz, 'Legal Principles and the Limits of Law' (1972) 81 *Yale Law Journal* 848.

[73] A Stone Sweet, 'Constitutional Politics in France and Germany' in M Shapiro and A Stone Sweet, *On Law, Politics, and Judicialization* (Oxford, Oxford University Press, 2002) 187. See also M Tushnet, *Taking the Constitution Away from the Courts* (Princeton, Princeton University Press, 1999) chs 6–7; J Waldron, *Law and Disagreement* (Oxford, Oxford University Press, 1999) chs 10–13; R Hirschl, 'Resituating the Judicialization of Politics: Bush v. Gore as a Global Trend' (2002) XV *Canadian Journal of Law and Jurisprudence* 191; and P Gabel, 'What It Really Means to Say "Law is Politics": Political History and Legal Argument in Bush v. Gore' (2002) 67 *Brooklyn Law Review* 1149.

[74] See Nonet and Selznick, *Law and Society in Transition* (n 37 above) 20 and the fundamental role in the development of the law played by the 'institutional logic'.

[75] See Weber, *Economy and Society* (n 3 above) 720–5; and D Trubek, 'Max Weber on Law and the Rise of Capitalism' (1972) 1972 *Wisconsin Law Review* 751. See also Raz, 'The Inner Logic of the Law' (n 55 above) 223; and R Summers, 'The Conceptualization of Good

Despite the similar effect of locating inside the legal arena the source of the law-making process, the weak and the strong legal withinputs have been kept separate in this work. The strong form of withinputs points out the phenomenon that legal actors deliberately give birth to legal political inputs and transform them into legal categories and concepts. The phenomenon of weak legal withinputs, in contrast, focuses on the features of contemporary Western legal culture where legal actors on their own activate the law-making process in order to give birth to new legal categories and concepts. In the legal actors' intentions, these categories and concepts should make the actual legal order only work better in its implementing the politically established goals, eg the categories should simply fill the systemic gaps or repair the errors in the legal machinery.

The boundary between weak and strong withinputs, however, is sometimes difficult to determine. This intricacy is mainly due to the fact that in the legal actors' very idea of limiting themselves in making the legal order work 'better', there sometimes is a politically loaded value hidden. In particular, this is the value of supporting the values chosen by the actors in the political arena and framing them into valid-and-therefore-binding legislation.[76] An extreme and well-known example is the one of Germany during the Nazi regime, where many judges certainly held the value of collaboration with the political authority. Such judges often were educated in a legal positivistic attitude to the political power and dutifully transformed Nazi values into legal categories in order to make such values fit flawlessly into the existing German legal system.[77]

Moreover, there is in operation that which Friedman defines as the 'legalistic' aspect of the legal culture.[78] Even in the strong form of

Faith in American Contract Law' in Summers, *Essays in Legal Theory* (n 21 above) 300–1, for the role played by the restatements of the American Law Institute in the development of the legal concept of good faith in American contract law.

[76] See D Trubek, 'Complexity and Contradiction in the Legal Order: Balbus and the Challenge of Critical Social Thought about Law' (1977) 11 *Law and Society Review* 540; Kennedy, *A Critique of Adjudication (fin de siècle)* (n 1 above) 155–6; and Evan, *Social Structure and Law* (n 64 above) 226. See eg, R Bork, 'The Judge's Role in Law and Culture' (2003) 1 *Ave Maria Law Review* 27; or the traditional model of administrative law as designed by R Stewart, 'The Reformation of American Administrative Law' (1975) 88 *Harvard Law Review* 1674.

[77] See I Ward, *Law, Philosophy and National Socialism: Heidegger, Schmitt and Radbruch in Context* (Frankfurt am Main, Peter Lang, 1992) 25–9. See also MD Dubber, 'Judicial Positivism and Hitler's Injustice (Book Review)' (1993) 93 *Columbia Law Review* 1825; and, on the South African judges' 'plain decisions', D Dyzenhaus, *Hard Cases in Wicked Legal Systems: South African Law in the Perspective of Legal Philosophy* (Oxford, Clarendon Press, 1991) 213–17.

[78] L Friedman, 'On Legalistic Reasoning: A Footnote to Weber' (1966) 1966 *Wisconsin Law Review* 150. See also Hart, *The Concept of Law* (n 16 above) 128–32; Habermas, *Between Facts and Norms* (n 8 above) 83, 448–9; N MacCormick, 'The Ethics of Legalism' (1989) 2 *Ratio Juris* 184; and LJ Wintgens, 'Legisprudence as a New Theory of Legislation' (2006) 19 *Ratio Juris* 5.

withinputs, legal actors often do not see themselves as autonomously activating a policy process for the transformation into law of their own values. They do not see themselves as having a leading role in the legal political moment of the law-making process, in the moment of the determination and selection of values that are to be implemented by the law. That which the legal actors actually do, or better, think they do most of the time, is fill the gaps caused in the legal system by a changed social reality, either by enacting a new statute or by reinterpreting an already existing one.

The history of French tort law in the nineteenth and early twentieth centuries offers an example of this possible intricacy between strong and weak forms of legal withinputs. French judges initiated and performed de facto an activity of law-making (withinputs). They progressively introduced into the national legal system an elaborated legal structure directed at implementing the typical values lying behind modern tort law (eg *neminem ledere*). However, the vast majority of the judiciary acted under the belief that what they were doing was simply their duty as the 'mouthpiece of the law', being as such the structure of the legal system. The large gaps left in the legal order by the Códe Civil, where only five articles originally were dedicated to torts, screamed for reparatory intervention by judges and scholars.[79]

Regardless of whether in their strong or weak form, the withinputs inside policy of law, together with the influence the actual legal system can operate on the choice of one legal category as opposed to another (mutual influences internal to the legal arena), have the same effect on the model: they point out the centrality of the legal arena and its actors in the law-making process in general and in the policy of law process in particular.[80]

VII. OVERLAPPING OF THE DIFFERENT ARENAS OF LAW-MAKING

The last example taken from French legal history introduces the third of the adjustments that has to be made to the model presented in Figure 4.2. Because of the presence of withinputs, it is very difficult in many cases to

---

[79] See A Tunc, *La responsabilité civile* (2nd edn, Paris, Economica, 1989) 56, 71–2; E Tomlinson, 'The Tort Liability in France for the Act of Things: a Study of Judicial Lawmaking' (1988) 48 *Louisiana Law Review* 1322; and F Lawson and B Markesinis, *Tortious Liability for Unintentional Harm in the Common Law and the Civil Law* (Cambridge, Cambridge University Press, 1982) vol I, x, 146–52. See also R David, *Le droit français. Le données fondamentales du droit français* (Paris, Librairie Générale de Droit et de Jurisprudence, 1960) vol I, 50.
[80] See L Friedman, 'Law, Lawyers, and Popular Culture' (1989) 98 *Yale Law Journal* 1579; and L Friedman, 'Legal Culture and the Welfare State' in Teubner (ed), *Dilemmas of Law in the Welfare State* (n 17 above) 17.

also truly determine whether the legal political inputs of a policy of law process have their place exclusively inside the political arena. For example, even if operating as legal actors, judges can be or could have been politically affiliated, corporate directors or members of a religious congregation.[81]

The adjustment one needs to make to the model then is derived from the consideration that in many cases, the same individual or group of individuals can act as key actors in different arenas of the same process of transformation of values into legal categories. For example, a member of a political party can be part of the procedure in a political congress leading to the proposal of implementing a certain value into law. He or she, at the same time, can sit as a member of a legislative committee having the task of transforming such values into a legislative draft. The same member of the political party acts then both in the formation of the legal political inputs and in their transformation into law.[82] A similar phenomenon of intersection also takes place between the legal and social arenas. Representatives of the community, eg spokespersons for larger corporations, trade unions, or civil society (as NGOs), often sit in a drafting committee set up by the legislature.[83]

It is often impossible, because of the overlapping roles played by the same individual or groups of individuals, to clearly demarcate where the formation of legal political inputs ends and the policy of law begins or where the latter ends and its policy of law outcomes begin. Contemporary legal theories under the embedded and, to some extent, the intersecting models, point to this impossibility in particular of a complete separation of the legal world from the different environments legislators, lawyers and judges live in when working.[84] The different moments of the law-making process actually therefore tend to intersect with each other. This phenomenon is represented in Figure 4.3, depicting the different squares as intersecting.

---

[81] See eg, Vago, *Law and Society* (n 33 above) 117.

[82] This overlapping is further stressed by the fact that the legal professions are by far the most represented in the US Congress (as in most Western national assemblies). See *ibid* 139. But see R Nelson and J Heinz, 'Lawyers and the Structure of Influence in Washington' (1988) 22 *Law and Society Review* 293.

[83] See eg, K Rokumoto, 'Law and Culture in Transition' (2001) 49 *American Journal of Comparative Law* 548; or the case of the California Senate Commission on Corporate Governance, Shareholder Rights and Securities Transactions, composed of state legislators, shareholder activists, business representatives, legal academics, state officials and corporate lawyers.

[84] See eg, I Ehrlich and R Posner, 'An Economic Analysis of Legal Rulemaking' (1974) III *Journal of Legal Studies* 277; or Frank, *Courts on Trial* (n 20 above) 147–9. See also M Klarman, 'What's so Great about Constitutionalism?' (1998–99) 93 *Northwestern University Law Review* 188.

The different moments are represented, however, as *partially* overlapping, that is they are not entirely coinciding. This specification is because individuals, or groups of individuals, tend to play different roles whether operating as political, legal or social actors. For example:

[a]s a political actor [government] assumes responsibility for deciding what ends are to be pursued and what resources it is prepared to commit in dealing with problems ... [G]overnment must then proceed as a legal actor, to establish the agencies and mechanisms by which public ends will be furthered.[85]

Playing a different role means that the individual or group tends to start from different premises (eg the choice of a judicial or in general legal career in public service vs a personal religious act of faith in favour of a certain belief). They also tend to use different means, eg the formal language of a statute or judicial decision vs passionate religious or political propaganda. Finally, they aim for goals of completely different natures, eg settling a dispute according to a statute vs convincing an audience of the rightness of beliefs.[86] These features of the specificity of each arena (different premises, different ways of reasoning, different goals to be gained) usually then allow the focal points of the arenas to be kept separate from each another.

Using the previous example, a party leader in the politics of law moment will stress the value aspects of a certain legislative proposal, eg its being 'good', 'just' or 'useful'. While an actor of the policy of law process (eg a member of the committee generating a final legislative draft), that party leader is obliged more or less to transform the role into one of a member of a legislative committee. In that new role, he or she will be constrained to employ a legal language, being obliged to use or shape new legal categories or concepts. The political actor, acting as a legal one, can very rarely bring into play concepts such as 'good' or 'just' as cornerstone categories or a justificatory basis of a legal reasoning contained in the draft of a statute.[87]

This feature, of the overlapping of the arenas while retaining distinct focal points, is strengthened by a further quality in the policy of law process. Here, however, the overlapping is not caused by the subjective coincidence of the same individuals or groups of individuals operating as different actors during different stages of the law-making process. In this case, the partial overlapping of the different stages is given by the fact that

---

[85] Nonet and Selznick, *Law and Society in Transition* (n 37 above) 112. See also T Parsons, 'The Law and Social Control' in Evan (ed), *Law and Sociology* (n 72 above) 72.

[86] See Habermas, *Between Facts and Norms* (n 8 above) 266; and J Raz, 'The Problem about the Nature of Law' in Raz, *Ethics in the Public Domain* (n 21 above) 191. For the double nature of the law-making (political and legal), see also Tuori, *Critical Legal Positivism* (n 4 above) 134.

[87] See Ross, *On Law and Justice* (n 9 above) 63–4. See eg, Jenkins, *Social Order and the Limits of Law* (n 62 above) 356. But see R Dworkin, '"Natural" Law Revisited' (1982) 34 *University of Florida Law Review* 183. Cf W Waluchow, *Inclusive Legal Positivism* (Oxford, Clarendon Press, 1994) 43–6.

it is often structurally difficult to draw a clear line separating values (legal political inputs), legal categories and concepts (policy of law outputs) and effects on the community (policy of law outcomes).[88] In a figurative sense, one can say that the two-way arrows, representing the mutual influences between the different moments, have the effect of pulling together the three squares in Figure 4.3.

Because of the above-mentioned mutual influences among the different arenas of the law-making process, values can assume, already during their formation and choice in the moment of legal politics, shapes and features typical of policy of law outputs. The actors operating in the politics moment, for example, can already make use there of the probable final product of the policy of law processes, ie of the legal categories and concepts they think correspond to their values, as an argumentative base for their reasoning. A political debate can make such an extensive use of legal terminology, such as 'strict liability', *habeas corpus* or 'private property' (instead of the economic, social or political values of which these legal categories are the transformation) that, in the end, it is fairly difficult to identify the borders between the originating legal-political values behind such legal concepts and the final results of the transformation.[89] Legal categories and concepts can become so charged with a direct value-political meaning that they are used directly in the political debate occurring in the political arena. This gives birth, for example, to an economic-political debate in which the discussion purely concerns the question of strict liability vs fault liability, rather than the economic values behind them.

This phenomenon is part of a larger process known as the *legalisation of politics*, identifying the process by which legal debates among the legal actors (eg in courts or in academic discourses) can dictate the conditions for the debates taking place in the political arena. As expressed by Loughlin:

> [t]he age-old controversies over the meaning of liberty, equality, democracy and the like are now taking place within a more explicit legal constitutionalist framework. The institution of courts will now play a more important role in giving precise meaning to the core values of society.[90]

---

[88] See eg, 'the minimum content of natural law' in Hart, *The Concept of Law* (n 16 above) 189–95 or 'wealth maximization' in R Posner, 'Utilitarianism, Economics and Legal Theory' (1979) 8 *Journal of Legal Studies* 103. See also C Lindblom, 'The Science of "Muddling Through"' (1959) 19 *Public Administration Review* 82.

[89] See Habermas, *Between Facts and Norms* (n 8 above) 151, pointing out an 'interpenetration of discursive law-making and communicative power formation', ie between legal regulation and collective goal setting. See also I Balbus, 'Commodity Form and Legal Form: an Essay on the "Relative Autonomy" of the Law' (1977) 11 *Law and Society Review* 582.

[90] Loughlin, *Sword and Scales* (n 18 above) 233. See eg, M Mandel, *The Charter of Rights and the Legalization of Politics in Canada* (2nd edn, Toronto, Thompson Educational Publishing, 1994) 61–4; or Luhmann, *Law as a Social System* (n 16 above) 421–2. See also

When applied specifically to the law-making process, the legalisation of politics affects the policy process in the sense that the values to be implemented through the law are already shaped in the form of legal concepts, and the alternatives on the political agenda can be (to a greater or lesser extent) set by the legal debate and by the legal actors' beliefs.[91]

A similar phenomenon can happen inside the legal arena when it comes to the moment of transforming values into legal concepts. The concepts chosen to mirror the choice of values made inside the political arena can be so affected by their political and ideological content and origins that they acquire a quasi-political nature. These are the legal concepts 'that appeal directly to one of the moral desiderata of our culture'.[92] Examples can be found in the use in statutory provisions of legal concepts such as '*fairness* in contractual relationships', which can be an expression of a will-value to have a more interventionist role by judicial organs in private contractual relations, or the '*rehabilitation* of criminals', referring to a highly political and ideological choice of a liberal tendency.

This *politicisation of the legal concepts* is the product of the more general process of the politicisation of the law as described in the Introduction and chapter three. Due to the tendency of a coinciding between the legal and political worlds, from a lawyers' perspective one can observe a process directed at attributing direct legal relevance to concepts created and selected outside the legal world. For example, a political party leader tries, as far as possible, to make use in the legislative drafting of a legal terminology closer to the political one. He or she argues convincingly for the use in the statute of expressions such as the 'social function of private property'. For an explanation of the social function of (the legal concept of) private property, the legal actors (eg judge) are then forced to search directly into the extra-legal reality. The legal actors are specifically compelled to embed the legal concept into the initial political environment and to make reference to the kind of political values (eg social-liberal vs socialistic) which are assumed to exist behind the concept of the social function of private property. In other words, the increasing overlapping of the legal world with the political one is revealed (and sometimes caused, in

---

Jenkins, *Social Order and the Limits of the Law* (n 62 above) 215; and the idea of 'legal moralism' in HLA Hart, *Law, Liberty, and Morality* (Stanford, Stanford University Press, 1965) 6–12.

[91] Already in the nineteenth century, Alexis de Tocqueville stated: 'There is hardly a political question in the United States which does not sooner or later turn into a judicial one. Consequently the language of everyday party-political controversy has to be borrowed from legal phraseology and conceptions.' A De Tocqueville, *Democracy in America* (New York, Anchor Books, 1969) 270 (reprint 1835). See also Cotterrell, *Law's Community* (n 19 above) 151–2.

[92] Kennedy, *A Critique of Adjudication (fin de siècle)* (n 1 above) 139. See also Bell, *Policy Arguments in Judicial Decisions* (n 2 above) 240–1. See eg, Canadian Charter of Rights and Freedoms (1982) s 7; and Waluchow, *Inclusive Legal Positivism* (n 87 above) 143–55.

particular in common law countries) by the increasing use by legal interpreters of social, political and economic evaluations.[93]

The legal arena, in its turn, can also structurally overlap with the social arena. The presence of several factors (eg a legal ideology of law-makers inspired by sociological jurisprudence) can deeply affect both the working of the legal actors in the policy process and their legal conceptual apparatus (policy of law outputs).[94] This conditioning usually expresses itself by incorporating into the very constitutive elements both of the policy process and of the policy outputs the (real or allegedly real) effects of the law-making on the community (or part thereof). For example, this can be the case when a statute chooses the legal category of general freedom of contracts with a prohibition for those that are *contra bonos mores*. Here, in order to find the actual meaning of the legal category 'freedom of contract', it is essential to take into consideration the outcomes the different types of contracts produce on the community (and in particular, on its morals).[95]

This *socialisation* of the policy of law process and its results is actually a part of a more general process where:

> [i]n our own period, [legal actors] are somewhat more likely to throw in references to other kinds of authority including ethical, economic, or social norms.[96]

In contrast, the distances between the legal and social arenas become greater (they overlap to a lesser extent in Figure 4.3), for example, if there is a formalistic approach to the law prevalent among the legal actors. The primary criterion by which the legal actors operate then is the formal legal rationality, ie with the idea that 'legal rules and procedures are generated from within the legal system, as opposed to external criteria such as

---

[93] See, Dworkin, *Taking Rights Seriously* (n 44 above) 122–3; and MDA Freeman, 'Positivism and Statutory Construction: an Essay in the Retrieval of Democracy' in S Guest (ed), *Positivism Today* (Aldershot, Dartmouth Publishing Company, 1996) 22. See eg, M Birnhack, 'The Idea of Progress in Copyright Law' (2001) 1 *Buffalo Intellectual Property Law Journal* 27. See also L Epstein *et al*, 'The Supreme Court as a "Strategic" National Policymaker' (2001) 50 *Emory Law Journal* 585.

[94] See R Pound, 'The End of Law as Developed in Legal Rules and Doctrines' (1914) 27 *Harvard Law Review* 225. See eg, L Edelman, 'The Transformation of Corporate Control by Neil Fligstein (Book Review)' (1991) 97 *American Journal of Sociology* 550.

[95] See N Palmieri, 'Good Faith Disclosures Required During Precontractual Negotiations' (1993) 24 *Seton Hall Law Review* 105. See also P Schwartz, 'Baby M. in West Germany (Book Review)' (1989) 89 *Columbia Law Review* 361 and Bürgerliches Gesetzbuch § 138 (FRG). But see G Teubner, 'Substantive and Reflexive Elements in Modern Law' (1983) 17 *Law and Society Review* 277.

[96] L Friedman, 'Taking Law and Society Seriously' (1999) 74 *Chicago-Kent Law Review* 535. See also Pound, *The Ideal Element in Law* (n 4 above) 167–8; and Hart's interpretation by J Coleman, 'Rules and Social Facts' (1991) 14 *Harvard Journal of Law and Public Policy* 724.

religious, ethical or political values'.[97] Consequently, the legal actors manoeuvre inside the boundaries established by the law itself, without paying attention to the outside social world.

There is not only an attraction of the legal arena towards the social arena. The social arena can also demonstrate a tendency of going through a process of the legalisation of its components, ie a process where the outcomes of the policy process in the social landscape are primarily determined not by how the community has received the policy of law outputs but by how the latter has been dispatched, ie by the choice or construction of legal concepts inside the policy moment.[98] Certain policy of law outcomes of a law-making process can occur just and only because a certain legal concept has been used instead of another. For example, a statute governs the transmissions of movies on the Internet under the general legal category of 'transmissions by air', and therefore those of the same legal types as radio or TV. This then can give rise to the practical outcome of closing down numerous webpages that do not pay the taxes or royalties due.

Actually, the political organisational form known as the welfare state has enormously increased the extension of the social landscape whose elements are essentially determined by law. One of the constitutive components of the welfare state is the fact that the law (ie legal concepts and categories) more and more shapes the basic components of society, a shaping that also goes under the name of 'social engineering'. This phenomenon of the absorption of the social arena into the legal world is part of a general tendency of contemporary law: the *legalisation of society*. As defined by Friedman, the legalisation of society means that 'there are fewer zones of immunity from law—fewer areas of life which are totally unregulated, totally beyond the *potential* reach of law'.[99]

---

[97] J Sterling and W Moore, 'Weber's Analysis of Legal Rationalization: a Critique and Constructive Modification' (1987) 1 *Sociological Forum* 72. See also Trubek, 'Max Weber on Law and the Rise of Capitalism' (n 75 above) 730; and E Weinrib, 'Legal Formalism: On the Immanent Rationality of Law' (1988) 97 *Yale Law Journal* 1013.

[98] See B Tamanaha, 'An Analytical Map of Social Scientific Approaches to the Concept of Law' (1995) 15 *Oxford Journal of Legal Studies* 533. But see Habermas, *Between Facts and Norms* (n 8 above) 307–8, pointing out the relative freedom of 'public opinion' from the constraints of the legal discourse.

[99] L Friedman, *The Republic of Choice: Law, Authority and Culture* (Cambridge, Harvard University Press, 1994) 15. See also N Bobbio, 'The Promotion of Action in the Modern State' in Hughes (ed), *Law, Reason, and Justice* (n 1 above) 199–202; M Galanter, 'Law Abounding: Legalisation around the North Atlantic' (1992) 55 *Modern Law Review* 13; Friedman, *Total Justice* (n 18 above) 147–52; R Pound, 'The Lawyer as a Social Engineer' (1954) 3 *Journal of Public Law* 292, 299–301; and A Peters, 'Law as Critical Discussion' in Teubner, *Dilemmas of Law in the Welfare State* (n 17 above) 252–4. Cf G Teubner, 'After Legal Instrumentalism? Strategic Models of Post-Regulatory Law' in Teubner, *Dilemmas of Law in the Welfare State* (n 17 above) 299, 310–12.

A. Some Exceptional Cases within the Policy of Law Process

In certain extreme cases, the three arenas tend to intersect each other at the same time (in Figure 4.3 this has been represented by the small area where the three arenas overlap). The values-choice, the legal categories-choice and the effects on the community (and their respective processes), tend all to subjectively and structurally coincide. This happens particularly in cases where the law-making process affects the basic fundaments of a community, eg in the case of the creation of a new constitutional document. The stipulating actors (political, legal and social) and the conceptual apparatuses to be used (politics, law and society) often tend to coincide there, making the transformational moment of policy very difficult to detect as a separate moment in the law-making process.

For example, it is very difficult to ascertain whether American founding fathers operate mainly as political, legal or social actors. Moreover, they often tended to use statements such as:

> Congress shall make no law respecting an establishment of religion, or prohibiting the free exercise thereof; or abridging the freedom of speech, or of the press; or the right of the people peaceably to assemble, and to petition the government for a redress of grievances.[100]

In these statements, as pointed out by Dworkin, it is very difficult to dissect the legal political inputs (values), the policy of law outputs (legal categories) and the policy of law outcomes (impacts on the community).[101]

Finally, in another extreme case of the Nazi regime in Germany, Figure 4.3 should depict the three arenas as almost entirely overlapping one another. This more or less complete correspondence of the policy of law process and results with their legal political inputs and policy of law outcomes is a consequence of the extension into the law-making process of the totalitarian nature of the Nazi regime. Due to the application of *Fuehrersprinzip* by the law-making authorities, the Nazi legal order set up a total and almost permanent submission of the choice of the sources (politics), the tools (law) and the effects (outcomes) of the law-making process to one person (the *Fuehrer*) and to a strong and unique ideological conceptual apparatus (the Nazi ideology). One example is the measures taken against the Jews, legally labelled as 'enemy of the State', a legal category heavily dependent and almost inseparable from the value-choice

---

[100]   US Const amend I.

[101]   See Dworkin, *Law's Empire* (n 18 above) 2–7. See also Habermas, *Between Facts and Norms* (n 8 above) 388–9; Sunstein, *Legal Reasoning and Political Conflict* (n 55 above) 82–3; and Kennedy, *A Critique of Adjudication (fin de siècle)* (n 1 above) 306. Another example can be found in the US legislation against Communist organisations, 50 USC § 781 (1964).

(Jews as mortal enemy of German people) and the policy of law outcomes (to treat the Jews as the enemy in wartime).[102]

VIII. CONCLUSION

The main task of this chapter has been the unlocking of the grey box located between politics and law, where values become legal categories and concepts: the policy of law. The analysis has been directed at opening a field between politics and the social consequences of the law. It is the field in which values take their legal dress, in which they will be presented to the members of the community and try to influence the latter's behaviours. It has been shown how it is possible to transfer into the legal phenomenon, with due modifications and adjustments, the concept of policy as developed by political scientists. Policy of law consequently has been defined as a web of processes and decisions. These processes and decisions are mostly located inside the legal arena, directed at transforming the values produced in the political arena (legal political inputs) into concepts and categories directly relevant in the legal world (policy of law outputs). As seen, the borders of the policy of law so defined tend often to cross the spaces where the decisions concerning values are taken (politics of law) and where the law-making results become a socially relevant phenomenon (policy of law outcomes).

In the policy of law, it is then possible to see how the dual tendencies stretching contemporary legal phenomenon in general towards and away from politics, have an effect on the law-making process and also on the policy process. Though differences in the extent of the overlapping can occur (eg according to the national legal system or the legal field under consideration), in Western legal systems the policy of law has always some (but never complete) common ground with both the formation of the political inputs and the policy of law outcomes. Having framed and briefly characterised the grey box in which values become legal concepts and categories, chapter five will establish the fundamental ambitions, objects and conceptual apparatus of the analysis of the policy of law.

---

[102] See R Miller, *Nazi Justiz: Law of the Holocaust* (Westport, Praeger Publishers, 1995) 11–20. See eg, the effects produced by the *Fuehrersprinzip* on the German administrative law-making in M Stolleis, *The Law under the Swastika* (Chicago, University of Chicago Press, 1998) 105–11.

5

The Policy of Law Analysis

In the previous chapter, a simple model explaining the position and function of the policy of law in the law-making process was developed. The policy of law process operates between the formation of values in the political world (politics of law) and the impact of the newly-made law on the social world (policy of law outcomes). The policy of law is the space in which values embedded in political decisions are transformed into law, having an effect on the existing legal system. It has also been illustrated how, in the contemporary legal order, this space occupied by policy of law is mainly (but not exclusively) the domain for the work and the reasoning of the legal actors.

This chapter will now move on to the identification of a branch of knowledge specifically devoted to the investigation of such moments in the law-making process: the policy of law analysis. This analysis will be characterised, both in its object and its investigative tools, in such a way as to distinguish it from the other two neighbouring types of studies: the politics of law analysis and the sociology of law. Finally, the extent to which policy of law studies can be encompassed within the traditional legal discipline and, more in particular, inside the area occupied by a jurisprudence defined by a Hartian terminology, will be explored.

I. THE POLITICS OF LAW ANALYSIS AND THE LAW-MAKING PROCESS

Once the different moments of the law-making process (legal politics, policy of law and policy of law outcomes) and their relations are established, it is possible to move towards the discovery of the branches of knowledge that correspond to these moments. Starting with the political arena, it seems appropriate to view its investigation as the main, although not the exclusive, domain of the politics of law analysis. The latter can be defined as that branch of human knowledge intended for the investigation of the processes of creation and selection of certain values-inputs that have to be realised by means of the law.[1] Among contemporary legal theories, CLS and its different spin-offs (in particular feministic jurisprudence and critical race theory) are those that, more than others, have worked in the direction of structuring a legal politics analysis as an autonomous field of investigation, an investigation focused on the criticism of 'the quest for consensus'.[2]

The political arena and its processes are not an exclusive domain of the politics of law because both the policy of law analysis and the sociology of law must take into consideration that which is happening inside the area where the politics of law is formed. However, in contrast to the politics of law analysis, policy of law and sociological investigations of the legal political inputs contribute to a better understanding of other moments of the law-making process (the policy of law moment and the policy of law outcomes of the law respectively).

The politics of law analysis obviously has strong connections with the hard-core of the legal discipline, that is with 'the sustained and systematic investigation of the field within which legal actions take place', performed in order 'to furnish a painstaking analysis and a reasoned explanation of the phenomenon in question'.[3] The legal-political scholar scrutinises, mostly from a critical perspective, not only the values behind the legal system but also the results reached by the legal analysis and explanations produced by legal scholars. The critical nature of the politics of law analysis results from the fact that it is usually performed in order to show the true political goals (ie values) lying behind the enactment of certain legal measures, certain judicial decisions or the promotion of certain legal theories:

> When people associated with cls assert that law is politics, I take them to mean that when one understands the moral, epistemological, and empirical assumptions embedded in any particular legal claim, one will see that those assumptions operate in the particular setting in which the legal claim is made to advance the interests of some identifiable political grouping ... It is in that sense that critical legal studies can be understood as a political location notwithstanding the disagreements among participants in the movement.[4]

---

[1] As samples of recent legal-political investigations, see I Ramsay, 'The Politics of Commercial Law' (2001) *Wisconsin Law Review* 568; or A Kanner, 'The Politics of Toxic Tort Law' (1997) 2 *Widener Law Symposium Journal* 163.

[2] See A Hutchinson and P Monahan, 'Law, Politics, and the Critical Legal Scholars: the Unfolding Drama of American Legal Thought' (1984) 36 *Stanford Law Review* 215. See also N Duxbury, *Patterns of American Jurisprudence* (Oxford, Clarendon Press, 1995) 504–9 for an analysis of the 'ambivalent' relations between the three legal streams as to this issue.

[3] I Jenkins, 'Legal Institutions, the Legal Profession and the Discipline of Law' (1966) 19 *Journal of Legal Education* 171.

[4] M Tushnet, 'Critical Legal Studies: a Political History' (1991) 100 *Yale Law Journal* 1517. See eg, Hutchinson and Monahan, 'Law, Politics, and the Critical Legal Scholars' (n 2 above) 201.

However, the politics of law analysis tends to have its main centre of gravitation outside the area occupied by the legal disciplines and, in particular, jurisprudence. First, the legal-political analysis tends to give a secondary position to the law-making process. In politics of law studies, the law-making process, and the legal system in general, are seen simply as channels through which the values pass in order to get the different political ideologies (or complex of values) realised into the society. The legal system is perceived simply as an intermediary step, being the real target of the legal political activity positioned after the law-making process. The basic reasoning grounding the analysis of the legal political activity is as follows: if one wants to implement some basic political values (eg equality between genders), then, by means of the law, one has to make certain factual situations happen (eg to have a workplace free from harassments based on gender).[5]

By giving a secondary position (mostly of an instrumental character) to the legal outputs and their process of formation, legal political investigations can then be seen as somehow falling out of the area occupied by the legal discipline and, specifically, by legal theory. A legal theoretical approach to law-making has as one of its specific features the focusing on the legal system in its explanatory models, regardless of the position the legal system then assumes towards the political arena. This targeting of the legal system is a consequence of the fact that legal theory is per definition an attempt to systematically explain the law.[6]

The secondary position occupied in the legal political analysis by legal outputs and their process of formation absolutely does not imply that legal political scholars neglect to analyse these. It simply means that legal political scholars analyse them functionally as to the creation of a link between values and outcomes. This functional role played by the policy of law process results in legal political scholars distancing themselves from that which is the peculiarity of the means known as legal concepts: their normative nature.[7]

---

[5] See eg, R Austin, 'Employer Abuse, Worker Resistance, and the Tort of Intentional Infliction of Emotional Distress' (1988) 41 *Stanford Law Review* 51-; or F Olsen, 'The Family and the Market: a Study of Ideology and Legal Reform' (1983) 96 *Harvard Law Review* 1498. See also Hutchinson and Monahan, 'Law, Politics, and the Critical Legal Scholars' (n 2 above) 217, 243–4; P Gabel, 'The Mass Psychology of the New Federalism: How the Burger Court's Political Imagery Legitimizes the Privatization of Everyday Life' (1984) 52 *George Washington Law Review* 265; and D Kennedy, *A Critique of Adjudication (fin de siècle)* (Cambridge, Harvard University Press, 1998) 1.

[6] See B Bix, *Jurisprudence: Theory and Context* (3rd edn, London, Sweet & Maxwell, 2003) 16–18.

[7] See D Kennedy, 'Form and Substance in Private Law Adjudication' (1976) 89 *Harvard Law Review* 1723; and R Posner, *The Problems of Jurisprudence* (Cambridge, Harvard University Press, 1990) 156–7. See also A Kronman, *The Lost Lawyer: Failing Ideals of the Legal Profession* (Cambridge, Harvard University Press, 1993) 264.

Legal political scholars centre their attention either on the original political battle for the values (ie the choice of the value) or, to a lesser extent, on their social effects (ie the outcomes). The functioning in itself of the legal system is often left to the periphery of their investigations, the legal system being simply the tool by which to transfer the values into actual situations. The opening sentences by Unger unequivocally are on this path:

> The critical legal studies movement has undermined the central ideas of modern legal thought and put *another conception of law* in their place. *This conception implies a view of society and informs a practice of politics.*[8] (emphasis added)

For example, legal-political scholars, on one hand, tend to focus their efforts on revealing that the implementation in society of a compulsory quota-system is actually a legal mantle covering the value of equality between the genders and the different powers (or political actors) behind it. On the other hand, the politics of law scholars marginalise the issue of why and how, in order to reach the goal of more equal employment for women, a compulsory quota-system has been chosen instead of incentives to employers through tax benefits.

A second reason pulls the politics of law analysis away from the traditional hard core of the legal discipline. Since the legal order is not the primary goal of its investigation, even when the policy of law outputs and processes are investigated, the conceptual tools used in such a task tend not to be taken from the realm of legal discipline. Instead, the legal-political scholar is inclined to look into other epistemological arenas, such as political science or political philosophy. The scholars of politics of law make vast use of categories such as 'ideology', 'power', 'legitimacy', 'oppression' or 'individualism'.[9] These explanatory categories are historically derived from conceptual apparatuses which, although perhaps present behind the legal language's scene, are usually felt as foreign (or at least exogenous) by the actors populating and working inside the legal arena. Few judges or lawyers would be keen in using, as an explicit reasoning in a decision, Kennedy's following statement:

---

[8]   R Mangabeira Unger, 'The Critical Legal Studies Movement' (1982) 96 *Harvard Law Review* 563. See also Kennedy, *A Critique of Adjudication (fin de siècle)* (n 5 above) 62; and P Gabel and J Feinman, 'Contract Law as Ideology' in D Kairys (ed), *The Politics of Law: a Progressive Critique* (3rd edn, New York, Basic Books, 1998) 508.

[9]   See eg, the definition of law as 'the condensation of social power' as in A Hunt, 'The Politics of Law and the Law of Politics' in K Tuori *et al* (eds), *Law and Power: Critical and Socio-Legal Essays* (Liverpool, Deborah Charles Publications, 1997) 68–70.

Nonetheless, I believe that there is value as well as an element of real nobility in the judicial decision to throw out, every time the opportunity arises, consumer contracts designed to perpetuate the exploitation of the poorest class of buyers on credit.[10]

This outside position of the politics of law analysis is valid, of course, under the condition of accepting the idea of the legal discipline as directed at investigating, explaining and teaching the law and law-making from a normative (or Hartian internal) perspective. If one takes as a starting point CLS' assumption as to the deep politicisation of the law, the final positioning of the politics of law analysis would probably be very different. The legal-political analysis would then be considered an integral and prominent part of the legal discipline.[11]

II. THE SOCIOLOGY OF LAW AND THE LAW-MAKING PROCESS

Moving on to the study of the social arena and its relationship with the law in the law-making process, this is covered primarily by the sociology of law. This is in particular true when the sociology of law is considered as that branch of knowledge concerning the mutual relationships between the legal order and society (seen either as a whole or in some of its components). Obviously this is a very general and, therefore, incomplete definition of the sociology of law.[12] However, it is sufficient for the purpose of this work: to point out the distinctiveness of its object of investigation from the one of policy of law analysis.

In a way similar to the studies of the politics of law, the sociology of law is also predisposed to moving its centre of investigation away from the law as seen through the eyes of lawyers. In particular, the legal-sociological studies focus their attention on society as a fundamental element determined by as well as determining the legal system and its constitutive elements. The law and legal system are considered, using a Hartian definition, from an external perspective. Even if the law and legal system constitute at least half of the object of the legal sociologist's work (the other being society), the legal phenomenon is seen from a perspective

---

[10] Kennedy, 'Form and Substance in Private Law Adjudication' (n 7 above) 1777. See also J Habermas, *Between Facts and Norms: Contributions to a Discourse Theory of Law and Democracy* (Cambridge, The MIT Press, 1998) 259.

[11] See Hutchinson and Monahan, 'Law, Politics, and the Critical Legal Scholars' (n 2 above) 227–31.

[12] See P Selznick, 'The Sociology of Law' (1960) 12 *Journal of Legal Education* 521; J Carbonnier, *Sociologie Juridique* (Paris, Presses Universitaires de France, 1978) 19–21; and R Cotterrell, *The Sociology of Law: an Introduction* (2nd edn, London, Butterworths, 1992) 4–6.

outside of the legal world, a perspective allowing the observer (sociologist) to consider the impact the normative system has on the population's social behaviours (and vice versa).[13]

Even Cotterrell, one of the strongest critics of such a distinction between 'insiders' (jurisprudence) and 'outsiders' (sociology of law) of the legal phenomenon, is forced to recognise that jurisprudence most of the time has concentrated on 'the abstract, conceptual, or "psychological" realm populated by legal values, symbols, concepts, principles, and rules'. In contrast, '[l]egal sociologists have concentrated heavily though not exclusively on the behavioral realm'.[14] For example, a study of the sociology of law focuses on whether and how the use of a compulsory quota-system in a legal system actually changes the concrete behaviours of employers in hiring women; or how the social reality has changed the way lawyers (eg judges) evaluate the gender-equality issue.[15]

Another factor distinguishes the sociology of law from the gravitational centre represented by the legal discipline and its normative vision of the law-making process. Legal sociologists make a broad use in their investigations not only of sociological methodologies, ie empirical investigations of both a quantitative and qualitative nature; they often also employ a terminology that clearly pays tribute to the dominant sociological root of the legal-sociological studies. Looking at the law-making processes with a conceptual apparatus loaded with sociological terms such as 'group interests' or 'fact beliefs', this moves the central points of the sociology of law into the conceptual fields of social sciences.[16] For example, even though the law and society movement with its empirical investigations has never fully crossed the legal sociological frontier, Friedman openly acknowledges that:

> The law and society movement relates to the legal order more or less the way the sociology of religion relates to religious life ... They can be studied as social phenomenon, without passing judgment on their normative content.[17]

---

[13]   See D Black, 'The Boundaries of Legal Sociology' (1972) 81 *Yale Law Journal* 1085. See eg, H McCammon, 'Disorganizing and Reorganizing Conflict: Outcomes of the State's Legal Regulation of the Strike Since the Wagner Act' (1994) 72 *Social Forces* 1017, 1021–40.

[14]   R Cotterrell, 'Jurisprudence and Sociology of Law' in W Evan (ed), *The Sociology of Law: a Social-Structural Perspective* (London, Collier Macmillan Publishers, 1980) 26–7. See also R Banakar, *Merging Law and Sociology: Beyond the Dichotomies in Socio-Legal Research* (Berlin, Galda and Wilch Verlag, 2003) 7–9, 166–9; KL Scheppele, 'Legal Theory and Social Theory' (1994) 20 *Annual Review of Sociology* 387; and N Luhmann, *A Sociological Theory of Law* (London, Routledge & Kegan Paul, 1985) 2–5.

[15]   The sociology of law, and political sociology, also investigate the mutual influences between the social reality and the political arena. See eg, R Schwartz, 'Moral Order and Sociology of Law: Trends, Problems and Prospects' (1978) 4 *Annual Review of Sociology* 591.

[16]   See eg, J Davis, 'Toward a Theory of Law in Society' (1978) 11 *Sociological Focus* 131.

[17]   L Friedman, 'Law and Society Movement' (1986) 38 *Stanford Law Review* 765.

During the law-making process, legal scholars, courts, legislative bodies and committees as well as lawyers in general make frequent and broad use of the data produced by sociological studies in their legal reasoning.[18] For example, a judge or legislative committee can refrain from imposing imprisonment in the case of a lesser robbery by a drug-addicted person. This avoidance can be based on sociological data demonstrating how such a measure does not prevent (or probably increases) addiction. However, in this case the legal actors use the sociological data more as 'scientific' support or decisional criteria for their legal reasoning. The legal actors tend to treat the data as questions of fact (as a photograph or a document) and not as a question of law. The sociological data, in the end, usually are considered as a helpful means but nevertheless foreign to the legal order, its reasoning and its argumentation.[19]

Of course, part of the sociology of law investigations is to analyse the legal arena. However, legal sociologists always tend to see it from the point of observation of social sciences, ie a point of observation external to the one shared by legal actors:

> Law can be seen as a thing like any other in the empirical world. It is crucial to be clear that from a sociological standpoint, law consists in observable acts, not in rules as the concept of rule or norm is employed in both the literature of jurisprudence and in every-day legal language. *From a sociological point of view, law is not what lawyers regard as binding or obligatory precepts.*[20] (emphasis added)

For example, the legal sociologist investigates legal actors such as judges and lawyers. He or she 'sees' them as far as they are socially relevant, that is as far as their work has an impact on the social arena. Judges and lawyers are not directly considered by the legal sociologist because of and according to their position and inputs into the legal system.[21]

---

[18] See S Vago, *Law and Society* (6th edn, Upper Saddle River, Prentice Hall, 2000) 192–5. See eg, a brief history of the wide use of social science data in the US Supreme Court's law-making in M Rustad and T Koenig, 'The Supreme Court and Junk Social Science: Selective Distortion in Amicus Briefs' (1993) 72 *North Carolina Law Review* 100.

[19] See eg, 29 American Jurisprudence 2d, Evidence § 27, defining sociological data as mere 'legislative facts' at the disposal of the law-making authority. See J Monahan and L Walker, 'Social Authority: Obtaining, Evaluating, and Establishing Social Science in Law' (1986) 134 *University of Pennsylvania Law Review* 477; and J Blumenthal, 'Law and Social Science in the Twenty-First Century' (2002) 12 *Southern California Interdisciplinary Law Journal* 47. See also A Aarnio, *Reason and Authority: a Treatise on the Dynamic Paradigm of Legal Dogmatics* (Cambridge, Harvard University Press, 1997) 75–6; and W Twining and D Miers, *How to Do Things with Rules* (4th edn, London, Butterworths, 1999) 160–4.

[20] Black, 'The Boundaries of Legal Sociology' (n 13 above) 1091.

[21] See N Timasheff, 'What is "Sociology of Law"?' (1937) 43 *American Journal of Sociology* 226. As an actual example of such sociological perspective of the legal phenomenon, see A Stinchcombe, *When Formality Works: Authority and Abstraction in Law and Organizations* (Chicago, University of Chicago Press, 2001) 140–57.

In summary, the politics of law analysis can be defined then as that branch of human knowledge dealing with the processes of the selection and formations of value-goals a certain legal order is expected to realise. The sociology of law deals with the actual impact of both the working and the resulting production of the legal order in the community's reality and vice versa. The focal points of both legal-political and legal-sociological studies, for different reasons, lie outside the fields occupied by the legal discipline.

The two analyses, politics and the sociology of law, naturally tend to intersect with each other in many aspects. This is primarily the result of the fact that on one side, legal-sociological studies need an investigation of ideologies (values), which play a determinant (although not exclusive) role in shaping the relations between law and society. For example, the different ideologies concerning racial discrimination need to be studied in order to understand the impact on society of the work of a legal actor.[22] On the other side, the legal political analysis always takes into consideration (often as a starting point) the actual socio-legal reality in which the value has to be inserted by means of the law.[23]

One should also add the fact that, because of historical common roots (eg Marx or Weber), most of the fundamental terminological apparatus of contemporary legal politics and sociology of law tends to be similar. Classic examples are the concepts of 'legitimacy', 'power' or 'institutions', which are widely used (although sometimes with relatively different meanings) both in political and sociological investigations of the legal phenomenon.[24]

There are, of course, other disciplines close to the legal ones which touch in their analyses upon the relationships of law and politics, and in particular the transformational moment in the law-making process. These are disciplines such as criminology, which is the discipline studying 'the processes of making laws, breakings laws, and reacting to the breakings of laws'.[25] These types of disciplines, although extremely useful for understanding certain crucial aspects of the policy of law process and of the

---

[22] See L Mayhew, *Law and Equal Opportunity: a Study of the Massachusetts Commission Against Discrimination* (Cambridge, Harvard University Press, 1968) 56–64. See also Cotterrell, *The Sociology of Law* (n 12 above) 91–3; and Davis, 'Toward a Theory of Law in Society' (n 16 above) 130–1.

[23] See O Weinberger, *Law, Institution and Legal Politics: Fundamental Problems of Legal Theory and Social Philosophy* (Dordrecht, Kluwer Academic Publishers, 1991) 224. For example, it can be a social reality of discrimination as in S Carter, 'When Victims Happen to be Black' (1988) 97 *Yale Law Journal* 421. See also Black, 'The Boundaries of Legal Sociology' (n 13 above) 1094.

[24] See R Smith, 'Political Jurisprudence, the "New Institutionalism", and the Future of Public Law' (1988) 82 *American Political Science Review* 92, as to the concept of 'institutions' linking the political and sociological approaches to the law.

[25] EH Sutherland *et al*, *Principles of Criminology* (11th edn, Dix Hills, General Hall, 1992) 3.

policy of law decisions, are actually not focused on investigating the feature of policy of law that makes it as it is: a moment of the law-making process where the internal perspective of the legal actors plays a fundamental role. For example, criminology deals both with the causes of crimes and the treatment of offenders (also central issues in criminal law theory); these two issues are, however, scrutinised according to criteria of a social sciences' nature (eg use of statistical data) and in light of different ideological-value positions (eg re-education of the offender vs compensation of the victim). The internal point of view of the legal actors, ie how they see the problems through the lenses of legal rationality, is left at the periphery of the criminological studies.[26]

III. THE POLICY OF LAW ANALYSIS

These definitions of the legal political analysis and the sociology of law leave a series of epistemological holes in the study of the law-making process. In particular, they leave open the possibility of having an investigation of the policy moment of the law. This type of investigation can insert itself between the study of the formulation of values (the politics of law analysis) and the actual implementation of their legal version into the community life (the sociology of law).

Based on the concept of policy studies as developed in political science, the policy of law analysis can be defined as that part of the legal discipline dealing with the question of how values produced in the political arena are transformed into legal categories and concepts. Moreover, it evaluates the kinds of impact these legal figures of values have on the legal system. The policy of law analysis is therefore a discipline focusing its investigation on two aspects of the transformational moment of the law-making process.

The policy of law analysis deals with the dynamic aspects of the transformation of values into law, studying the processes which values undergo in order to be inserted into the existing legal system (policy of law process). It deals with the general issue of explaining the modalities through which values are transformed into legal categories and concepts (in Figure 4.3, how from f the legal arena arrived at l(f)). The policy of law analysis also focuses on why, in this transformational process, certain legal tools are used (or produced ex novo) instead of others. By doing this, the policy of law analysis also takes into consideration the modalities through

---

[26] See eg, P Carlen, 'The Staging of Magistrates' Justice' (1976) 16 *British Journal of Criminology* 48. See also R Akers, 'Linking Sociology and its Specialties: the Case of Criminology' (1992) 71 *Social Forces* 5.

which the existing legal order influences the transformational process (in Figure 4.3, the effects of two-way arrow l(f) on the policy processes).[27]

The other aspect of the transformational moment that the policy of law analysis investigates is the structural consequences the transformation of values into law has on the legal order (policy of law outputs). The policy of law analysis researches the imprinting of the transformational processes on the existing law or, in other words, the consequences the adoption of a legally binding concept has on the legal system (in Figure 4.3, l(f)).[28]

For example, a policy of law analysis aims at investigating why and how the value of the 'protection of the society from inherent risks of certain economic activities' has been transformed into the statutory concept of 'strict liability', using then the legal tool of 'liability' instead of 'negligence'.[29] Moreover, it deals with the issue of how and whether this new concept of strict liability has been imprinted onto the existing tort law system (and the legal order as a whole). Finally, the policy of law analysis has the major task of evaluating, and somehow predicting, whether statutory sanctioned strict liability would decrease the legal space assigned to the judges in tort issues, in particular with respect to evidentiary matters. This decrease in the judge's discretion can be due to the fact that it is now the legislator that imperatively determines whether and when a certain causal relationship exists from the presence of a certain activity (eg mass manufacturing of certain products) and a certain fact (eg injuries of the consumer while using the product).[30]

A. Separation of the Policy of Law from Legal-Political and Legal-Sociological Studies

The adoption of this definition of a policy of law analysis as dealing with the transformational dynamics and outputs in a law-making process then allows one to distinguish this kind of investigation from both legal political analysis and the sociology of law. The policy of law analysis is different from the politics of law analysis mainly for two reasons. First, the policy of

[27] See eg, focusing on the influence of drafted legislation on judge-made law, A Hartkamp, 'Interplay between Judges, Legislators, and Academics: the Case of the New Civil Code of the Netherlands' in S Markesinis (ed), *Law Making, Law Finding and Law Shaping: the Diverse Influences* (Oxford, Oxford University Press, 1997) 96–104.

[28] As to the idea of imprinting, see M Hannan, 'Rethinking Age Dependence in Organizational Mortality: Logical Formalizations' (1998) 104 *American Journal of Sociology* 132.

[29] See eg, G Priest, 'The Invention of Enterprise Liability: a Critical History of the Intellectual Foundations of Modern Tort Law' (1985) 14 *Journal of Law Studies* 518.

[30] See S Presser, 'How should the Law of Products Liability be Harmonized? What Americans Can Learn from Europeans' (2002) 2 *Global Liability Issues* 9-. See eg, S Saltzburg et al, *Federal Rules of Evidence Manual: a Compete Guide to the Federal Rules of Evidence* (6th edn, Charlottesville, Michie Corporation, 1994) 482–3.

law analysis does not have as its primarily goal showing the formation and selection of values occurring in the political arena (formation of f in Figure 4.3). The policy of law scholar starts the investigation from the entrance of the values into the legal arena, aiming instead at scrutinising how such political values became legally relevant in their legal forms.[31] Secondly, the policy of law investigation proceeds along a legal pattern. The analysis is mostly devoted to studying from a normative perspective how and why certain legal tools have been chosen by legal actors to transform a certain value into law.

A normative perspective means that the policy of law analysis must focus mainly on the legal argumentations and legal reasonings developed by the legal actors in choosing one legal category over another.[32] The normative perspective adopted by the policy of law analysis helps create a distance from those studies developed by legal politics, which also scrutinise the policy of law process. These studies always have a non-normative perspective of such processes, that is a perspective focused on the idea of the 'actual' (in the sense of socio-political) powers and ideologies which are behind and control the process of transformation of values into law.[33]

The policy of law analysis is also different from the sociology of law. The policy of law scholar does not have the investigation of the impact of certain legal choices on the community and its life (policy of law outcomes in Figure 4.3) as a primary target. The major object for a policy of law investigation instead is to evaluate the impact on the legal order of the choice of using a certain legal tool for the transformation of a value into a legally relevant concept or category (policy of law outputs). Moreover, in this evaluation, the policy of law analysis must use empirical research (of both a quantitative and qualitative nature) as a secondary source, while always keeping as the main perspective the normative view of the 'legal insiders'.[34]

For example, the politics of law analysis focuses on the moral and social values as pushed forward by environmental grassroots organisations, through which the subjectively fragmented interests as to having a clean

---

[31] In this sense, the extent of the aims of the policy of law analysis adopted in this work is narrower than the one embraced by Weinberger, *Law, Institution and Legal Politics* (n 23 above) 242–6.

[32] See eg, HLA Hart, 'The House of Lords on Attempting the Impossible' in HLA Hart, *Essays in Jurisprudence and Philosophy* (Oxford, Clarendon Press, 1983) 371–85.

[33] This non-normative angle, typical of legal political analysis, can be traced eg in K Klare, 'Labor Law as Ideology: Toward a New Historiography of Collective Bargaining Law' (1981) 4 *Industrial Relation Law Journal* 452. Compare R Duvin, 'The Duty to Bargain: Law in Search of Policy' (1964) 64 *Columbia Law Review* 250.

[34] See Cotterrell, 'Jurisprudence and Sociology of Law' (n 14 above) 21–9. Compare with the complete reliance on empirical investigations by general policy studies as, eg, in D Hensler et al, *Class Action Dilemmas: Pursuing Public Goals for Private Gain: Executive Summary* (Santa Monica, Rand Corporation, 2001) 4–5.

environment, through the legal order, somehow unify and are heard in a community.[35] The policy of law's attention instead is directed at revealing, on one side, the reasoning that led the legal actors (either in their judicial, legislative or jurisprudential roles) to import into the field of environmental law, the legal procedural concept of class action, as a unifying legal device for what originally were scattered individual claims. On the other side, the policy of law analysis aims at bringing to the surface the impacts that the introduction of such a new legal category has on the existing legal order (eg it now recognises in its turn the existence of a general category known as 'collective interests', legally relevant for future legislation).[36] In his or her turn, the legal sociologist evaluates, based mainly on empirical data, whether and to what extent the legal innovation represented by the class action (and more generally, the recognition of the legal existence of collective interests) has promoted, for example, the growth and strength of the role of grassroots organisations in a community and/or whether the latter development has influenced any changes in the procedural law concept of 'standing'.[37]

Before concluding this part, two clarifications are necessary. First, it is true that there actually are other branches of knowledge that also deal specifically with the intermediary space in the law-making represented by policy of law. The most evident example in political science is the movement known as political jurisprudence. Started in the 1960s, political jurisprudence immediately clarified its perspective: '[A] vision of courts as political agencies and judges as political actors.'[38] On this basis, the movement developed in two directions: towards the rationalisation of 'the role of courts and law within a theory of democratic legal process' and towards the relativisation (to the contingent political reality) of the meaning of constitutional and statutory provisions.[39] However, with such

[35] See J Cooley and T Lemly, 'The Federal Class Action in Environmental Litigation: Problems and Possibilities' (1973) 51 *North Carolina Law Review* 1388. See also, more in general on the beliefs behind the legal category of class action, S Yeazell, *From Medieval Group Litigation to the Modern Class Action* (New Haven, Yale University Press, 1987) 239–45.

[36] See eg, K Rivlin and J Potts, 'Proposed Rule Changes to Federal Civil Procedure may Introduce New Challenges in Environmental Class Action Litigation' (2003) 27 *Harvard Environmental Law Review* 530; or Yeazell, *From Medieval Group Litigation to the Modern Class Action* (n 35 above) 11–21, 256–7.

[37] See eg, K Orren, 'Standing to Sue: Interest Group Conflict in the Federal Courts' (1976) 70 *American Political Science Review* 724.

[38] M Shapiro, 'Political Jurisprudence' (1964) 52 *Kentucky Law Journal* 296. See also the foundational work for political jurisprudence, M Shapiro, *Law and Politics in the Supreme Court: New Approaches to Political Jurisprudence* (New York Free Press, 1964) 6–17.

[39] M Shapiro, 'Recent Developments in Political Jurisprudence' (1983) 36 *Western Political Quarterly* 542, 544. See also J Segal and H Spaeth, *The Supreme Court and the Attitudinal Model Revisited* (Cambridge, Cambridge University Press, 2002) 343–9.

premises, political jurisprudence then overlooks one of the essential features of the policy of law moment, its normative nature. By stating that courts are simply a 'subset of political institutions', this movement inevitably pays no (or very little) attention to the very core of the policy of law process: its coming into existence because legal actors work and think as part of a world (more or less) different from the political arena.[40]

Secondly, both the legal-political and the legal-sociological analyses actually stretch their investigations of law-making also in directions other than towards the legal arena (the space where sociology of law and politics of law analysis overlap in Figure 5.1). Since this work is from a normative perspective, it aims at limiting and discussing the boundaries that the legal discipline (among which, as will be seen immediately below, the policy of law analysis has to be counted) has with other disciplines. The analysis of how the sciences bordering the legal discipline's domain interact with each other is then outside the scope of this work.

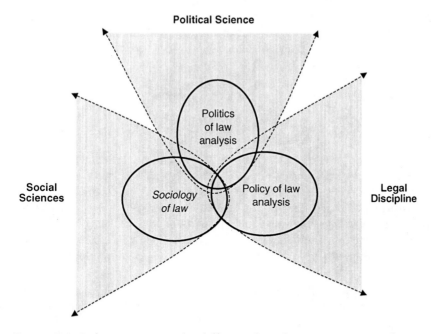

Figure 5.1: Relations among the different disciplines investigating the law-making process

---

[40] M Shapiro, 'Judges as Liars' (1994) 17 *Harvard Journal of Law and Public Policy* 156. See also Smith, 'Political Jurisprudence, the "New Institutionalism", and the Future of Public Law' (n 24 above) 97–8, 101–5.

B. The Policy of Law Analysis as a Distinct Legal Discipline

As has now been established, the policy of law analysis has as the main object of its investigation the transformational moment of the law-making process. It now remains to locate the place such policy of law analysis has on the map of human knowledge, or, in other words, to ascertain which perspective the policy of law analysis needs to embrace in approaching the policy of law phenomenon. As seen above, the policy moment of law-making in Western legal orders can be seen as having a strong legal imprint: done mainly by legal actors (or political actors acting as such), usually according to a legal rationality (either formal or substantive) and for a legal purpose (to change the legal system). As the policy of law is a legal phenomenon, it then seems appropriate that its analysis should begin with, or at least take into major consideration, the internal perspective of the legal actors:

The policy of law analysis can be defined as a constitutive part of the general field of jurisprudence and, in particular, of legal theory. This inclusion is particularly valid if one accepts the Hartian description of legal theory, that is a theory of what the law is in terms of generally seeking (ie not being bound to any particular legal order or legal culture) 'to give an explanatory and clarifying account of law as a complex of social and political institutions with a self rule-governed (and in that sense "normative") aspect.'[41]

Looking at the ambition, object and conceptual apparatus of the policy of law investigation, one can draw the conclusion that the hard core of such knowledge has to be positioned inside the realm of jurisprudence in general, and of legal theory, in particular.

Starting with the aim of the policy of law analysis, its hard core can be considered as located inside jurisprudence. The main purpose of the policy of law analysis is to offer a theoretical explanation and clarification of the transformational process and the results of law-making.[42] In particular, the policy of law investigation looks into the conceptual and categorical apparatus employed in the law-making process and deployed in legal forms by legal actors. For example, it certainly can be extremely valuable for the

---

[41] HLA Hart, 'Postscript' in HLA Hart, *The Concept of Law* (PA Bulloch and J Raz (eds), 2nd edn, Oxford, Clarendon Press, 1994) 239. See HLA Hart, 'Problems of the Philosophy of Law' in Hart, *Essays in Jurisprudence and Philosophy* (n 32 above) 103–5; N MacCormick, *H.L.A. Hart* (Stanford, Stanford University Press, 1981) 37–40; and K Tuori, *Critical Legal Positivism* (Aldershot, Ashgate Publishing, 2002) 320. See also the criticism in R Dworkin, *Law's Empire* (Cambridge, Harvard University Press, 1997) ch 2; and Hart's defence by J Raz, 'Two Views of the Nature of the Theory of Law' in J Coleman (ed), *Hart's Postscript: Essays on the Postscript to the Concept of Law* (Oxford, Oxford University Press, 2001) 27–36; and by T Endicott, 'Herbert Hart and the Semantic Sting' in *ibid* 41–7.

[42] See eg, J Waldron, *The Dignity of Legislation* (Cambridge, Cambridge University Press, 1999) ch 6, although he adopts a legal philosophical orientation rather than a legal theoretical one.

policy of law scholar to use legal sociological data showing that juries of laymen are not favourable to plaintiffs in tort cases. These data, however, simply state a factual situation (concrete behaviours of juries) and can be used by the policy of law analysis only to explain the legal theoretical issue that is central for the policy of law: the role played by the legal actor known as the jury in the transformational process that results in the legal category of damages as having a (hypothetical) secondary role inside the tort system.

Most (but not all) the work of the policy of law analysis has to be focused on the description, and not on the prescription, of a particular moment in the law-making process, ie the transformation of values into legal categories and concepts. This aim of being descriptive results in the aspiration for policy of law studies of being relatively value neutral, in the sense that their efforts are directed at analysing the way values are transformed (or not) into law without either sharing them or endorsing them.[43] It is, of course, only a relatively value-free position since the policy of law analysis accepts as taken-for-granted certain values, eg that a legal order must exist in order to regulate human behaviour.[44] The most suitable solution of the issue of the prescriptive/descriptive nature of the policy of law is perhaps the one given by Raz as to the aim of jurisprudence in general: to provide 'interpretative explanations'.[45] The aim of a policy of law analysis can then be identified as giving interpretative explanations since, in providing an explanation of the transformational process during the law-making, policy of law analysis seeks the improvement of the understanding of the 'law-that-is'.

Despite this legal theoretical hard core of describing the legal reality, policy of law as a discipline tends to locate itself in the nebulous boundaries typical of jurisprudential studies in general. It is in the very policy of law analysis in which one finds one of the places where jurisprudence tends to overlap extensively with other non-legal disciplines,

---

[43] See Hart, 'Postscript' (n 41 above) 244. See also HLA Hart, 'Introduction' in Hart, *Essays in Jurisprudence and Philosophy* (n 32 above) 8–12; and J Raz, 'Legal Validity' in J Raz, *The Authority of Law: Essays on Law and Morality* (Oxford, Oxford University Press, 1979) 156. Compare P Soper, 'Legal Theory and the Obligation of a Judge: the Hart/Dworkin Dispute' (1977) 75 *Michigan Law Review* 473.

[44] In the end, as highlighted also by MacCormick, there is always a value choice in choosing a normative perspective. See N MacCormick, *Legal Reasoning and Legal Theory* (Oxford, Clarendon Press, 1997) 63–4, 139–40. See also Tuori, *Critical Legal Positivism* (n 41 above) 300–4; I Jenkins, *Social Order and the Limits of Law: a Theoretical Essay* (Princeton, Princeton University Press, 1980) 60; W Waluchow, *Inclusive Legal Positivism* (Oxford, Clarendon Press, 1994) 29–30; and J Raz, 'Authority, Law and Morality' in J Raz, *Ethics in the Public Domain: Essays in the Morality of Law and Politics* (Oxford, Clarendon Press, 1994) 219–21.

[45] See Raz, 'Two Views of the Nature of the Theory of Law' (n 41 above) 30–1. See also R Summers, 'On Identifying and Reconstructing a General Legal Theory: Some Thoughts Prompted by Professor Moore's Critique' (1984) 69 *Cornell Law Review* 1024.

in particular sociology and political science. The ambition of policy of law studies tends to lead into more legal political topics. Similar to the position of policy studies inside political science, the policy of law analysis has one foot in 'pure research' of a theoretical nature and another in applied sciences directed at 'the nuts and bolts of detailed problem-solving'.[46] This two-fold ambition of the policy of law actually can be inserted in a more dual nature of the functions attributed to legal theory:

> Legal theory has both a theoretical and a practical goal. On one hand it answers a theoretical need by explaining the phenomenon of law and by reducing its complexity through a globalizing, systemic approach. On the other hand, legal theory answers practical needs in that it helps to improve the methodology of legal technique and legal practice.[47]

The policy of law analysis explains and clarifies the legal conceptual apparatus, in particular looking at its political and social origins, in order to understand (and make understood) the reasons behind any 'discrepancies' in the functioning of the legal order. The task of policy of law analysis then belongs to the clarificatory task that Hart attaches to researchers working with jurisprudence in general.[48] For example, the policy of law analysis points out some of the reasons why the value of equality between men and women, so largely embraced in the words of the political actors, is not implemented or is implemented with different meanings in a legal system.

Moreover, the policy of law analysis has the ambition of actively intervening in the legal-political debate in order to offer choices of legal measures that can remedy such discrepancies. The policy of law analysis can suggest, for example, the linking of the value of gender equality to a statutory interpretation of the category of equal opportunity in a substantive key. Using Pound's words, one could state that the policy of law analysis offers to the legal world both 'practical expositions of [the formation of] its precepts' and 'considerations of what its precepts ... ought to be'.[49]

This function as played by the studies of policy of law is part of the larger function performed by jurisprudence in contributing to 'the development of legal technology—that is the invention or creation of concepts,

---

[46] A Heidenheimer *et al*, *Comparative Public Policy: the Politics of Social Choice in America, Europe and Japan* (3rd edn, New York, Saint Martin's Press, 1990) 2.

[47] M Van Hoecke, 'Jurisprudence' in CB Gray (ed), *The Philosophy of Law: an Encyclopedia* (New York, Garland Publishing, 1999) 460.

[48] See Hart, 'Introduction' (n 43 above) 3.

[49] R Pound, *Jurisprudence* (St Paul, West Publishing Company, 1959) 23. See also N MacCormick, 'Reconstruction after Deconstruction: a Response to CLS' (1990) 10 *OJLS* 558; and A Ross, *On Law and Justice* (London, Stevens & Sons, 1958) 46–8.

devices, institutions, and procedures as solutions to practical problems'.[50] These remedies, offered by the policy of law analysis, must remain however of a legal character. The policy of law analysis must investigate and operate within legal concepts and categories, and not (at least not directly) with aspects of a social or political nature of the legal phenomenon. For example, while a policy of law analysis can offer a new interpretation of the legal concept of vicarious criminal liability, extending it to corporations, it must not address the issue of increasing economic costs in the social arena due to higher environmental standards. The policy of law analysis also stays away from the promotion in the political arena for more 'justice' in environmental issues.[51]

It is, however, clear that the proposals coming from the policy of law analysis can, indirectly, significantly influence the proposals formulated in both the social and the political arenas. Remedies of a social or political nature require (or at least presuppose) a receptive, or at a minimum, non-hostile legal order. For example, it would be harder, via the mass media, to promote in the social arena the idea of complete acceptance of same sex partnerships if the courts consider homosexuality a criminal offence.

This hurdling over the boundaries of jurisprudence by the policy of law analysis and entering into the legal-political fields of problem-solving activities is strictly connected with the mixed character of the object of the investigation. The policy of law analysis finds its centre of investigation in a typical jurisprudential target: law as a complex of binding rules, in their turn merged around concepts and categories. Law is not simply regarded as an (authoritative) means among others (eg economic measures) to gain certain results, a depiction that is common in the vast majority of the political science literature. Neither is the legal phenomenon considered, as in most sociological investigations, as a complex of behaviours and actions influencing and influenced by the social surroundings.[52]

The main focus of the analysis of policy of law must instead be on the law and the legal system perceived as a normative system of rules. It builds its exploratory work on the internal aspects of the legal phenomenon, on the perception by the participants of the legal game as a binding system of categories and concepts, on idea of concepts and categories as providing

---

[50] W Twining, *Globalisation and Legal Theory* (London, Butterworths, 2000) 12. See also Weinberger, *Law, Institution and Legal Politics* (n 23 above) 212–13; and Tuori, *Critical Legal Positivism* (n 41 above) 285.

[51] See eg, N De Sadeleer, *Environmental Principles: from Political Slogans to Legal Rules* (Oxford, Oxford University Press, 2002) 333–9. See also M Weber, *The Methodology of the Social Sciences* (E Shils and H Finch (eds), New York, Free Press, 1949) 53.

[52] See eg, C Campbell and P Wiles, 'The Study of Law in Society' in Evan (ed), *The Sociology of Law* (n 14 above) 16–18; and A Stone Sweet, 'Judicialization and the Construction of Governance' (1999) 32 *Comparative Political Studies* 148.

the legal actors 'with reasons for acting and with grounds for criticizing the behaviour of those who fail to comply'.[53] The policy of law analysis concerns the transformational process and evaluates its results through the eyes and the discourses of lawyers or, in other words, through the matrix of legal (formal or substantive) rationality superseding such discourses.[54]

In this way, the policy of law analysis also shares the three-dimensional aspects typical of the concept of jurisprudence as described by Dreier and Alexy: it is an analytical investigation of legal concepts and categories, from a normative perspective resulting in concrete problem-solving proposals.[55] The policy of law analysis in general has a (Hartian) normative object of investigation because it starts from the assumption of the existence of a 'great anomaly' of the legal language: its 'inability to define its crucial words in terms of ordinary factual counterparts'.[56] As a consequence, the policy of law analysis has as the main object of its work the argumentations and reasonings that have led legal actors to produce or modify certain legal concepts, more than the sociological or psychological counterparts of the legal concepts.[57]

It is true that Hart in general stresses the need for legal analysis to contextualise the law. This contextualisation, however, is meant in its restrictive meaning. It is the necessity, in order to fully understand a certain legal concept, of positioning the legal concepts and categories inside the framework represented by the internal point of view of the legal actors. For example:

> the expression 'a right'... does not describe or stand for any expectation, or power, or indeed anything else, but has meaning only as part of a sentence the function of which as a whole is to draw a conclusion of law from a specific kind of legal rule.[58]

One can posit that the policy of law analysis has a normative hard core as it does not have as its central object the social or political reality behind the

---

[53] J Coleman, 'Rules and Social Facts' (1991) 14 *Harvard Journal of Law and Public Policy* 706.

[54] See Tuori, *Critical Legal Positivism* (n 41 above) 291. But see P Soper, *A Theory of Law* (Cambridge, Harvard University Press, 1984) 1–3.

[55] See R Dreier and R Alexy, 'The Concept of Jurisprudence' (1990) 3 *Ratio Juris* 9.

[56] HLA Hart, 'Definition and Theory in Jurisprudence' in Hart, *Essays in Jurisprudence and Philosophy* (n 32 above) 25. See also A Ross, 'Tû-tû' (1957) 70 *Harvard Law Review* 822; K Olivecrona, *Law as Fact* (2nd edn, London, Stevens & Sons, 1971) 88–9; and A Marmor, *Interpretation and Legal Theory* (Oxford, Clarendon Press, 1992) 93–7.

[57] See eg, S Gottlieb, 'The Paradox of Balancing Significant Interests' (1994) 45 *Hastings Law Journal* 829. For a similar kind of investigation (though about the law-applying moment of the legal phenomenon), see also MacCormick, *Legal Reasoning and Legal Theory* (n 44 above) 8–13; and J Bell, *Policy Arguments in Judicial Decisions* (Oxford, Clarendon Press, 1983) 36–9.

[58] Hart, 'Definition and Theory in Jurisprudence' (n 56 above) 28. For a different interpretation of Hart, see eg, N Simmonds, *The Decline of Juridical Reason: Doctrine and Theory in the Legal Order* (Manchester, Manchester University Press, 1984) 8–9.

legal concept, for example, of a corporation. The policy of law analysis primarily investigates, instead, the legal context of the creation of the concept of a corporation, ie the reasoning and arguments that have brought the law-making judge to extend to corporate bodies legal concepts (such as criminal liability) originally designed for individuals.[59]

The very embracing of a normative perspective makes the policy of law investigation a discipline that can contribute to certain of the debates traditionally ascribed to jurisprudence: values and the law, the separation of law and morals, as well as the theory of law-making.[60] Policy of law analysis focuses, from a normative perspective, on the modalities and reasons as to why a certain legal category or concept has been chosen to represent, in the legal order, a certain value produced inside the political arena. The policy of law scholars dissect and analytically investigate the formation processes that lead to the construction of the legal concepts and categories of a legal order, a necessary operation that can contribute considerably to enhancing the role of general jurisprudential investigations in the modern law-making process.[61]

C. Partially Mixed Nature of the Policy of Law Analysis

Since the object of the policy of law analysis is the transformational process conducted in order to introduce, in a legal format, certain values into the social reality of a certain community, it is inevitable that the policy of law inquiry actually opens its field of investigation to realities other than the law and the legal system. In particular, attention is expanded to both the political and social arenas. In order to better understand the value-background behind the process of the formation of as well as the resulting legal categories and concepts, a policy of law analysis needs to take into consideration the formation of inputs, ie realities external to the legal arena but nevertheless fundamental to the latter's working. Policy of law analysis must consider the legal political forces present in a certain community (eg political parties, grassroots organisations or lobbyists), both the procedural and substantive values they stand for and the battles occurring inside the political arena. As pointed out generally by Pound:

---

[59] This is a modification of an example given by Hart, 'Definition and Theory in Jurisprudence' (n 56 above) 43.

[60] See Summers, 'On Identifying and Reconstructing a General Legal Theory' (n 45 above) 1022.

[61] See Weinberger, *Law, Institution and Legal Politics* (n 23 above) 24. In this sense, a policy of law analysis can also contribute to a more complete development of a *legisprudence*, ie a rational investigation of legislation. See LJ Wintgens, 'Legislation as an Object of Study of Legal Theory: Legisprudence' in LJ Wintgens (ed), *Legisprudence: a New Theoretical Approach to Legislation* (Oxford, Hart Publishing, 2002) 39.

[t]here is no escape in the science of law from the problem of values. Every adjustment of relations and ordering of conduct has behind it some canon of valuing conflicting and overlapping interests.[62]

For example, in order to fully understand the creation in a legal order of 'separate but equal' treatment as a primary legal category with respect to differences in treatment based on race, the policy of law analysis cannot ignore the actual values behind such a category. Only this background knowledge allows the scholar to distinguish a policy of law directed at fulfilling the value of discriminatory treatment of a minority (as with African-Americans in the United States) to the opposite direction of protecting a minority (as with the German-speaking population in the Italian South Tyrol).

This attention to the legal political inputs in the policy of law analysis also comprehends those values that, for several reasons, apparently did not find a directly corresponding space in the legal arena, those that were not transformed into legal concepts or categories. The grasp of such legally infertile values can help the policy of law scholar to better understand other legally fertile values. In particular, the latter can perhaps be better understood when considered as a compromise solution, agreed upon in order to also give some legal space to certain tenets of the non-prevailing political party.[63]

The object of a policy of law investigation is, moreover, also unlocked as towards the social arena. In particular, an opening occurs at the moment of the investigation when the scholar suggests legal remedies to that which previously have been defined as 'discrepancies' between values and legal outputs. It is often only in light of the social consequences of a certain legal category (policy of law outcomes) that the policy of law analysis can discover that the legal outputs are a transformation of values (legal political inputs) other than those originally introduced into the law-making process.[64] For example, it was only after decades of waiting for congressional action with respect to the actual discriminatory policy of law

---

[62]   R Pound, *The Ideal Element in Law* (Calcutta, Calcutta University Press, 1958) 90. See also Hart, 'Problems of the Philosophy of Law' (n 41 above) 111; Raz, 'Authority, Law and Morality' (n 44 above) 221; and MDA Freeman, *Lloyd's Introduction to Jurisprudence* (7th edn, London, Sweet & Maxwell, 2001) 50–1. Aginst H Kelsen, 'Science and Politics' in H Kelsen, *What is Justice? Justice, Law, and Politics in the Mirror of Science* (Berkeley, University of California Press, 1957) 367–8. As to the importance of also taking into account procedural values in the investigation of the law-making process, see R Summers, 'Evaluating and Improving Legal Process: A Plea for "Process Values"' (1974) 60 *Cornell Law Review* 3.

[63]   An example in this sense can be seen in the policy of law analysis by W Pedersen, '"Protecting the Environment": What Does that Mean?' (1994) 27 *Loyola of Los Angeles Law Review* 969. See also C Sunstein, *Legal Reasoning and Political Conflict* (Oxford, Oxford University Press, 1996) 41; and C Sunstein, 'Constitutional Agreements without Constitutional Theories' (2000) 13 *Ratio Juris* 122–4, 128–30, stressing in particular *the constructive uses of silence.*

[64]   See Vago, *Law and Society* (n 18 above) 186–7.

outcomes of the legal category of 'separate but equal treatment' in the US community, that the US Supreme Court finally re-interpreted the constitutional principle of the prohibition against discrimination (Equal Protection Clause) into a new legal category of 'separation as inherently unequal' in the field of education.[65]

This expansion of the policy of law analysis to other disciplines does not suggest the loss of its fundamental normative nature. First, the analysis of policy of law still looks to the outside worlds from the legal internal point of view. The other two worlds (political and social) are scrutinised only if and to the extent they affect the system of binding categories and concepts known as law. In this way, the policy of law analysis avoids the criticism of being a sort of breakfast-jurisprudence of the law-making process. The policy of law analysis needs not take into consideration elements such as a bad breakfast for a legal actor, since this does not directly affect the system of legal categories but only the state of mind of the legal actor.

Secondly, policy of law scholars take into consideration the political and social arenas. They do not however base their work on such extra-legal dimensions. The focus of the policy of law analysis is still on the legal arena while giving a peripheral look at the surrounding political and social arenas. In a few words, to deprive the policy of law analysis of its normative status because of these openings would be like depriving Hart's jurisprudence of its normativity because of his recognition of the existence of a contingent minimum content of natural law in every legal system.[66]

Thirdly, central for the policy of law analysis are the legal outputs, ie the changes in the legal system directly relevant to the legal actors as normative and therefore binding. The indirect effects of a new legal category or concept on the legal world, ie via the social or the political arenas, remain outside this area. In particular, outside the area of investigation of the policy of law scholar are those cases of newly-made legal categories that, for several reasons, have not become legal outputs, ie they have not yet left any direct imprint either on the legal system or on the legal discourse in general.[67]

---

[65] See *Plessy v Ferguson*, 163 U.S. 551 (1896) and *Brown v Board of Education*, 347 U.S. 495 (1954). See also M Klarman, *From Jim Crow to Civil Rights: the Supreme Court and the Struggle for Racial Equality* (Oxford, Oxford University Press, 2004) 292–312. As to some of the problems of tracing the original legal political inputs introduced into the legal arena, see eg, R Dworkin, *A Matter of Principle* (Cambridge, Harvard University Press, 1985) 48–50. See also R Dworkin, *Freedom's Law: the Moral Reading of the American Constitution* (Cambridge, Harvard University Press, 1996) 155–62; and R Bork, *The Tempting of America: the Political Seduction of the Law* (New York, Touchtone/Simon and Schuster, 1990) 107–10.

[66] See HLA Hart, 'Comment' in R Gavison (ed), *Issues in Contemporary Legal Philosophy: the Influence of H.L.A. Hart* (Oxford, Clarendon Press, 1987) 35–6. See also Bix, *Jurisprudence* (n 6 above) 46–7.

[67] See eg, the symbolic function played by an ineffective law-making on the social arena as in M Edelman, *The Symbolic Uses of Politics* (Urbana, University of Illinois Press, 1964) 37.

IV. CONCEPTUAL APPARATUS OF THE POLICY OF LAW SCHOLAR

This distinctiveness as to the nature and object of the policy of law analysis, a jurisprudential hard core with extensive overlapping into the political and social sciences, does not leave the conceptual apparatus employed in the policy of law analysis unaffected. The conceptual apparatus to be used in a policy of law analysis has its focal point inside jurisprudence. In analysing the transformational moment, the policy of law analysis takes a position inside the legal order. It evaluates the phenomenon, making use for cognitive purposes largely of both the conceptual and types of legal rationality shared by the legal actors.[68]

The inputs, the transformational process and the final legal outputs are scrutinised making use of key legal concepts such as 'legal validity'. These legal concepts allow the researcher to consider whether and to what extent the value inputs, the transformational process and the legal outputs are directly relevant for the legal order or, generally, whether and how they somehow will imprint or have imprinted the legal culture shared by the legal actors.[69]

For example, in investigating a new statute obliging monopolistic corporations to refrain from entering into certain contracts in order to break their monopoly, the policy of law scholar will tend to avoid the use of non-legal conceptual tools, such as those of an economic or moral nature. He or she will avoid the issue of the effect on the supply/demand of the market for the monopolised goods, or the 'justice' for a single customer against a large corporation. Instead, both the formation and the imprinting that the new legal concept of the 'obligation to refrain from entering into monopolistic contracts' has or will have on the actual contractual legal system, and in particular with respect to the legally valid concept of freedom of contract, will be scrutinised and evaluated.

Despite this jurisprudential hard core, the conceptual tools at the disposal of the policy of law analysis tend to glide into other epistemological fields, in particular those of the political and social sciences. The policy of law analysis concerns, as seen before, the legal phenomenon positioned

Despite this 'invisibility' in the legal arena, the new and ineffective legal concept can, however, become indirectly relevant to the policy of law investigation because it can stimulate (eg in the form of debates) both the social and the political actors to send into the legal arena new values in order to be transformed into law. See V Aubert, 'The Rule of Law and the Promotional Function of Law in the Welfare State' in G Teubner (ed), *Dilemmas of Law in the Welfare State* (Berlin, Walter de Gruyter, 1986) 32.

[68] See eg, Rivlin and Potts, 'Proposed Rule Changes to Federal Civil Procedure' (n 36 above) 530–9. See also MacCormick, *Legal Reasoning and Legal Theory* (n 44 above) 292.

[69] See eg, K Greenawalt, 'Religious Convictions and Lawmaking' (1086) 84 *Michigan Law Review* 400. See also HLA Hart, *The Concept of Law* (Oxford, Clarendon Press, 1961) 95–6; and, as to the idea of legal culture, T Grey, 'Judicial Review and Legal Pragmatism' (2003) 38 *Wake Forest Law Review* 478.

in both a structural and functional intermediary position between the political and the social arenas. It is then unavoidable that the policy of law scholar, because of this bridging position taken by the object of the investigation, is equipped with at least some of the conceptual and epistemological apparatus built up by the disciplines dealing specifically with the two ends of the construction, political science and sociology.[70]

Of course, it is possible to investigate the ramifications of the policy process into the social or political arenas by using a purely legal conceptual apparatus. However, by keeping the conceptual legal purity, a scholar runs the high risk of missing one central point of policy of law: that policy of law concerns the transformation into law of something which is not law. In order to then understand the transformational process, one needs not only look into the final result (legal category), but also to have an idea of the beginning of the process (value). Although mainly making use of a legal conceptual apparatus, the policy of law analysis cannot ignore concepts and investigative tools such as 'discourse', 'power', 'legitimacy', 'groups of interests', 'arenas', 'networks' and 'coupling'. Concepts such as 'power' and 'legitimacy' have been widely used in the legal discipline, in particular by those jurisprudential scholars that have embraced an embedded model in explaining the relationships between law and politics. Moreover, Hohfeld already in the early 1900s considered 'power' and 'privilege' to be two of the fundamental concepts of the legal discipline, or, in his words, as 'the lowest common denominators of the law'.[71]

Despite this legal theoretical open-mindedness, it is generally true that concepts like these do not have a direct relevance for the legal order. The lack of the direct legal relevance of concepts such as 'arenas' or 'groups of interests' denotes that the conceptual apparatus developed by the political and social sciences is usually not accepted as having a normative status in legal reasoning. For example, few judges (and even less drafting committees) dare to base decisions (at least explicitly) on concepts such as 'coupling', 'discourse' or 'legitimacy'. Even in the legal theoretical debate,

---

[70] This necessity of opening the conceptual tool kit of jurisprudence in general to other branches of human knowledge is felt by many contemporary legal scholars. See eg, the political concept of 'interests groups' in D Farber and P Frickey, 'The Jurisprudence of Public Choice' (1987) 65 *Texas Law Review* 883; or the sociological concept of 'institutions' in K Llewellyn, 'Law and the Social Sciences: Especially Sociology' (1949) 62 *Harvard Law Review* 1305; and more recently in N MacCormick and O Weinberger, *An Institutional Theory of Law: New Approaches to Legal Positivism* (Dordrecht, D Reidel Publishing Company, 1986) 2–5, 11–12. See also Tuori, *Critical Legal Positivism* (n 41 above) 134–5.

[71] W Hohfeld, 'Fundamental Legal Conceptions as applied in Juridical Reasoning' (1916–17) 26 *Yale Law Journal* 710. See also Kennedy, *A Critique of Adjudication (fin de siècle)* (n 5 above) 15–16; and J Raz, 'Government by Consent' in Raz, *Ethics in the Public Domain* (n 44 above) 341–2.

the intrusion by Hohfeld into other conceptual fields, for example, has always been viewed with some sort of suspicion by the generality of the legal scholars.[72]

These concepts nevertheless can have an indirect relevance; that is they can present strong and deep links with the formation of concepts traditionally considered as belonging to the legal arena. For example, the idea of legitimacy (and in particular in its rational version) is today strictly connected to the idea of a 'legally competent' authority, ie to the 'belief in the legality of enacted rules and the right of those elevated to authority under such rules to issue command'.[73] They can then be extremely helpful and necessary to the investigation of the relations between the legal arena and the two other arenas, ie the social and the political ones.[74] In particular, only with concepts such as 'actors', 'legitimacy', 'culture' or 'ideology' is it possible not only to thoroughly analyse the entire policy of law process and its results but also to produce problem-solving solutions with a higher degree of success.

As stated not only by empirically orientated legal scholars (such as legal realists) but also by contemporary legal positivists (such as McCormick and Weinberger) and representative of the embedded model (such as law and economics), law at the end is not done for its own sake but in order to regulate a social reality.[75] Therefore, the policy of law analysis, although it has to keep its gravitational centre inside the legal discipline, can only benefit from the extension of its conceptual apparatus. This expansion ends up also including those investigative categories and definitions built up for instance by social sciences for the very purpose of better understanding the social reality the law is to regulate.[76]

These concepts from the political and social sciences are fundamental to fully grasp which values lie behind certain legal concepts, to understand whether and to what extent the legal concepts are the legal version of the values and, finally, to have a clearer depiction of the social environment in which the legal concepts are or have been operating. For example, a scholar can investigate the policy process that has led the value of protecting the community from significant environmental damage to be

---

[72] See eg, H Randall, *Hohfeld on Jurisprudence* (1925) 41 *LQR* 90; or T Spaak, 'Norms that Confer Competence' (2003) 16 *Ratio Juris* 89 n 2. See also A Stone Sweet, 'Constitutional Politics in France and Germany' in M Shapiro and A Stone Sweet, *On Law, Politics, and Judicialization* (Oxford, Oxford University Press, 2002) 187.

[73] M Weber, *Economy and Society* (G Roth and C Wittich (eds), Berkeley, University of California Press, 1978) 215.

[74] See Tuori, *Critical Legal Positivism* (n 41 above) 278.

[75] Exemplary as to this common point of departure for many contemporary legal scholars is the initial statement in R Pound, 'My Philosophy of Law' in *My Philosophy of Law: Credos of Sixteen American Scholars* (Boston, Boston Law Book, 1941) 249.

[76] See eg, W Twining, *Law in Context: Enlarging a Discipline* (Oxford, Clarendon Press, 1997) 110.

transformed into the legal concept of the 'protection of diffuse interests'. The purely legal conceptual apparatus here is unable to grasp the fundamental role played by the environmental organisations and their value of considering the environment as 'common good of the community' in the formation of such legal concepts.[77] The insufficiency of the legal analytical tools can be caused by the fact that these organisations lack a legally recognised place in the law-making process. For example, their opinions are not required by administrative law in the procedure which grants permission for the establishment of a factory in an area.

If one only uses the internal legal perspective in the policy of law analysis, then one runs the risk of considering as non-existing for the transformational process these actors and their value of 'common good' (because they both are not 'legally valid' or, in other words, not recognised by the legal system). This lack of consideration can produce a hole in the explanation of the transformational process, particularly in the case where it is the environmental organisations' very value that succeeds in getting transformed.

The risk of a gap can then be avoided by using parts of the conceptual apparatus from the political and social sciences. The tools from these sciences can help clarify for the policy of law analysis the central role played by the environmental organisation (and its values) in the transformational process into the legal arena, a central role built upon the fact that the organisation is considered a 'legitimate' voice in the environmental discussion at least in both the political and social arenas.[78]

In the policy of law analysis, its normative hard core then co-exists with several important socio-political segments (see Figure 5.1), a co-existence mainly due to the crossing in the reality of the processes of policy of law into the political and socio-legal phenomena. For example, the multiplicity and often conflictual character of the value-inputs coming out from the political arena have to be taken into consideration by the policy of law scholar when they become directly relevant for the transformational moment. This is the case when the battle among opposite and equally strong values at the political level results in empty legal categories and concepts. The latter already from the beginning can lack the necessary legal tools for their implementation; the legal competence for monitoring the actual execution of the legal category is, for instance, not delegated to any organ. Always keeping in mind these structural and conceptual overlappings, the fundamental features distinguishing the policy of law analysis

---

[77] See Gottlieb, 'The Paradox of Balancing Significant Interests' (n 57 above) 847. See also MacCormick, *Legal Reasoning and Legal Theory* (n 44 above) 239; and Freeman, *Lloyd's Introduction to Jurisprudence* (n 62 above) 14–15.

[78] See C Schroeder, 'Prophets, Priests, and Pragmatists' (2003) 87 *Minnesota Law Review* 1065.

from her sister investigations, legal politics and the sociology of law can nevertheless be summarised as in Table 5.1.

Table 5.1: Politics of law analysis, policy of law analysis and sociology of law

	Main perspective in evaluating the legal phenomenon	Main objects of investigation	Main conceptual apparatus
Analysis of the politics of law	Political arena	The formation of and resulting inputs to be transformed into law in order to be implemented in a community.	Political science
Analysis of the policy of law	Legal arena	The transformational process of the legal political inputs into legal outputs inside the legal arena, the imprinting such outputs have on the legal order (and vice versa).	Legal discipline
Sociology of law	Social arena	The outcomes from the legal arena and their actual effects on the community (and vice versa).	Social sciences

V. SOME FINAL COMMENTS ON THE POLICY OF LAW ANALYSIS

The phenomenon of the implementation of values into the society has been the object of many studies, both in political science and the social sciences.[79] Moreover, the investigation of how, in general, the law is used to make people follow certain patterns of behaviours (or in other words, for introducing into the community values or authoritative models of behaviours) is certainly not new to jurisprudence.[80]

The policy of law analysis, however, can open for itself an autonomous position in the investigations of the law-making process, a position

---

[79] See eg, A Blumrosen, 'Legal Process and Labor Law: Some Observations on the relation between Law and Sociology' in W Evan (ed), *Law and Sociology* (New York, Free Press of Glencoe, 1962) 191–212.

[80] See eg, Hart, 'Postscript' (n 41 above) 249.

between the approaches of political science and sociology. In contrast to the political and social sciences, the policy of law analysis aims at opening the grey box represented by the transformational processes and its results with the keys of jurisprudence. The policy of law analysis takes into primary consideration the use and the construction of conceptual legal tools created by the legal actors as the decisive (but not sole) factors in introducing certain values into the legal order.[81]

The policy of law analysis also distances itself from the previous jurisprudential studies as to the issue of the policy moment of the law-making. For the latter studies, the analysis of such a moment tends to actually be a part of a more general investigation of how the law relates to its surrounding environment. In the end, not much attention has been specifically paid to understanding the processes occurring inside the transformational moment, the focus mainly being on discovering which parts of the law correspond to which pieces of either the political or social realities.

The analysis of the policy of law, on the contrary, has as a primary target the very investigation of the transformational moment. Specifically, it studies how and to what extent the three main arenas (political, legal and social) interact in the transformation of the values into a specific language, the legal language (the policy of law process). Secondly, the policy of law analysis has as its main object (and not as a consequence or presupposition) of the investigation the impact the results these interactions have on the legal system; in other words, the effects of the chosen or invented legal categories on the existing law (policy of law decisions).

This, of course, does not mean that the policy of law analysis is the sole and correct perspective from which to observe the moment of policy of law in the law-making process. However, this is a space where the legal actors and their ideas of law have a prominent role. The transformational moment is one of the first places in the law-making process where the normative perception of the legal phenomenon becomes decisive.[82] Therefore, it is necessary to strengthen the role and the position of this branch of knowledge, the policy of law analysis, that, although taking into consideration both the social and political dimensions of the policy process and

---

[81] On the contrary, as pointed out by Tuori, '[i]n the division of labour between the branches of science, the exploration of the external determinants of legal dynamics falls within the domain of social sciences, such as politology or the sociology of law'. Tuori, *Critical Legal Positivism* (n 41 above) 199.

[82] See eg, R Summers, 'Policy on the Anvil of Law' in R Summers, *Essays on the Nature of Law and Legal Reasoning* (Berlin, Duncker & Humblot, 1992) 193–6, though his 'policy' and legal 'desideratum' stands for legal political inputs and policy of law outputs respectively in this work.

its results, is still able to give an account of the transformational moment from the perspective of the main actors, the legal ones.[83]

This is furthermore helpful if one considers the fact that disciplines are often carried out not only in order to explore the object of the investigation. A discipline (and in this, the legal ones are not an exception) also aims, in light of the results of such exploration, to change the object. In this case, the policy of law analysis can contribute considerably, offering both explorations and proposals in a language and in a rationality which is understood (and shared) by one of the most important makers inside the law-making process: the legal actor.

VI. CONCLUSION

The main task of this chapter has been to establish of the fundamental ambitions, objects and conceptual apparatus of the analysis of the policy of law. As a preliminary step, it has been seen how both the politics of law analysis and the sociology of law, despite their close connections with the policy of law studies, primarily aim at moments in the law-making process other than the transformational one. These divergences, moreover, are strengthened both by the different perspectives from which they investigate the phases of the law-making processes and results, and by the different conceptual apparatus legal politics and legal sociology use. Having framed the external (and often unclear) borders of the policy of law studies, attention has been shifted inwards, in the challenge of identifying the basic elements of the policy of law analysis.

The policy of law investigation looks at the transformation of values into law from the legal perspective, that is the perspective of the actors belonging to the legal arena. From this point, the policy of law analysis studies both the transformational process of the legal political inputs into legal outputs inside the legal arena, and the imprinting such outputs have on the legal order (and vice versa). These legal inquiries tend to have their programmatic, ontological and conceptual focal points inside the legal discipline, in particular inside the legal theoretical dimension of jurisprudence. Nevertheless, subsequent to the open nature of its object of investigation, the analysis of policy of law must often intersect with political and sociological studies.

---

[83] See eg, C Grant Bowman and E Schneider, 'Feminist Legal Theory, Feminist Lawmaking, and the Legal Profession' (1998) 67 *Fordham Law Review* 249. The authors investigate in particular the central role played by the interrelations between legal scholars and lawyers in the law-making process dealing with gender issues.

The next and final chapter will, after a brief summary, sketch the possible uses of policy of law analysis in the solution of some of the major problems the legal world nowadays faces: globalisation and gender. Moreover, some directions of future development of policy of law studies will be presented.

6

The Policy of Law Analysis: What is the Point?

I N THE FAMOUS decision, *Bush v Gore*, the US Supreme Court states:

> None are more conscious of the vital limits on judicial authority than are the Members of this Court, and none stand more in admiration of the Constitution's design to leave the selection of the President to the people, through their legislatures, and to the political sphere. *When contending parties invoke the process of the courts, however, it becomes our unsought responsibility to resolve the federal and constitutional issues the judicial system has been forced to confront.*[1] (emphasis added)

This statement epitomises one of the major difficulties confronting legal actors today. Educated universally in the belief that law and politics are two separate worlds, and that lawyers should avoid political issues as much as possible, legal actors realise when faced with real issues not only that they are forced to deal with politics but also that, occasionally, the very responsibility of choosing a political course for an entire community will fall onto their shoulders. The present work has attempted to contribute to clarifying one of the spaces in which legal actors meet political issues. The aim in particular has been to fence off such a space by providing a theoretical framework for the moment in the law-making process in which political issues become directly relevant for the legal world and its inhabitants: the policy of law.

I. A SYNOPSIS

The construction of this theoretical framework began by investigating how the relationship of law and politics has been considered and treated in contemporary legal theory. Chapter one loosely applied Weber's ideal-types as a heuristic device in order to show how contemporary legal theory has

[1] *George W. Bush v Albert Gore, Jr*, 531 U.S. 112 (2000).

depicted the relationship of law and politics according to three fundamental models: the autonomous model, the embedded model and the intersecting model. The criteria used for assembling the legal theories into these ideal-typical models are the answers they give to three main issues with respect to the relationship of law and politics: how contemporary legal scholars view the concept of law in relation to politics (the *static* aspect), law-making in relation to the political order (the *dynamic* aspect) and the position of the legal discipline towards the political material (the *epistemological* aspect).

If the legal theory postulated a sharp distinction between the legal phenomenon and the world of politics, it was categorised as within the autonomous model. Examples of such theories are legal positivism (as posited by Kelsen) and analytical jurisprudence (in the writings of Hart). Although with different modalities as well as several exceptions and mitigations, both Kelsen and Hart tend to endorse a vision of the law as *rigid* toward politics, produced by a law-making *closed* to the discourse and rationality of the political order, to be studied by a *pure* legal discipline, leaving politics to the other disciplines.

The legal movements adopting an embedded model have been positioned on the other side of the map, depicting positions as endorsed by contemporary legal theories as to law and politics, CLS, John Finnis' natural law theory, as well as law and economics. These theories tend to exhibit a *flexible* nature of the law towards the political phenomenon, the law-making tends to be *open* to the political discourses and political rationalities, and legal studies must endorse a *mixed* nature, integrating the legal discipline with categories and concepts belonging to sociology, psychology, political sciences and economics.

The American and Scandinavian legal realisms have been placed under the third ideal-typical model in which law and politics are two intersecting phenomena. Both these legal realist theories, despite their differences, aim at retaining the specificity of the nature of law towards politics, a law which remains *partially rigid* in its relations to the political phenomenon, created by a law-making *open* to the political actors' discourse, to be investigated by a legal discipline, *partially mixed* with material coming in both generally from non-legal disciplines and specifically, from the political world.

The fact that the contemporary legal theories covered by these three models operate on a common field, from which their different perspectives all commence, is highlighted at the end of chapter one. The issue of the relations between law and politics is first one of the central concerns for contemporary legal theories, no matter how such theories then answer the question. Secondly, each theory recognises that law and politics are two different objects, regardless of where legal scholars then position the law with respect to politics (separated, embedded or intersecting). Thirdly, the legal and the political phenomena necessarily interact with each other within each theory, although the range of the frequency of such interaction varies considerably from a zenith (as in the embedded model) to a nadir (as in the autonomous model).

Based on these considerations, chapter two explores the possibility of framing one of the bridges connecting the legal boundary to the political one. In particular, the focus is on one of the areas in which law and politics meet, the *transformational moment*. This is the moment at which the values produced inside the political arena are transformed into legal categories and concepts. The majority of contemporary legal theories depict this moment as mirroring the general dilemma currently faced by the law. On one side, due to the high degree of politicisation of the legal phenomenon, legal scholars are forced to give the transformational moment (although attaching to it a different nature as well as functions) a central position in their visions of the law and its creation. On the other side, because of the accelerating tendency towards a more specialised law, most legal scholars (with the partial exception of legal realists and certain others) tend to leave any systematic analysis of this moment at which values are transformed into legal categories and concepts at the periphery of their investigation.

In order to open a wider space in the legal-theoretical discussion as to such a crucial transformational moment in the life of the law and law-making, the distinction as made by political scientists between the *politics* and the *policy* dimensions of the process of formation and implementation of political decisions is highlighted in chapter three. If the definition of policy as postulated by political scientists, a *network* of both *processes* and *decisions* with a *conversional function* of inputs into outputs is accepted, this concept of policy becomes the most suitable analytical tool to assist legal theories in penetrating the transformational moment of the law-making process.

Furthermore, this characterisation as developed inside political science has brought to the surface the deficiencies of the idea of policy as used today by legal actors (both scholars and practitioners) or, in other words, the deficiencies of the normative perspective of policy. This perspective by legal actors has limited the meaning of policy to only one part of the phenomenon as identified by political scientists: the final result (standards) in the form of political evaluations and decisions affecting the legal world.

Chapters four and five redesign the theoretical frameworks of the transformational moment and its analysis respectively in accordance to the above. This begins with an enlargement of the normative idea of policy in the directions indicated by political scientists (policy as conversional processes and results). In particular, the possibility of defining the transformational moment as the moment at which the policy of law takes place is tested.

The redesign of the policy of law takes the following two-step path. In the first step, a model explaining the position and function of the transformational moments in the law-making process is developed. A space can be opened up in the law-making activity between the formation of values in the political world (politics of law) and the impact of the newly-made law on the social world (policy of law outcomes). This space is defined as *the policy of law*, a space in which values entrenched in political decisions are transformed into law, having an effect on the existing legal order. The policy of law has been furthermore defined as a web of conversional processes and decisions located inside the legal arena. These processes and decisions are directed at transforming the values produced in the political arena (legal political inputs) into concepts and categories directly relevant into the legal world (policy of law outputs). In contemporary law-making, this space of the policy of law is mainly the domain for the work and reasoning of the actors belonging to the legal world. However, the borders of the policy of law as so defined often tend to cross into the spaces in which decisions about values are taken (politics of law) and where the law becomes a socially relevant phenomenon (policy of law outcomes).

After the establishment of the existence of such a moment of 'policy of law' in the law-making process, the second step, as explored in chapter five, consists of setting up the fundamental ambitions, objects and conceptual apparatus of *the analysis of the policy of law*. This analysis is characterised, both in its object and its investigative tools, as different from the other two neighbouring types of studies: the *politics of law analysis* and the *sociology of law*. The latter, despite their close connections with the policy of law studies, aim primarily at different moments in the law-making process. These divergences, moreover, are strengthened both by the different perspectives and by the different conceptual apparatus adopted by legal politics and the sociology of law in investigating the phases of the law-making processes and results.

Further, in meeting the challenge of identifying the basic elements of the policy of law analysis, it has been demonstrated that the policy of law investigation should be encompassed among the legal disciplines, in particular inside jurisprudence. Nevertheless, subsequent to the intermediary nature of its object of investigation (located between the political choices and the social impacts on and of the law), the policy of law analysis often intersects with studies, data and conceptual apparatus of a political and sociological nature.

II. LOCAL, SUPRANATIONAL AND INTERNATIONAL DIMENSIONS OF THE POLICY OF LAW

The discussion presented here focuses on policy of law processes and results occurring solely at the national level for reasons of clarity and space.[2] More importantly, national law-making has been presupposed as hypothetically waterproof to impacts coming from non-national law-making, namely from local (eg in a federal system), supranational (eg European Union) or international law-makings (*eg* World Trade Organisation). For example, the issue of whether and to what extent the harmonisation of a national law-making with the European community law affects its law-making processes and results, and in particular its policy of law, has not been taken up in this work.

The importance of the policy of law, however, does not cease upon the introduction in the analysis of these local, supranational and international dimensions of the law-making process. In contrast, the importance of considering the policy moment, the moment at which values become legal categories, increases considerably if one positions national law-making into a broader context of influences (of a political, social or legal character) coming from institutional actors other than the domestic ones.

In investigating an actual law-making process taking place at the national level, the policy of law analyst cannot only consider the horizontal structures and developments of the policy process and results, ie the interactions between the different national arenas (political, social and legal). He or she must also investigate the policy moments at their vertical dimension, ie in their interactions with 'superior' (eg at the EU or UN level) and 'inferior' (eg at the federal state or regional level) law-making processes, institutional actors and arenas.[3]

This enlargement does not contradict that which has been stated in this work. First, the localisation, supernationalisation or internationalisation of the policy of law processes, ie their being affected by that which happens outside the national dimension, does not concern the entire spectrum of national law-making. For example, while the importance for the national policy of law of the international political, social and legal arenas in matters such as monetary policy and environmental issues is evident, the phenomenon is much more limited in areas such as taxation or labour disputes. Secondly, the enlargement, when it occurs, seems to influence

---

[2] The concept of policy is widely used in the literature and practice of international and supranational law. Although this perspective has not been investigated in the present work, the international and supranational legal environments tend to employ the concept with the same meaning and limitations as described for the national dimension as examined in chapter three.

[3] See eg, A-M Slaughter, 'Judicial Globalization' (2000) 40 *Vanderbilt Journal of International Law* 1103.

more the quantitative aspects of the policy processes and results rather than their qualitative features. The result is that no total subversion of the essence of the policy processes and results as framed in this work can be detected. In other words, the policy moment of the law-making process is still present and maintains its central position in determining the techniques and reasons behind the transformations (both at national and non-national levels) of values into legal categories and concepts.

The number of actors and interactions certainly multiplies. Actors such as the European Commission or the London Maritime Arbitrators' Association must be taken into account in order to fully understand the reasons behind a certain act as adopted in a national legal order directed at regulating the transportation of goods.[4] However, the essence of the policy process does not change. The focus simply has to expand to the modalities and the results (and their reception by the national law-makers) through which at a European or international level the economic value of favouring the exchange of goods has been transformed into a limited liability for carriers. Moreover, persons specially trained to work with the law and its specific way of reasoning will usually make (or propose) policy of law decisions both in Brussels and London. Even at the local, supranational or international levels, political actors constantly make use of legal experts when placing their ideas and values into law.

Therefore, even if at a higher (or lower) level, national legal actors usually interact with other (international, supranational or local) legal actors, actors sharing the same or a similar rationality of legal discourse (at least in the Western legal world), playing the same central role in transforming values into local, supranational or international law. This introduces another reason for not dismissing the policy of law and its analysis when discussing local, supranational and international levels of the legal phenomenon. The policy of law, its processes and results are not simply fundamental at a national level, ie when it comes to integrating into a national legal system legal categories developed somewhere else. The processes and results of policy of law can also play a fundamental role in the law-making processes occurring at the local, supranational and international levels.

It is true that in the local, supranational and international law-making processes, the role of non-legal actors (and their value-rationality as opposed to legal rationality) often appears to be dominating (almost monopolising) the production or adoption of new legal categories and concepts. Legal provisions as written by a county council or by the European Commission are often cited as purely political products, ie

---

[4] See R Cotterrell, *The Sociology of Law: an Introduction* (2nd edn, London, Butterworths, 1992) 37.

simply as a purely political (value) discourse printed on legal paper. One recent example is the decision by the US President to invade Iraq, endorsed into a legally relevant decision as taken by Congress. The desire to 'neutralise' a long-time opponent was certainly one of the major political values heavily inundating the legally relevant decision taken by the President together with Congress, legally authorising the employment of US troops on Iraqi soil.

This highlighting of the central role of non-legal actors in the law-making process is certainly correct, but only to a certain extent. Even in the most politically characterised outputs of a local, supranational or international law-making process, the actors promoting or pushing for the implementation of certain values into a (local, supranational or international) community, most of the time feel the need of transforming or, in other words, of justifying their values behind a curtain of legal categories and concepts. In the case of Iraq, for example, both the US President and Congress repeatedly felt the necessity of transforming their value of eliminating a possible enemy by making use of legal categories based either on different interpretations of previous UN resolutions or on a legal right to self-defence. Once this failed to find support among the majority of the actors in the international community, the US government tried, from the already settled legal category of 'pre-emptive self-defence', to construct a new legal category in international public law, namely the concept of 'preventive war'. In both cases, the attempts have been in the direction of a policy of international law: to transform a purely political value (to punish enemies of the United States) into a legal category in order to then implement such values into the international community.[5]

In summary, the policy of law and its investigation does not lose its validity once the fact that the law-making process of a national legal order normally operates inside a web of relations with local, supranational and international actors as well as laws is taken into consideration. On the contrary, the policy of law process remains central in order to understand not only the relations of the national law-making process with the legal categories produced above or below it, but also for comprehending and explaining why and how certain legal categories and concepts have been produced and/or adopted by the very law-making processes occurring at the local, supranational and international levels.[6]

---

[5] See GW Bush, 'Introduction' to the National Security Strategy of the United States of America (last accessed 30 May 2006) www.whitehouse.gov/nsc/nss.htlm and M O'Hanlon et al, 'Policy Brief 113: the New National Security Strategy and Preemption' (accessed 30 May 2006) www.brook.edu/comm/policybriefs/pb113.htm.

[6] For an example of an analysis of the policy process occurring at the supranational level, see O Lando, 'Comparative Law and Lawmaking' (2000) 75 *Tulane Law Review* 1015.

III. THE POLICY OF LAW ANALYSIS AND CERTAIN
CONTEMPORARY PHENOMENA

Now that the main theoretical frameworks for the policy of law and its investigation are established, the centrality of the transformational process must be briefly examined in order to understand certain phenomena which heavily affect the legal world today and, in particular, the law-making processes. The main goal here is to offer a framework within which to develop a possible middle-range theory concerning the law-making process, explaining only components of the phenomenon, in this case the moment of policy of law. In this way, this middle-range theory of the law-making process can serve as a bridge between the 'detailed workaday hypotheses' and the 'comprehensive analytical schemes'.[7]

The policy of law analysis, by inserting the single contributions of legal actors into the more general phenomenon of law-making, can function as a channel permitting the insertion of the micro-theories of legal phenomenon (eg those explaining, for example, the behaviours of appellate courts) into macro-theories dealing with the law (eg those theories establishing the general positions the law has or should have towards values). If one considers two major developments affecting contemporary legal work as well as thought, namely globalisation and the gender analysis of law, the importance of such a middle-range theory of the law-making process clearly emerges not only in helping macro-theories in explaining larger events. This middle-range theory of the law-making process can also offer solutions to certain problems that can accompany such contemporary phenomena into the legal world.

A. The Policy of Law Analysis and Globalisation

The phenomenon of globalisation from a legal perspective can be defined as the circulation of legal models (ie legal categories and concepts) in a way that has rendered many different aspects of the different national legal systems homogeneous.[8] This 'homogenisation of legal problems and of

---

[7] R Merton, 'The Role-Set: Problems in Sociological Theory' (1957) 28 *British Journal of Sociology* 108.

[8] See W Twining, *Globalisation and Legal Theory* (London, Butterworths, 2000) ch 1. See also E Heger Boyle and J Meyer, 'Modern Law as a Secularized and Global Model: Implications for the Sociology of Law' in Y Dezalay and B Garth (eds), Global Prescriptions: the Production, Exportation, and Importation of a New Legal Orthodoxy (Ann Arbor, University of Michigan Press, 2002) 66–9.

legal responses to these problems' has occurred in particular with respect to such issues as human rights, capital punishment and numerable commercial issues.[9]

Once globalisation is defined in these terms, the fundamental contribution which a policy of law analysis can bring to the understanding of the phenomenon becomes evident, in particular if the analysis is taken from a normative perspective. The circulation of legal models receives a form of sanction, either *ex ante* or *ex post*, by the national or international legal actors. Legislative bodies, judges, arbitrators and lawyers become the central (although not exclusive) figures in this law-making process, allowing the transformation of global legal categories and concepts into legal categories and concepts with a legal status in their own (international, supranational or national) communities. One example is the increasing role played by national labour courts, in the face of the declining importance with respect to union membership, as the principal route for employees to enforce their fundamental 'floor of rights' as recognised at an international level.[10]

In addition to this function of increasing the understanding of the process of globalisation, policy of law studies can also help to solve certain problems connected thereto. Far from being a developmental and linear phenomenon in general, globalisation also raises many issues and problems in the legal world. One is the difficulty encountered by many global legal categories and concepts in actually having a concrete effect on the daily life of the receiving community; for example, the failure of many typically capitalistic economic legal tools to actually implement a capitalistic mindset in the business communities of traditionally non-capitalistic countries attempting to take on many of the features characterising Western legal systems (eg Russia).

This 'malfunction' of the phenomenon of globalisation can partially be explained with a policy of law analysis. First, it is necessary to distinguish, within the phenomenon of globalisation, between the *globalisation of the policy of law* and the *globalisation of the politics of law*. By the *globalisation of the policy of law* is meant that there presently is a tendency by which the same legal categories and concepts are received in many national and international legal orders. In other words, legal actors around the world tend to use the same kind of legal tools, eg the legal category of 'limited financial liability' as a quality attached to the legal position of a

---

[9] C Baudenbacher, 'Judicial Globalization: New Development or Old Wine in New Bottles?' (2003) 38 *Texas International Law Journal* 505. See also generally the assorted contributions in V Gessner and A Cem Budak (eds), *Emerging Legal Certainty: Empirical Studies on the Globalization of Law* (Aldershot, Ashgate Publishing, 1998).

[10] See S Adler, 'The Role of Judges in the Implementation of Social Policies' (2002) 18 *International Journal of Comparative Labor Law and Industrial Relations* 374.

shareholder. Not necessarily corresponding to this general tendency is an underpinning general *globalisation of the politics of law*. The latter indicates the phenomenon according to which various national and international communities similarly share values underlying these global legal categories and concepts.

The relatively centralised and authoritative feature of contemporary law-making processes usually facilitates the adoption in a legal system of global legal categories. Few members of a drafting committee, for example, quickly decide to embrace and impose upon an entire national community a foreign legal category such as limited financial liability for shareholders. The introduction of new 'foreign' values into a community is more difficult, as the value-making process lacks authoritative force and often the centralised character typical for the legal phenomenon. In Habermas' words, 'the political transformation of values and attitudes is not a process of blind adaptation', a blind adaptation which, in contrast, is expected by the members of a community facing new categories as embraced in a legal text.[11] Changes in a community's values are often the result of a long and complex process of 'constructive opinion and will-formation'.[12]

These structural differences exist between the legal politics and the policy of law of globalisation. For example, in the receiving country, the value underlying the adoption of a limited financial liability for shareholders can actually not be the one (global) of promoting a flux of new financial resources in economic activities but simply the one of promoting financial speculations. By identifying the possibility of such gaps between the policy and the politics moments of legal globalisation, the policy of law analyst can then recommend that more attention be paid to the intentions of the political and social arenas (legal inputs) behind the adoption of a law-making process suggested and/or promoted by globalising forces (eg the WTO).

Even if one assumes that the globalisation of legal categories (policy of law) mirrors a parallel and simultaneous globalisation of the underpinning values (legal politics), the observation of the phenomenon from the standpoint of the transformational moment can help to explain some of the failures of the process of globalisation.[13] The political and social arenas can present favourable and encouraging conditions for the acceptance of new legal categories and concepts. They can both agree on a true globalised politics of law, ie they promote and sustain the transformation

---

[11] J Habermas, *Between Facts and Norms: Contributions to a Discourse Theory of Law and Democracy* (Cambridge, The MIT Press, 1998) 336.

[12] *Ibid* 337.

[13] As an example of overlapping between globalisation of legal categories and globalisation of values, see A Seita, 'Globalization and the Convergence of Values' (1997) 30 *Cornell International Law Journal* 465.

of certain global values (eg encouraging the taking of risks in new economic activities) into global legal categories (eg the legal category of limited financial responsibility for shareholders). In other words, there is a situation in which the national environment is ready and sympathetic to the policy of law outcomes of a certain law-making process.

Despite these favourable conditions, globalisation processes can fail in actually implementing certain values when using global legal categories. This can happen because of the central role played by the legal world and its actors in the policy of law processes directed at transforming certain (already existing at global level) values into (also already existing at the domestic level) legal categories. The legal world can reject such categories for several reasons by stopping the production of any policy of law output. For example, the judges of a country, educated according to a Marxist legal tradition, can consistently and generally maintain the legal irrelevancy of a new category of limited financial liability for certain economic enterprises.

Moreover, the circulation of legal models can also be stopped by conditions peculiar to the receiving legal system. When legal actors transform global legal categories into binding categories for the community, ie the law-making process produces some legal outputs, because of the shape of the legal order, such outputs can be unable to have an impact on the social arena (no policy of law outcomes). For example, the receiving legal order lacks mechanisms of legal protection for financial institutions that are supposed to supply credit to newly established enterprises with limited financial liability.

It is just in this type of *impasse* that the policy of law analyst can intervene and offer a contribution. Focusing mainly on the legal actors and their transformational role, the policy of law analyst can point out where the process of introducing new legal categories in a legal order has been blocked. If the globalisation of the legal system has stopped, for example, before the production of legal inputs, then the solution should start with re-educating the legal actors. Reforming teaching in the law faculties, compulsory continuing legal education courses for judges, sabbaticals abroad for legal consultants working for the legislature, are some possible ways of re-invigorating and recommencing the law-making process.

In contrast, if there are legal outputs but they are ineffective, ie they do not produce any outcomes in the social arena, then the solutions of the policy of law scholar should probably be sought in more traditional directions: more attention to the panorama of legal scholarship during the law-making process (with contributions of well-established law professors to drafting committees), the simultaneous reform of the surrounding legal areas, longer transitional periods in which both the old and the new legal categories are allowed.

B. The Policy of Law Analysis and Gender

Starting in the early 1980s, gender has increasingly become a fixed standpoint in contemporary legal studies. The basic assumption of a gender perspective with respect to the legal phenomenon is that the law is far from being gender neutral and objective. On the contrary, the law is structured and expressed in a way, in the best of cases, which ignores the perspective of women or, in the worst cases, disadvantages their positions inside the legal system.[14] Several studies (mostly of socio-legal origin and under the roof of the different branches of the feminist legal theories) have proved not only the basic validity of such statements. They have also pointed out the failure of many of the legal reforms directed at recalibrating this lack of balance in the law in favour of men as the privileged object of attention and protection by the legal order in areas such as family law, employment law, domestic violence law and discrimination law.[15]

The policy of law analyst can also contribute here with respect to a better understanding and/or solutions to some of the problems arising as to gender issues attached to the law. He or she in particular can point out the reasons why certain values shared by a certain part of a community are not able to find their space in the legal system and, consequently, are unable to be implemented by law into a larger sector of the same community.

Two points of the policy process are of particular relevance for gender issues. The first concerns the already described difference between the politics and the policy dimensions of the law-making process. Many of the reforms in gender-related issues are condemned to failure from the beginning by the fact that the legal political inputs into the legal arena are already unclear.[16] This 'original sin' of the politics of law then imprints the entire policy of law process, giving birth to empty legal categories, ie to legal categories that potentially are carriers of conflicting legal outputs.

For example, the political arena can agree on the implementation by law of a 'my-body-my-choice' value. The latter is then transformed into a legislative measure sanctioning that women are the only legitimate holders of 'reproductive rights'. However, legal actors often lack a unified position as to the meaning of such a legal category. For some actors, the recognition of women as the only holder of reproductive rights simply means the

---

[14] See C Dalton, 'Commentary: Where We Stand: Observations on the Situation of Feminist Legal Thought' (1988) 3 *Berkeley Women's Law Journal* 2.

[15] See eg, L Frohmann and E Mertz, 'Legal Reform and Social Construction: Violence, Gender, and the Law' (1994) 19 *Law and Social Inquiry* 830.

[16] See Dalton, 'Commentary: Where We Stand' (n 14 above) 5–8. For a distinction between 'liberal' and 'social-welfare' values inside feminist legal thinking, see Habermas, *Between Facts and Norms* (n 11 above) 420–7. See also R Posner, 'Conservative Feminism' in DK Weisberg (ed), *Feminist Legal Theory: Foundations* (Philadelphia, Temple University Press, 1993) 99–117.

disruption of the barriers that impede women as to deciding when and whether to have a child. These legal actors then interpret such a legal category as a mere legalisation of abortion or anti-contraceptive advertisements, ie that hospitals are legally allowed to perform abortions or private broadcasting networks to permit advertisement as to day-after pills. In contrast, for other legal actors, the 'promotion by legislative measures of the reproductive rights of women' also means that women have the right to a more active role in both the public and private sectors in implementing their reproductive rights.[17] This can imply, for example, the duty of hospitals to perform abortions or the duty of private broadcasting networks to devote a certain amount of hours per year as to contraceptive advertisements.

The policy of law analyst can then intervene in such a situation suggesting a wide variety of solutions, ranging from a more specific and clearer text of the legislation (eg with non-binding explanatory appendixes) to the issuing of co-ordinated (in the sense of embracing one or the other line of interpretation) administrative acts of implementation by the competent governmental bodies (eg the Ministry of Health or the Ministry of Communication).[18]

In addition to this role in promoting an elucidation with respect to the passage from the legal politics to the policy of law dimensions of gender issues, the policy of law analyst can also play a major part in understanding and 'repairing' the law-making process by operating on its legal outputs. At times, the failure of efforts to modify by law the actual situation of a community are neither due to adverse political conditions (not permitting the formation of legal inputs) nor to any resistance to the legal reforms traceable at a social level (not allowing the legal outputs to become policy of law outcomes). The law-making process can give birth to legal categories and concepts that are unable to produce any concrete impact on the life of the community because they are unable to produce any impact on the legal system itself (ie no legal outputs).

This problem is particularly evident with respect to gender-related issues, fairly recently recognised issues confronting the legal system, a system that up to the present has tended to consider its main actors and target as male. The introduction into the legal system of legal categories expressing the value of gender often requires a change not only of the specific legal area the law-making process endows, but also of many surrounding legal areas.

---

[17] See K Kolbert, 'A Reproductive Rights Agenda for the 1990s' (1989) 1 *Yale Journal of Law and Feminism* 3.

[18] See eg, the policy of law measures suggested in J Hochberg, 'The Sacred Heart Story: Hospital Mergers and their Effects on Reproductive Rights' (1996) 75 *Oregon Law Review* 958. See also HLA Hart, 'Abortion Law Reform: the English Experience' (1972) 8 *Melbourne University Law Review* 409.

For example, problems can arise even when the legal category of reproductive rights is interpreted unanimously by different legal actors as including active participation of public and private actors. The activation of these actors for ensuring women's reproductive rights requires a transformation of the legal system which is broader than simply the imposition of a legal duty on the shoulders of some private or public actors. Otherwise, the legal category of reproductive rights runs the risk of becoming merely a ceramic crucible between iron pots of well-established legal categories.

Reproductive rights, interpreted as inclusive of the right to an active role by public and private actors, can conflict with those legal categories such as ensuring religious liberties (and, in particular, the legal right of Catholic doctors and/or hospitals to refuse to perform medical procedures conflicting with their religious beliefs) or freedom of speech (under which broadcasters can claim a right to choose which advertisements to air).[19] In such a case, the policy of law analyst can offer a large spectrum of suggestions directed at allowing the new legal category of reproductive rights to have an impact on the legal order (ie to produce some policy of law outputs). The use of special work-groups by legislative committees drafting statutes in which reproductive rights are recognised is one suggestion. Each work-group can be specifically devoted to analysis and legislative solutions to problems caused by the impact of the new legal category on different legal areas, eg health or telecommunication law.

The policy of law analyst can also suggest the insertion of reproductive rights into already more settled legal categories. For example, the law-maker can solve the problem by giving a statutory definition of abortion as an 'emergency medical measure'. In this way, medical staffs have the legal duty to perform an abortion, regardless of religious beliefs. Similarly, birth control advertisements could be moved by statute to the legal category of 'public health service' and, therefore, broadcast networks would have a duty to provide for messages concerning birth control as an issue of public health.

IV. THE POLICY OF LAW ANALYSIS: SOME QUESTIONS TO BE ANSWERED

The ambition of this work has been to frame, inside the relationship of law-politics, a field in which values are transformed into legal categories and concepts. A secondary aim has been to propose a branch of future studies, whose goal is primarily the analysis of this field from a normative

[19] See, for a similar actual case, I Chettiar, 'Contraceptive Coverage Laws: Eliminating Gender Discrimination or Infringing on Religious Liberties' (2002) 69 *University of Chicago Law Review* 1870.

perspective. It must be stressed that the purpose has simply been one of charting the external borders both of a field (policy of law) and of its analysis. In order to do this, a depiction of this field and its analysis as distinct from the surrounding phenomena (politics of law and social impact of the law) and their investigations (politics of law analysis and sociology of law) has been proffered.

Once the external frames are established, a faithful application of this theory should focus the attention inwards, into the policy of law process and its results and, at the same time, in establishing the main tools at the disposal of the policy of law analyst with respect to any scrutiny. In particular, the next steps should be in a direction of building one or several models aimed mainly at answering two major questions following the recognition of the existence of a transformational moment in the law-making process: How does the policy of law work? Why do legal actors choose one legal category instead of the other?

A. How Does the Policy of Law Work?

In answering the first question, any theory of the policy of law will have to identify the specific modalities through which the transformational proc-esses take place. It will need to specifically categorise and explain the mechanisms through which political, economic, cultural or religious values become legal categories and concepts. In particular, this theory of the policy of law will have to be developed along two major converging lines of work.

First, the investigation of the modes of the working of a policy process needs to take as a central point of observation the perspective of the legal actors. These actors play the leading (although not exclusive) part in such processes. In particular, the Weberian distinction between a formal and a substantive legal rationality should be invoked. With it, a line can be drawn between actors working from within the legal system, whose coherence or consequentiality they are to preserve, and those social and political actors that, although active in the law-making process, strive for goals external to the internal logic of the legal system (eg the realisation of a certain political ideology or the improvement of the efficiency of an economic system).

In drawing this line, the policy of law analyst, however, will have to always keep in mind the relative nature of this distinction between legal and non-legal institutional actors (as well as their goals). Considering the vast variety of guises a legal actor can take, it is often unclear where the latter ends and the social or political actor begins. One example is in-house corporate attorneys. Moreover, legal actors themselves (judges *in primis*), even when embracing as unique a value as the maintenance of the internal logic of the legal system, often are carriers of messages also of a political nature; messages that are likely to surface in particular in the presence of hard cases. Even the most obedient judge with respect to the letter of the positive law must sometimes 'go beyond the law and (without sacrifice of impartiality) consult his own sense of moral and political rightness or equity'.[20]

There is a second major process a theory of policy of law will have to address in order to answer the question of how the policy of law works. This starts from the channels through which, in the law-making process, the communications occur among the different actors. In particular, a future model explaining the policy of law should include a deep investigation of the legal language. The latter already has been a central focus of the legal phenomenon as seen by many contemporary legal theories, from Finnis to Hart, from CLS to the legal realists. As pointed out by movements such as postmodernism or feminist legal theory, it is, however, necessary in order to fully understand the point of the passage from political to legal languages, to substitute the concept of legal language with the broader one of 'legal discourse'.[21]

A possible model of the policy of law needs to focus on the legal discourse since:

> the concept of legal discourse is a methodology for the reading of legal texts which places the communicative or rhetorical functions of law within their institutional and socio-linguistic contexts.[22]

Legal discourse then allows the policy of law analyst to investigate the policy process by placing the legal phenomenon in the centre of its ontological web of relations with the political and social arenas.[23]

B. Why Do Legal Actors Choose One Legal Category instead of the Other?

The centrality of the legal discourse for any future model of the policy process then introduces the viable paths the policy of law analyst needs to

---

[20] N MacCormick, *H.L.A. Hart* (Stanford, Stanford University Press, 1981) 126. See also C Varga, 'Kelsen's Pure Theory of Law: Yesterday, Today and Tomorrow' in C Varga, *Law and Philosophy: Selected Papers in Legal Theory* (Budapest, Faculty of Law of Lórand Eötvös University, 1994) 292.

[21] For example, Habermas states the necessity of moving from the 'logicosemantic' idea of legal discourse to a more 'pragmatic conception' of it. See Habermas, *Between Facts and Norms* (n 11 above) 225–8.

[22] P Goodrich, *Legal Discourse: Studies in Linguistics, Rhetoric and Legal Analysis* (New York, St Martin's Press, 1987) 205.

[23] See B Bix, *Law, Language, and Legal Determinacy* (Oxford, Clarendon Press, 1993) 2–6. See Habermas, *Between Facts and Norms* (n 11 above) 191–2.

follow in order to answer the second question: what are the motives driving legal actors in the choice (or in the construction) of a legal category or concept? Since the policy process is positioned inside the legal world but has strong relations with the political and social dimensions of the legal phenomenon, it seems reasonable to expect that a model for the explanation of such a process would go beyond the mere consideration of the legal reasoning along which the law-making develops.

If the values behind a certain legal category are the starting point of a policy of law analysis, and if a central role in such a process is played by the legal discourse, then it seems sound to expect that a model of the policy process will also sieve through the different moral, political, social, economic and cultural aspects underlying the legal reasoning. The policy of law analyst will have to take a step into the world of moral reasoning because, for example, the law-maker (either as a legislator, scholar or judge) will always reason and arguably rationalise his/her choices in terms of finding the *correct* legal category for a certain value. The law-making authority will transform a value into law trying to be as faithful as possible to some criteria to which the authority itself (and hopefully the addressees) attributes an a priori validity, ie a value-status.[24] These criteria can be of a different nature; they can be economic criteria (eg the economic efficiency of the legal order), formal legal criteria (eg the consistency and logic of the legal order) or *stricto sensu* political criteria (eg the idea of democracy). Regardless of the kind of criteria the law-making agencies opt for, they are all perceived and used by the legislator, judge or scholar as moral axioms, ie as assumed-to-be-valid lights guiding the work of law-makers.[25]

A model of the policy process therefore should be able to penetrate and expose the axioms underpinning the law-maker's choices in favour of one or the other legal category. The illumination of such economic, formalistic or moral axioms is necessary not only for a better understanding of the process of policy of law, since they 'establish a procedure of legitimate lawmaking ... [and] *steer the production of the legal medium itself*'.[26] (emphasis original) The descent into the value-roots is necessary also in investigating the results of the policy process. Only by first openly recognising the political, moral, social or economic original backgrounds of the legal categories and concepts made or used in the law-making process can the policy of law analyst then proceed to identify that which is normative as left in the legal phenomenon.[27]

---

[24] See *ibid* 226–9.
[25] See M Moore, 'The Need for a Theory of Legal Theories: Assessing Pragmatic Instrumentalism: A Review Essay of "Instrumentalism and American Legal Theory" by Robert S. Summers (Book Review)' (1984) 69 *Cornell Law Review* 1003, in particular point (3).
[26] Habermas, *Between Facts and Norms* (n 11 above) 111.
[27] See J Bell, *Policy Arguments in Judicial Decisions* (Oxford, Clarendon Press, 1983) 270.

In conclusion, as stated by Habermas:

> In academia we often mention law and politics in the same breath, yet at the same time we are accustomed to consider law, including the rule of law, and democracy as subjects of different disciplines: jurisprudence deals with law, political science with democracy, and each deals with the constitutional state in its own way, one side in normative terms, the other from an empirical perspective.[28]

In this spirit, the findings of this work point in the direction of a suitable location on the normative side, namely the policy of law, where the construction of a bridge allowing the legal discipline to access the political dimension of the legal phenomenon can begin. Now all that remains is to build this bridge.

---

[28] J Habermas, 'On the Internal Relation Between the Rule of Law and Democracy' (1995) 3 *European Journal of Philosophy* 12.